Library of Congress Cataloging-In-Publication Data

kamp, Bernard J. (Bernard Joseph), 1938-
   The evolution of religion: A re-examination / by Bernard J.
      Verkamp.
         p.   cm.
   Bibliographical references and index.
   ISBN 0-940866-48-X (hard). – ISBN 0-940866-49-8 (pbk.)
   1. Religion. 2. Evolution–Religious aspects. I. Title.
BL430.V47   1995
200–dc20
                                                95-5902
                                                   CIP

University of Scranton Press
Chicago Distribution Center
11030 S. Langley
Chicago   IL   60628

THE EVOLUTION OF RELIGION

THE EVOLUTION OF REL[I

A Re-Examination

by

BERNARD J. VERKAMP

Ve

Scranton: University of Scranto[n

To my friend and colleague --
Phillip E. Pierpont

CONTENTS

ACKNOWLEDGEMENTS

Quotations from Donald T. Campbell, "Variation and Selective Retention in Socio-Cultural Evolution," in Herbert R. Barringer, George I. Blanksten, and Raymond W. Mack, *Social Change in Developing Areas* (Cambridge: Shenkman, 1965). Quoted with permission from Shenkman Publishing Company, Inc.

Quotations from Robert Bellah, *Beyond Belief: Essays on Religion in a Post-Industrial World*. Copyright (c) 1991 The Regents of the University of California. Quoted by permission of the University of California Press.

Quotations from Descartes, *The Philosophical Works*, translated by Elizabeth S. Haldane and G. R. T. Ross. Copyright 1983 The Press Syndicate of the University of Cambridge. Reprinted with the permission of Cambridge University Press.

Quotations from D. Bruce Dickson, *The Dawn of Belief*. Copyright 1990 by The Arizona Board of Regents. Quoted by permission of The University of Arizona Press.

Quotations from Alister Hardy, *The Biology of God* (London: Jonathan Cape, 1975), by permission of the Estate of Alister Hardy and Random House UK Limited.

Quotations from *The Collected Works of C.G. Jung*, Volume 9, Part I (Princeton: Princeton University Press, 1959). Reprinted with permission from Princeton University Press.

Quotations from George Lindbeck, "The A Priori in St. Thomas' Theory of Knowledge," in *The Heritage of Christian Thought*, ed. by R. E. Cushman and E. Grislis (New York: Harper and Row, 1965).

Quotations from Rudolf Otto, *The Idea of the Holy* (New York: Oxford University Press, 1958). Quoted by permission of Oxford University Press.

Quotations from Rudolf Otto, *The Philosophy of Religion* (London: Williams and Norgate Ltd., 1931).

Quotations from Rudolf Otto, *Religious Essays* (London: Oxford University Press, 1931). Quoted by permission of Oxford University Press.

Quotations from Roy A. Rappaport, "The Sacred in Human Evolution." Reproduced, with permission, from the *Annual Review of Ecology and Systematics*, Volume 2, copyright 1971, by Annual Reviews Inc.

Quotations from V. Reynolds and R. E. S. Tanner, *The Biology of Religion*. Copyright 1983. Quoted with permission from the publishers, Longman House.

Quotations from Robert J. Richards, *Darwin and the Emergence of Evolutionary Theories of the Mind and Behavior*. Copyright 1987 The University of Chicago Press. Quoted by permission of The University of Chicago Press.

Quotations from Robert J. Richards, *The Meaning of Evolution*. Copyright 1992 by The University of Chicago Press. Quoted by permission of The University of Chicago Press.

PREFACE

For years I have listened to what scholars from every field have been saying about the origin and nature of religion. That many of them seemed to be contradicting each other did not especially bother me. It was, I assumed, part and parcel of any genuinely dialectical encounter. More disturbing, however, was the suspicion that not a few of them were simply talking past each other, with little or no attention to how their own specialized views might be combined with those of others to develop a larger picture of where religion came from, how it developed, and what it really is. And so, mainly for the sake of clarifying matters for myself and my students, I set out to investigate whether and how the material from disparate fields might be brought together into a more coherent, unified theory. The result is the book at hand. In reality, it is little more than a study guide, indicating a frame of reference within which to proffer some tentative answers to a set of questions that will require more than a single lifetime of research. Venturing as I have across so many different fields in which I have no special expertise, I know only too well how vulnerable I am leaving myself on every flank. As Donald T. Campbell once observed, only "marginal scholars who are willing to be incompetent in a number of fields at once" could attempt such interdisciplinary work.[1] Given the risks involved and the controversial nature of so much of the material presented, readers might wonder why the author has not delayed airing it until such time as he had thought it through more thoroughly, and arrived at a higher degree of certitude than he can now claim. But if philosophy is, as I suppose it to be, an ongoing conversation, there may be some value in the injection of half-digested, still rather raw material that participants, like avian nestlings, might do not find the author's interpretation of the material palatable, will thereby have at least some morsels on which to feed their own hermeneutic interests, and to construct perhaps a more reliable theory of their own.

Notes

1. D. T. Campbell, *Descriptive Epistemology: Psychological, Sociological, and Evolutionary* (unpublished William James lectures, given at Harvard University, and cited in Michael Ruse, *Taking Darwin Seriously* [Oxford: Basil Blackwell, 1986], xiii).

INTRODUCTION

It will be a primary objective of this book to show that, far from falling ready-made from the heavens above, religion, like any other cultural entity, has evolved from below. The reader will note that, although the book is entitled "Evolution of Religion," it carries also the subtitle: "A Re-examination." The latter was chosen purposely by the author to set some distance between his own work and earlier studies on the origin of religion by late nineteenth and early twentieth century "evolutionists." The conclusions they drew will, in fact, be challenged by this book at almost every juncture.

To start with, the author does not share the assumption of past evolutionists, like Auguste Comte and Sigmund Freud, that religion can be explained along empirical lines as being nothing more than a product of nature and culture. Being open to the religious view himself, the author is inclined rather to think that the ascension of religion in various and sundry niches would never have begun or gone anywhere, except for some ontologically (albeit not necessarily chronologically) prior event that Jews and Christians like to call "creation," or that another religion like Buddhism might refer to as a process of "trans-descension," whereby ultimate Reality has "emptied" itself into everything temporal and spatial.[1] The author shares the conviction, in other words, that in the final analysis, the evolution of religion can be fully appreciated only when it is viewed also from a "theological" perspective. And throughout this book, but especially in chapters two and six, some attention is paid to theological questions about the relation of body and soul, divine *concursus*, supernatural selectivity, and so forth. The author would hope that all readers will give serious consideration to these theological points. Those who do not find them convincing, however, might still benefit from a reading of the rest of the book. For although the author does not consider empirical observation the sole source of knowledge, he does highly respect the scientific method, and sees in theology no excuse for neglect or manipulation of the facts. Indeed, the author was motivated to write this book primarily by a conviction that religion cannot possibly make any sense unless it is linked up with the rest of biological and cultural evolution that has been shown by the life and social sciences to be unfolding all around it. Notwithstanding its theological orientation, therefore, or perhaps precisely because of it, this book also contains much information of an empirical sort about the origin and nature of religion that can be read and appreciated apart from any theological perspective.

By insisting upon the "mysterious" nature of religious evolution, the author of this book also has in mind to reject the assumption of most earlier evolutionists that religion can be reduced to something other than itself, or to one or another of its component parts. In the first chapter, the book will attempt to show that religion has been an extremely complex part of human experience from the very beginning, and that, far from being derived from mere experience, religion is an innate structure of the human soul. What sense this latter conclusion might possibly make is discussed in an appendix through a review of what various thinkers have said down through the centuries about the innateness of the religious category. Such insistence upon the autonomy of religion is not taken to mean, however, that religion has no roots in the animal world, or that, once established, it has undergone no change. Chapters two, four and five of this book suggest the contrary, with chapter two tracing the soul's "prehistory," and the latter two sketching the historical course of religious evolution. But here again, major departures from past evolutionist assumptions (e.g., about the unilinear nature of all evolution) can be expected. And, in chapter three an attempt will be made to explain what past evolutionists generally ignored, namely, the mechanism by which religious evolution might have occurred.

Finally, this book will also take issue with past evolutionist tendencies to write religion off as belonging merely to man's infantile, pre-scientific stage of intellectual development. It assumes instead that religion has been, and will always be around, so long as there are human beings. This assumption rests to some extent upon the aforementioned identification of religion as an innate structure of human consciousness. But it is based also upon what will be described in chapter six as the adaptive value of religion. What will be seen therein is that far from being a threat to, or a drag upon science, religion has in fact contributed significantly to the survival of mankind, and might even, if its own doctrine about ultimate reality warrants any credence, prove to be mankind's best hope for rescuing science and technology from themselves.

Notes

1. See Masao Abe, "Kenotic God and Dynamic sunyata," in John Cobb and Christopher Ives, eds., *The Emptying God* (Maryknoll, N.Y.: Orbis, 1991), 14-19. In an unpublished paper entitled "Beyond Buddhism and Christianity — 'Dazzling Darkness'," and recently shared with me by the author, Masao Abe uses the Pseudo-Dionysian expression "dazzling darkness" to refer to such an instance of creativity.

Chapter One

The Origin of Religion

A search for the origin of things has always been counted among the chief functions of religion.[1] It would be rather ironic, therefore, to exempt religion itself — as some today seem inclined to do — from the kind of scrutiny modern Western Man has afforded the origin of the human species, the earth, the universe, life, and other human institutions, like art and language.[2] This recent reluctance to investigate the origin of religion may derive in part from what William James referred to as a confusion of existential and evaluational questions.[3] Some may suspect, in other words, that by seeking out the origin of religion, doubts will be raised about its worth. James himself tried to counter such suspicions with the pragmatic reminder that the value of religion is to be judged not so much by its roots, as by its fruits.[4] Among scholars of religion, however, the reluctance to investigate the origin of religion is due mainly to what is perceived to have been the failure of past efforts in this regard. Robert Brockway has noted, for example, that "the origins of the religion problem were abandoned shortly after World War One by virtually all anthropologists,"[5] and "avoided" by all but a few scholars, because reliable information was so hard to come by, and the problem seemed so unsolvable.[6] And if indeed the task is, as some nineteenth century evolutionists conceived it to be, one of demonstrating scientifically exactly what religion was like in the beginning, it would, of course, be impossible to meet. For, as will be seen, there simply is not enough archeological evidence to support the kind of definitive accounting of early religion they tried to give. Pursued on its own, the "archeological path" may, in fact, be, as Brockway claims, "a dead end route."[7] But that does not mean that the task is altogether hopeless. An intelligent analysis of what fragments of archeological evidence exist, along with a more enlightened use of ethnographical analogues and, as Brockway himself advocates, some reliance on ethological and psychological inference, not to mention philosophical and theological speculation, can shed at least some light on the origin of religion. To achieve this goal, it will be helpful to break the problem down in accordance with the various meanings of the English word 'origin.' As any dictionary will reveal, the latter can refer to the chronological 'beginning,' or the date when one or another phenomenon originated. It can also connote a 'starting point' in the sense of the 'initial stage' of development. Or, finally, it can refer to the 'source' from which something arises. The problem about the origin of religion brings all of these connotations into play. It really involves three separate questions: when religion originated, what it originally was, and how it all began. Only the first and third of these questions will be dealt with in this chapter. The second will be addressed in our subsequent discussion of the course of religious evolution.

I. The Chronological Beginning

Not infrequently in the past, some theorists have been inclined to argue that mankind was not initially religious. One of the more blatant claims of this sort was made in John Lubbock's 1870 work, *The Origin of Civilization and the Primitive Condition of Man*. Relying rather naïvely on reports from sailors and merchants about the apparent lack of any religious belief or practice among certain "primitive" peoples, who were assumed to be similar in every respect to the first humans, Lubbock concluded that the latter, too, must have been atheists.[8] The same conclusion was at least implied by ancient Greek and Roman theorists, like Critias, Statius, Epicurus, and Polybius, and some seventeenth and eighteenth century thinkers, who argued that religion originated when some shrewd individuals invented the gods to frighten the vulgar masses into civil obedience,[9] or by many other theorists, from Euhemerus to Herbert Spencer, who have argued that the gods are mere mortals raised to divine rank after death because of their superior deeds.[10]

Since "no documents of a primordial humanity without religion" have ever been found, it is unlikely that those making claims of this sort will ever be able to meet the "burden of proof" which Mircea Eliade claims lies with them.[11] But is there any positive evidence that early man was religious? The answer to this question will depend to some extent upon how we identify 'early man.' The family of hominids originating out of the Primate order around 3.8 million years ago eventually (c. 2.2 million years ago) divided into two genuses: the now extinct *Australopithecus* and *Homo*, from which would descend *Homo habilis* (c. 2.2 million years ago), *Homo erectus* (c. 1.9 million years ago), *Homo sapiens* (c. 600,000 B.P.), *Homo Neanderthalis* (c. 130,000 B.P.) and the fully modern hominids *Homo sapiens sapiens* (c. 35,000 B.P.).[12] In a later chapter, it will be seen that there is some anthropological and ethological evidence to suggest that because of their development of a cerebral cortex, the *Australopithecines* and the earliest homines (habilis and erectus) may have enjoyed a capacity for abstraction and symbolic thinking, or perhaps even supernaturalist ideation.[13] The use of fire, and the manufacture of "naturefacts" and stone tools by *Homo habilis* probably remained at what Piaget would call a childlike "pre-operational level" (i.e., without any clear picture of the end product), but might still have involved a nascent "aesthetic appreciation" of form and color for their own sake, or even a latent sense of magico-religious values.[14] Some have found religious significance, too, in the gradual assumption by *Homo habilis* of an erect posture, to the extent that by thus walking around on hind legs, *Homo erectus* gained a more anthropocentric view of reality, and was in a better position to organize, in an "operational" manner, the division of land, dwellings, and so forth.[15] Ethological studies of contemporary primates show a similar tendency toward social discipline, and re-enforce the assumption of the latter among primeval hominids.[16] Given the occasional function of religion as an instrument of social control, it is not unreasonable, some say, to see therein the roots of religion.[17]

Actual archaeological evidence of religious behavior during the Lower Paleolithic Period (2,900,000 -90,000 B.P.), however, is hard to come by, and difficult to interpret. One bit of evidence of a "concern [by *Homo erectus*] with realities transcending mere biological needs" found at Olduvai Gorge (occupied c. 1,500,000 B.P.), Terra Amata (c. 300,000 B.P.), Becov (c. 250,000 B.P.) and other sites from the Lower Paleolithic period, is the apparently "intentional collection and use of ochre or other red-colored rocks and minerals."[18] Because ochre had "no apparent practical or technological use until the development of iron metallurgy" (c. 2,000 B.C.), it has been argued that its collection by the early hominids was for aesthetic or ritualistic purposes, and contributed toward their religio-magical development of self-mastery and self-actualization, as well as a belief in life beyond the grave[19]. Further evidence of a concern beyond simple survival from the Lower Paleolithic period is the "cult of skulls" that is thought to have occurred some 500,000 years ago in the Chou-k'ou-tien caves near Beijing, and

several hundred thousand years later at sites, like
Steinheim and Swanscombe, in southern Germany and
England.[20] The skulls and lower jawbones found may
have been amulets or the debris of cannibal feasts, and to
that extent imply a ritual treatment of the dead or the
veneration of ancestral spirits.[21] Such an interpretation
has not been accepted by most scholars.[22] Recent
taphonomic studies have also called it into question, on
grounds that the breakage of bones that was thought to be
so significant may have been caused by scavenging
animals, water, or other natural, postmortem processes.[23]
Much the same might be said about the Cult of Skulls
supposedly practiced during the Middle Paleolithic period
(90,000 - 35,000 B.P.) at the cave site of Monte Circeo
near Rome.[24] Furthermore, even if there were such cults,
they would "offer no proof of any deliberate burial."[25]
Remains and grave goods found at La Ferrassie,
Regourdou, and other European and Eurasian middle
Paleolithic sites do suggest, however, that death was very
much on the mind of *Neanderthal* man, that at least some
Neanderthals intentionally buried their dead, and to that
extent showed some concern for life after death.[26]
Whether the *Neanderthals* also worshipped the animals
they hunted, or made offerings to some supreme being or
Lord of Wild Beasts, as the discovery of piles of bear
skulls in cave sites at Drachenloch and Petershoehle
seemed to imply, is now in considerable doubt, because
the bones in question may have been accumulated
naturally.[27] With the start of the Upper Paleolithic Period
(c. 35,000 B.P.) and the "replacement" of *Neanderthal* by
modern *Homo sapiens sapiens*,[28] the process of
"hominization" or the "gradual emergence of thought and
self-consciousness" is accelerated,[29] and "tantalizing
evidences of prehistoric religion"[30] begin to abound in the
form of more elaborate burial rites, sacrificial offerings,
and an outpouring of representational parietal and

portable art.[31]

There is much about the burial rites of Upper Paleolithic peoples whose meaning is still unclear — e.g., burial of the deceased in a fetal position, edging of graves with animal skulls, etc. But the care taken in the disposal of the corpses (cushioning of the skulls with rocks, for example), ornamentation of the corpses with bone, shell, horn, tooth, and ivory, "life-bestowing" jewelry, or the coating of the corpse with blood-red ochre, as in the case of the "Red Lady of Paviland," would seem to suggest that Cro-Magnon and other human types of the period harbored "a respect and regard for the departed that goes beyond fear," and that the grave itself was viewed not so much as a prison, as "a portal to an after-life."[32]

Among the portable art objects from the Upper Paleolithic period are many expendable weapons, utensils, and ornamental pendants that might also, nothwithstanding their functional nature, "manifest the sacred." Especially "hierophanous," however, are statuettes, like the Venuses of Willendorf and La Mouthe, or decorated stone and bone slabs depicting human females, animals, and ovals (symbolic, perhaps, of the female vulva). Whatever other function such objects may have enjoyed, they seem primarily to have been material expressions of a religious veneration of mother-goddesses, and a celebration of female fertility and the life-giving, animating role of the male-female polarity.[33]

The Upper Paleolithic wall-paintings and carvings found primarily in caves around southwestern Europe depict everything from large mammalian game animals, enigmatic macaroni or meander lines, birds, elk, imaginary animal forms, man-animal combinations (like the dancing "sorcerer" found in the Les Trois Frères Cave in France), drawings of the human face, outlines of the human hand, and stick-figures of human beings engaged in one or another activity (like the "Dead Man" discovered in the shaft of a cave at Lascaux in Spain).[34] Exactly what, if anything, all these parietal works of art tell us about the original nature of religion is very hard to say. But in view of their "floating otherworldly quality" and "contextual circumstances" (darkness, depth, remoteness, etc.) suitable for a sanctuary or temple, it seems likely that they were related to some kind of mythological and ritualistic system, or a "religion of the caves," as Leroi-Gourham refers to it.[35]

To be sure, some theorists in the past, like Sir James G. Frazer, have looked at the same evidence and concluded that primeval man was given to magic before turning to religion.[36] The rituals being practiced, and their concrete expression in the form of the aforementioned parietal and portable art objects, it was argued, were all part of an attempt by primitive man to dominate the forces of nature by exploiting the "sympathy" established through "contagion" and "imitation." By drawing an image of a bison pierced by arrows, for example, the Upper Paleolithic people were supposedly trying to assure themselves a successful hunting of the real animal.[37] Or by portraying female animals followed or covered by rutting males, the prehistoric hunters were said to be seeking by magic "to bring about couplings among the bison of the region."[38] Only when this infantile "science" failed, or, in other words, only when it was discovered that the supposed causal connections between the forces of nature and certain rites or incantations did not exist, did they become religious and begin to pray to the powers of nature that they now recognized as lying beyond their control.[39] The high incidence of game animals portrayed, their correlation to species indigenous to southwestern Europe during the Upper Paleolithic period, the fact that most are depicted as targets of traps, arrows, spears, etc., or as actually being dead, and the superimposition of images, all, along with a comparison to hunting rites of contemporary "primitive" peoples, lend some credence to this once widely-accepted interpretation of cave art as being part of hunting and fertility magic.[40]   More recently, however, some scholars have begun to question whether hunting peoples were ever so "anxiety-ridden" about the hunt as such an hypothesis assumes.[41]   Others, like Johannes Maringer, have pointed out that "magic plays a very small part in the most primitive societies, while the belief in a supreme being is well-nigh universal."[42] Magic, he says, comes into play "only among the more advanced hunters" after belief in the supreme god to whom "purely primitive man" had prayed, sacrificed, and offered first fruits to gain "hunting luck" had degenerated.[43] While admitting, therefore, that Upper Paleolithic hunters engaged in magic, Maringer argues that the latter was in fact derivative from more primordial religious beliefs.[44]   In any event, no chronological sequence from magic to religion, such as Frazer assumed, has ever been documented.[45] Furthermore, even if one assumes, as some scholars now do, that religion and magic, though different in nature, became inextricably intertwined from the start, with the one same ritual, like the shamanic dance, for example, often being exploited simultaneously for both magical and religious purposes,[46] it could still be argued that the experience of religion is at least logically prior to the practice of magic to the extent that any attempt to dominate the forces of nature rests upon "an implicit assumption of a transcendent dimension of invisible reality."[47]   "To seek to derive numinous power from magical," therefore, is, as Rudolf Otto has noted, "altogether to invert the situation, since long before the magician could appropriate and manipulate it, it had been 'apperceived as numinous' in plant and animal, in natural processes and objects, in the horror of the skeleton, and also independently of all these."[48]

II. The Source of Religion

Assuming that religion has been around since the beginning of mankind, a second, closely related, question arises about how the first humans came to be religious. Down through the centuries, all kinds of theories have surfaced in an attempt to answer this latter question. Some ancient Greeks, like Theagenes and the Stoics, or later Romantic theorists, like Friedrick Creuzer, have argued that it arose out of man's tendency to allegorize the forces of nature.[49] Plato and Giambattista Vico noted similarly that religion resulted from man's proclivity for imaginative, mythological talk in symbolic terms about nature.[50] For Aristotle, the source of religion was to be found in the respect for eternal cosmic laws aroused in primeval man by the observation of the regular order and beautiful harmony of natural phenomena, like the sky.[51] Others, however, like Democritus and Epicurus, argued that it was not so much respect as fear of natural phenomena that gave rise to religion.[52] Fear of another sort (i.e., of eternal punishment), spawned by a combination of greed and ignorance, was said by Critias and other aformentioned ancient Greek and Roman and eighteenth — century theorists to be the source of religion.[53]

Some of these theories were obviously based on hostility toward religion, and were motivated by an atheistic or agnostic assumption that religion is altogether illusory.[54] A similar attitude was undoubtedly operative in the thinking of many nineteenth and early twentieth century theorists, especially those of an evolutionist bent. Because they doubted the reality of the objects of religious experience, they were all the more inclined to concoct some "biological, psychological, or sociological theory of how everywhere and at all times men have been stupid enough to believe in [souls and spirits and gods]."[55] Ludwig Feuerbach and Karl Marx blamed man's self-alienation, arguing that the gods and eternal life were nothing but the projection of the better part of his individual and social self.[56] According to Auguste Comte, religion, with its worship of gods and infantile storytelling, was rooted in mankind's prescientific lack of intellectual maturity.[57] Sigmund Freud agreed that religion was entirely illusory, and proceeded to reduce it to an obsessional neurosis. Primeval totemism, he claimed, could be explained psychogenetically in terms of the Oedipus complex, with the ambivalent feelings toward the father eventually being projected onto a provident god.[58] For E. B. Tylor, the roots of animism lay in "the reasonable inference that effects are due to causes;" the "spirits are simply personified causes."[59] Spencer thought that the basis of all religion was fear of the dead man's phantom.[60] Wilhelm Wundt also saw fear as the source of totemism.[61] Others would find the source of religion in the idealization of human values. Emile Durkheim, for example, claimed that religion in general, and totemism in particular, arises "out of the nature of social life itself;" it is the "way in which a society sees itself as more than a collection of individuals, and by which it maintains its solidarity and ensures its continuity."[62] Thus, as deVries wrote, "what no one had ever dared to do with poetry or music — except in some circles of historical materialism — was done to the *summum bonum* of men: religion was divested of its autonomy in human life and regarded as a mental illusion or as the product of social conditions."[63] Just as man was thought to have evolved out of something other and lower than man, so, Eric Sharpe points out, it was assumed that "religion must have evolved out of something other and lower than religion," out of "that which was not religion."[64]

These reductionist theories were rooted to some extent in what Peter Harrison has described as David Hume's refusal to recognize any kind of religious *a priori*, such as the Cambridge Platonists and a few Deists will be seen in the appendix to have been championing during the eighteenth century.[65] They assumed, in other words, that religion is nothing but a product of human experience. This assumption has carried over into our own time. Typical of the modern behaviorist view, for example, is the suggestion made by J. J. Smith to the effect that "the human being at birth is nonreligious in the same sense that he is nonscientific, nonmoral, or nonaesthetic," because "he inherits none of these qualities in a functional form but acquires them gradually through experience."[66] Jean Piaget, whose views have dominated child psychology in recent decades, has rejected such raw empiricism, on the grounds that it does not pay enough attention to the "active role of the subject."[67] Piaget himself, however, also denies that "the subject possesses from the start endogenous structures which it imposes on objects,"[68] and concludes instead that if there is anything innate in the human mind, it is only "certain modes of interacting with the environment," i.e., "adaptive" and "organizational functions."[69] Religious "structures," therefore, are interpreted by Piaget and disciples of his, like Lawrence Kohlberg and James Fowler,[70] as being "constructed" out of the interaction of the subject and the environment — specifically, as Pierre Bovet had earlier suggested,[71] out of the child's transfer, at about the age of six, of parental "omnipotence" and "omniscience" onto the "gods" or "ideal figures" it has learned about in religious instruction.[72] On the further, nineteenth-century assumption that "ontogeny recapitulates phylogeny," Piaget was inclined to think that by thus describing the development of the individual child's latent awareness of religious ideas, he had also provided some insight into the "origin" of mankind's religion.[73] In other words, he was convinced that he had added weight to the view of nineteenth century evolutionists that the religion of early man was altogether the result of a "learning" process.[74]

That much of what we now call religion is "learned" has been generally supported by recent studies.[75] There is some evidence to suggest, however, that the whole of the religious phenomenon cannot be explained in such a way. In a work entitled *The Children's God*, David Heller has recently noted, for example, that while the child's representation of God bears the mark of a tremendous socialization impact of family, age, gender, personality, and religion,[76] there are also "strikingly universal . . . common themes" (e.g., intimacy, omnipresence, anxiety, connectedness),[77] "which cannot be so readily explained by theories of socialization"[78] or by "developmental change."[79] How they can be explained, Heller leaves "for the individual observer to decide."[80] Like Robert Coles' *The Spiritual Life of Children*,[81] however, he does at least hold out the possibility that the children might be "tapping into something uniquely spiritual."[82] This is a suggestion that sounds remarkably similar to the conclusion drawn earlier by Andrew Lang, Rudolf Otto, Joachim Wach, Mircea Eliade, and other modern scholars of religion, to the effect that in the final analysis, religion is something 'given' in the human soul that precedes, and cannot be reduced to, human experience alone.

Convinced of the lack of evidence for the reductionist theories being propounded by Max Mueller and other nineteenth century evolutionists, Lang concluded that "the beginning of religion is an inscrutable mystery," whose historical inquiry can only lead back to "an unanalysable *sensus numinis*."[83] Arguing against Hume and the evolutionists along Kantian lines, Otto stated that it is impossible to derive "the category of the holy" from sense experience or from other categories.[84]   The religious disposition, he insisted, is unique and autonomous. "It is just the same," he says, "with the feeling of the numinous as with that of moral obligation."[85] Just as "the idea 'ought'" cannot be said to "gradually evolve" out of any other feeling, but "is only 'evolvable' out of the spirit of man itself,"[86] so the numinous feeling "is not to be derived from any other feeling," but is rather "qualitatively *sui generis*."[87] It is simply "given" as part of man's nature, and we have "to take him for granted as he is."[88] "To profess to give a history of religion," he concluded, "is to presuppose a spirit specifically qualified for religion."[89]

Following Otto's lead, Joachim Wach and Mircea Eliade also concluded that religion is a "primal condition of life, not a cultural product,"[90] "an element in the structure of consciousness and not a stage in the history of consciousness."[91] The shamanic ecstatic experience, for example, is, according to Eliade, "coexistent with the human condition, in the sense that it is an integral part of what is called man's gaining consciousness of his specific state of being in the world."[92] It is "a constitutive element of the human condition" to the extent that "it is impossible to imagine a period in which man did not have dreams and waking reveries and did not enter into 'trance' — a loss of consciousness that was interpreted as the soul's traveling into the beyond."[93] And what is true of shamanic ecstacy, he says, applies to all the "major religious attitudes;" "they came into existence once and for all from the moment when man first became conscious of the position he stood in within the universe."[94]

How such an innate, irreducible category of religion might be, or, down through the centuries, has been conceived, and what evidence there is for its existence, will be discussed at length in an appendix to this book. Suffice it at this point simply to note that many social and life scientists, philosophers, and theologians have lent their support to such a notion, and will be seen later to have collectively understood it as referring to a genetically-founded structure of human consciousness, which leaves the individual so endowed not only with a tacit sense of the sacred and an innate "knowledge" about how to pursue survival in the long run, but also with an instinctive propensity or predisposition toward an ontological idea of the holy that categorizes and structures the data of experience in such wise as to render reality symbolically meaningful. In what follows, we will assume the existence of a religious given so defined as a working hypothesis for our investigation of the evolution of religion. We will be asking, in other words, how it is that human consciousness came to be structured in such wise, and how it has evolved subjectively and objectively down through the millennia.

Notes

1. See Mircea Eliade, *The Sacred and the Profane* (New York: Harper and Row, 1961), 8-85; M. Eliade, *A History of Religious Ideas* (Chicago: The University of Chicago Press, 1978), vol. I, *From the Stone Age to the Eleusinian Mysteries*, 26-27.

2. See M. Eliade, *The Quest: History and Meaning in Religion* (Chicago and London: The University of Chicago Press, 1969), 44.

3. William James, *The Varieties of Religious Experience* (New York: The New American Library, 1958), 23-25.

4. Ibid., 32-34.

5. Robert W. Brockway, "The Origins of Religion Debate and its Implications: A Psychological Perspective," in *International Symposium on the Intellectual Expressions of Prehistoric Man: Art and Religion*, ed. Antonio Beltran and others (Capo di Ponte and Milan: Edizione del Centro and Editoriale Jaca Book Spa, 1979), 55.

6. See Ibid., 56, 518-521; Eliade, *Quest*, 50.

7. Brockway, "Origins," 59.

8. See Edward E. Evans-Pritchard, *Theories of Primitive Religion* (Oxford: Clarendon Press, 1959), 107; Eric J. Sharpe, *Comparative Religion: A History* (London: Gerald Duckworth, 1975), 51-53; Jan de Vries, *Perspectives in the History of Religions* (Berkeley, Los Angeles, and London: University of California Press, 1977), 99-101.

9.   See de Vries, *Perspectives*, 7-10; Peter Harrison, *'Religion' and the Religions in the English Enlightenment* (Cambridge: Cambridge University Press, 1990), 16.

10. See de Vries, *Perspectives*, 9, 10, 14-15, 21-23, 25, 26, 32, 34, 53; Sharpe, *Comparative Religion*, 6, 33; Harrison, *Religion*, 16-18, 140-44.

11. Eliade, *History* I: 5; see also: *New Catholic Encyclopedia NCE* henceforth, ed. W. J. McDonald (New York: McGraw-Hill, 1967), XII: 253-54. In his introduction to Max Weber's *Sociology of Religion*, Talcott Parsons notes that it was "a first crucial point in Weber's theory that there is no known human society without something which modern social scientists would classify as religion," and that the "view that belief in the supernatural is universal has been completely confirmed by modern anthropology" (M. Weber, *The Sociology of Religion* [Boston: Beacon Press, 1964], xxvii-xxviii).

12. See D. Bruce Dickson, *The Dawn of Belief: Religion in the Upper Paleolithic of Southwestern Europe* (Tucson: The University of Arizona Press, 1990), 31-35. Prior to recent news releases, the earliest known hominid was thought to be *Australopithecus afarensis*, who supposedly developed an erect posture for the sake of carrying food back home (see John Pfeiffer, "Current research casts new light on human origins," *Smithsonian* [June, 1982]: 91-103).

13. See Brockway, "Origins," 60.

14. See Dickson, *Dawn of Belief*, 41, 45; Eliade, *History*, I: 4.

15. See Eliade, *History*, I: 3; Denise Lardner Carmody, *The Oldest God: Archaic Religion Yesterday and Today* (Nashville: Abingdon, 1981), 22; Dickson, *Dawn of Belief*, 41.

16. Brockway, "Origins," 56-57.

17. Ibid., 57.

18. See Dickson, *Dawn of Belief*, 42, 43.

19. Ibid., 42, 43-44; Eliade, *History*, I: 9.

20. See Johannes Maringer, *The Gods of Prehistoric Man* (New York: Alfred A. Knopf, 1960), 14-15, 16-21; E. O. James, *Prehistoric Religion: A Study in Prehistoric Archaeology* (New York: Frederick A. Praeger, 1957), 17-18; Dickson, *Dawn of Belief*, 44-45.

21. Maringer, *Gods*, 19-21; James, *Prehistoric Religion*, 17.

22. See Eliade, *History*, I: 9.

23. Dickson, *Dawn of Belief*, 45, 93.

24. Ibid., 51-52.

25. Maringer, *Gods*, 15; Brockway, "Origins," 55.

26. Maringer, *Gods*, 21-29; Dickson, *Dawn of Belief*, 49, 50.

27. Maringer, *Gods*, 38-62; Brockway, "Origins," 55; Dickson, *Dawn of Belief*, 51.

28. See Dickson, *Dawn of Belief*, 35.

29. Ibid., 91.

30. Brockway, "Origins," 55, 520.

31. Maringer, *Gods*, 274.

32. James, *Prehistoric Religion*, 25-30; Maringer, *Gods*, 74-84; Dickson, *Dawn of Belief*, 93-95; Eliade, *History*, I: 9-13.

33. Dickson, *Dawn of Belief*, 95, 99, 101-103, 211-14; Carmody, *Oldest God*, 26-29; Maringer, *Gods*, 153-60; Eliade, *History*, I: 20-22.

34. Dickson, *Dawn of Belief*, 111-19; Maringer, *Gods*, 117-52; Eliade, *History*, I: 22-23.

35. See Dickson, *Dawn of Belief*, 111, 113, 119; Carmody, *Oldest God*, 30; Eliade, *History*, I: 17.

36. For a summary of Frazer's *The Golden Bough* in this regard, see: de Vries, *Perspectives*, 189-91; Evans-Pritchard, *Theories*, 27-29.

37. Maringer, *Gods*, 110-15, 274-77; Dickson, *Dawn of Belief*, 126-29.

38. Maringer, *Gods*, 141, 138-42, 276-77; Dickson, *Dawn of Belief*, 128-29.

39. de Vries, *Perspectives*, 190; Evans-Pritchard, *Theories*, 28.

40. Dickson, *Dawn of Belief*, 126, 127-28; Maringer, *Gods*, 53-62; Eliade, *History*, I: 17.

41. Dickson, *Dawn of Belief*, 129.

42. Maringer, *Gods*, 115, 151.

43. Ibid., 116, 278.

44. Ibid., 117, 127-28, 151-52, 278.

45. Evans-Pritchard, *Theories*, 28; John B. Noss, *Man's Religions* (London: Macmillan, 1969), 12.

46. See Gerardus van der Leeuw, *Religion in Essence and Manifestation* (New York and Evanston: Harper and Row, 1963), II: 545; de Vries, *Perspectives*, 195-96; E. O. James, *The Beginnings of Religion* (Westport, Conn.: Greenwood Press, 1973), 46-48.

47. NCE 9: 65.

48. R. Otto, *Gefuehl des Ueberweltlichen*, 56, as quoted in van der Leeuw, *Religion*, I: 25 n.2.

49. See de Vries, *Perspectives*, 5-6, 8-9.

50. Ibid., 34-35.

51. Ibid., 8-9.

52. Ibid., 9.

53. Ibid., 7-10.

54. Evans-Pritchard, *Theories*, 15, 121.

55. Ibid., 121.

56. See Hans Kueng, *Does God Exist?* (Garden City, N.Y.: Doubleday, 1980), 191-261.

57. See Ibid., 169-71.

58. See Hans Kueng, *Freud and the Problem of God* (New Haven: Yale University Press, 1979), 36, 38; Robert Coles, *The Spiritual Life of Children* (Boston: Houghton Mifflin, 1990), 2-21; *NCE* 12: 252.

59. de Vries, *Perspectives*, 102.

60. Ibid., 103.

61. Evans-Pritchard, *Theories*, 37-38.

62. Ibid., 55, 56; Emile Durkheim, *The Elementary Forms of the Religious Life* (New York: The Free Press, 1965), esp. 390. See also: George Santayana, *Interpretations of Poetry and Religion* (Cambridge: The MIT Press, 1989), 33-34, 38, 67, 70, 105, 171-72.

63. de Vries, *Perspectives*, 221.

64. Sharpe, *Comparative Religion*, 58, 62.

65. Peter Harrison, *Religion*, 169. Hume, it should be noted, does,

according to Michael Ruse, recognize "propensities" that "correspond precisely to Wilson's epigenetic rules" (M. Ruse, *Taking Darwin Seriously*, 184). For further discussion of Hume and the "epigenetic rules," see *Infra*, Appendix, note 56.

66. J. J. Smith, "Religious Development of Children," in *Child Psychology: Child Development and Modern Education*, ed. Charles E. Skinner and Philip L. Harriman (New York: Macmillan, 1941), 274. Smith adds later: "The human being at birth holds a neutral status as regards religion; the baby is neither religious nor anti-religious" (Ibid., 276).

67. See. J. Piaget, *The Principles of Genetic Epistemology* (London: Routledge and Kegan Paul, 1972), 10-11; *Language and Learning, The Debate between Jean Piaget and Noam Chomsky*, ed. Massimo Piattelli-Palmarini (Cambridge: Harvard University Press, 1980), 23, 24, 241.

68. Piaget, *Principles*, 19, 56, 91; J. Piaget, *Biology and Knowledge* (Chicago and London: University of Chicago Press, 1971), 269-71; Piattelli-Palmarini, *Language and Learning*, 30, 59, 231, 238.

69. J. Piaget, *The Moral Judgment of the Child* (New York: The Free Press, 1965), 399; Piaget, *Principles*, 91; J. Piaget, *The Origins of Intelligence in Children* (New York: International Universities Press, 1975), 2-3. Dan Sperber, incidentally, accuses Piaget and his followers of "prejudice" against "any kind of innatist hypothesis" (See his comments in Piattelli-Palmarini, *Language and Learning*, 78-79).

70. See L. Kohlberg, *The Philosophy of Moral Development* (San Francisco: Harper and Row, 1981), 294-307; *Moral Development, Moral Education, and Kohlberg*, ed. Brenda Munsey (Birmingham, Ala.: Religious Education Press, 1980), 130-160, 269-358; J. Fowler, *Stages of Faith* (San Francisco: Harper and Row, 1981).

71. Pierre Bovet, *The Child's Religion* (New York: E. P. Dutton and Co., 1928), esp. 33-47; David Elkind, "The Development of Religious Understanding in Children and Adolescents," in *Research on Religious Development*, ed. Merton P. Strommen (New York: Hawthorn Books, 1971), 662.

72. J. Piaget, *The Child's Conception of the World* (Totowa, N.J.: Rowman and Littlefield, 1983), 268, 354, 378, 381-85; Piaget, *Moral Judgment*, 371, 375, 376.

73. See Brockway, "Origins," 57-58.

74. Ibid.

75. See Ronald Goldman, *Religious Thinking From Childhood to Adolescence* (New York: Seabury Press, 1968), 19-33; Elkind, "Development of Religious Understanding," 655-685.

76. D. Heller, *The Children's God* (Chicago and London: The University of Chicago, 1986), 18-104.

77. Ibid., 105-28.

78. Ibid., 106.

79. Ibid., 129.

80. Ibid.

81. Coles, *Spiritual Life of Children*, 4-9.

82. Heller, *The Children's God*, 129.

83. Sharpe, *Comparative Religion*, 61.

84. Rudolf Otto, *The Idea of the Holy* (New York: Oxford University Press, 1967), 114, 115, 160.

85. Ibid., 44.

86. Ibid., 43.

87. Ibid., 44.

88. Ibid., 114. William James seemed to imply the same when he wrote: "We hear, in these days of scientific enlightenment, a great deal of discussion about the efficacy of prayer; and many reasons are given us why we should not pray, whilst others are given us why we should. But in all this very little is said of the reason why we do pray, which is simply that we cannot help praying. It seems probable that, in spite of all that 'science' may do to the contrary, men will continue to pray to the end of time, unless their mental nature changes in a manner which nothing we know should lead us to expect" *Principles of Psychology*, GB 53: 203.

89. Otto, *Idea of the Holy*, 176.

90. J. Wach, *Introduction to the History of Religions*, ed. Joseph Kitagawa and Gregory Alles (New York: Macmillan, 1988), xxiii.

91. Eliade, *History*, I: xiii, 5, 19; Eliade, *Quest*, i.

92. M. Eliade, *Rites and Symbols of Initiation* (New York: Harper and Row, 1965), 100–101.

93. Eliade, *History*, I: 19.

94. M. Eliade, *Patterns in Comparative Religion* (Cleveland and New York: The World Publishing Co., 1967), 463.

Chapter Two

The Soul's Prehistory

To argue that the religious disposition is a unique and autonomous element in the structure of human consciousness is not to say that it is altogether beyond the influence of evolutionary and historical forces. Both Otto and Eliade themselves readily admitted that a variety of social, economic, and geographic factors have affected the way *homo religiosus* has viewed and reacted to reality.[1] Before taking notice in a subsequent chapter of their views in that regard, however, some consideration will need to be given to what Karl Rahner has called the soul's "pre-history."[2] For even if we agree with Otto and Eliade that the roots of religion lie hidden in the "*fundus animae*"[3] or with traditional Christian theology that the soul is in some sense the creation of God,[4] we are still left with the possibility of the human body having undergone evolution toward its proper disposition for truly religious behavior.[5]

How significant the body's development is seen to be for the creation of the soul itself depends to some extent upon how the soul is conceived. Richard Swinburne and other modern thinkers, like John C. Eccles,[6] have argued that even in dualistic conceptions such as their own, or Descartes',[7] there is still room to take seriously the body's evolution toward consciousness. Thus, even while claiming that the soul, as an essential, substantial part of the human person, is independent of what is only contingent to the latter, namely, the body,[8] and denying from a Creationist perspective that the human soul "develops naturally from the genetic material" (as some Traducianists claim),[9] Swinburne still acknowledges the significance of the body's evolution for "structuring" of the soul in such wise as to allow for the pursuit of long-term goals.[10] In a strictly Platonic or Neoplatonic (e.g., Bergsonian)[11] interpretation, however, the human soul is viewed as a pre-existent fragment of some universal cosmic soul that has "fallen" into alien matter.[12] Within such a negative context, the body's own history can only serve to remind the "materially individuated"[13] soul of how far it has sunk, or how high it must climb to regain its pristine, pure spirituality. To achieve a more positive appreciation of the intrinsic significance of the body's evolution for creation of the soul itself, therefore, it will be necessary, Rahner and other modern Christian thinkers have argued,[14] to move away from any Platonic-Cartesian dualism toward a Judaeo-Christian conception of the human soul as a vital principle,[15] or, in other words, as a "principle of humanity, which brings material, spatial-temporal being to its own perfection, allows it to determine itself, and thus to rise above the mere determinatedness proper to material being."[16] Viewed in such wise as the substantial principles of the "whole man," Rahner notes, the soul and the body are seen to "stand in reciprocal relationship," and it becomes clear that "the history of the body is the pre-history of the soul, even though the soul has an immediate and transcendental relation of origin to God."[17] An authentically Christian interpretation of the "immediate creation of the soul" will, in fact, Rahner argues, play up the "history of the body," to the extent that God will be seen to have created in and through the natural process of "becoming" itself, rather than by way of some special act of intervention.[18] This does not mean for Rahner that man is merely a product of nature that differs only by degree from the brutes.[19] Like Teilhard de Chardin,[20] Rahner insisted that any real "becoming" must involve a "qualitative leap" from the old to the new; it cannot consist of a mere re-organization or duplication of already existing elements; it must involve "something more" — i.e., an increase in "being."[21] But again like Teilhard,[22] Rahner will claim that "matter" is not altogether "passive" in this regard.[23]

Although "negative" by virtue of the spatial-temporal "limits" it sets, matter also has its "positive" side, namely, its "being."[24] Animate and sensitive matter especially "has an intrinsic affinity to consciousness, immanence, and spirit."[25] While, therefore, the material creature, as a "solidified" but "limited" spirit, can never strip itself of its negativity and on its own leap beyond itself into the "noosphere," it does have the potential of co-operating in its "liberation."[26] It can play an "active" role in its becoming. Under the influence of its intimate, yet distant, relation to absolute Being (established by way of the latter's conservation and *concursus*) it can, as a secondary cause, transcend itself and give rise to "more 'reality' than itself is and possesses."[27] On the assumption, then, that ontogeny does to some extent recapitulate phylogeny,[28] and the further medieval assumption that "the spiritual soul only comes into existence at a later stage in the growth of the embryo, [with] several pre-human stages [lying] between the fertilized ovum and the organism animated by a spiritual soul," the origin of the human soul may, Rahner concluded, be compared to the creation of the individual soul: "In both cases a not yet human biological organism develops towards a condition in which the coming into existence of a spiritual soul has its sufficient biological substratum."[29]

It will not do, therefore, for religionists simply to assume that the human soul, with all its structures, was created by God out of nothing. If the origin of religion is to be properly understood, the pre-history of the religious category will also need to be investigated. We will need to ask, in other words, how it came about that human beings were endowed by birth with a capacity or predisposition for mythological interpretation of reality, in the context of which the performance of rites (worship, sacrifice, prayer, etc.) could, along with related moral behavior, offer some hope of survival in the long run.

We can best begin such an investigation by recalling that among the earliest expressions of the religious category was the ceremonial burial of the dead by *Neanderthal* Man some 100,000 years ago. Such burial practices were uniquely human.[30] To be sure, death is "normal and innate in most organisms."[31] But not all conscious organisms have an awareness of their mortality. The eating of cadavers by termites, for example, or the removal of dead members from their nests by ants, bees, and other colonial insects, represent "instinctive sanitation measures," but bear "no resemblance to the living practicing burial rites for dead members of their own species."[32] Nor does the protracted carrying of their deceased infants by female apes and monkeys.[33] It would make no sense, therefore, to try to find some "ancestral model"[34] of human burial customs among the lower animals, or to suggest that the *Neanderthals* were somehow genetically determined to behave in such a specific manner. Whether death-awareness was universal at the *Neanderthal* time level is not known.[35] But even if it had been, this would not in itself require us to think, Dobzhansky argues, that the early burial rites were "due to a special instinct or to an inborn drive," or that the "death-awareness" of the early humans was a "primary, irreducible, or unitary genetic or psychological entity."[36] For death-awareness, he says, seems to be of little immediate adaptive value. Its dawning during the Middle Paleolithic period may have contributed significantly to the arousal of "ultimate concern," and left the first humans with such metaphysical and religious inklings of infinite Being as might have enhanced their chances of final salvation.[37] As far as immediate survival was concerned, however, it may even have been detrimental, and to that extent might better be described as a "curse," or as the "bitter fruit of man's having risen to the level of consciousness and functioning ego."[38]   Still, the self-awareness of which death-awareness is said to be an "integral part" is, according to Dobzhansky and other biologists, of "primary adaptive significance" in that "it serves to organize and to integrate man's physical and mental capacities by means of which man controls his environment."[39]   And although such "self-awareness" may also lack a "special gene," its component parts, namely, "symbolic thinking, communication, symbolic language, intelligence, and reasoning," were no doubt "conditioned" by the "whole of the human genetic endowment."[40]   That death-awareness and its expression in burial ceremonies was an "evolutionary novelty" that set *homo sapiens sapiens* and successive generations of human beings apart from the brutes,[41] does not mean, therefore, that the gap between the two is unbridgeable, or that "rudiments" of "components" of the "*humanum*" could not be found among the lower animals.[42]   A consideration of the ritualistic-mythological dimension of the aforementioned burial customs, or of other early religio-magical activities, like the trance-producing shamanistic dances, will show the contrary.

In that regard, notice might first of all be taken of what has been viewed by some as an "anticipation" of religious ritual or religious sensitivity in general among lower animals. Darwin himself thought, for example, that he had found several such patterns in the fierce growling and barking of his dog at a parasol blowing in the wind, and in the devotion of any dog to its master. The former, he said, was not unlike the religious phenomenon of animism in which inexplicable movement gives rise to the suspicion of the presence of some strange living agent.[43] The latter, Darwin noted, may be compared to man's devotion to God, in that the "love, complete submission to an exalted and mysterious superior, a strong sense of dependence, fear, reverence, gratitude, and hope for the future" that accompanies man's religious devotion, is not unlike the "complete submission . . . fear, and other feelings" that are associated with a dog's devotion to its master.[44]   Darwin was neither the first nor the last to compare canine loyalties to religious devotion.   Both Francis Bacon and Robert Burns had done so earlier[45] and not long after Darwin, Friedrich von Huegel would do so too.[46]   More recently, Alister Hardy devoted a whole chapter of his book, *The Biology of God*, to the "parallel" between "Dog and man: man and God."[47]   Following the lead of Carveth Read and Konrad Lorenz, Hardy concluded that "the behavioral relation of the dog to man is not just an illustrative analogy" of man's relation to God.[48]   Rather, "it is a clear demonstration that the same biological factors, resulting from the same kind of social development (that of the [hunting] pack), have become involved in the formation of man's images of God."[49] With Lorenz, Hardy argued that the dog becomes attached to man first by transferring the submissive attachment every wild dog feels toward its pack-leader to a human being, and secondly, through a neotenous process of preserving a puppy's instinctive love of its mother and transforming it into a love for the human master.[50]   "This is not altogether unlike the almost sudden 'conversion' that occurs in the religious life of many human adolescents," Hardy noted, before going on to say that "the faithfulness, love, and devotion of a dog for his master or mistress shows us . . . the same elements that make up the essentials of man's attitude to his personal God."[51]   "I am not trying to suggest," Hardy added, "that there is any direct relationship between dogs and man in any genetic evolutionary sense; they are members of two quite different orders of mammals whose distinct ancestral stocks go back at least to the beginning of the Paleocene period of nearly a hundred million years ago."[52] "What I am suggesting," he concluded, "is that the principles operating in these two widely separated species are in fact the same biological principles; and they are the same just because primitive man, the hunting hominid, is closer in social behavior to the hunting dog than he is to any other member of the animal kingdom," and "the emotions that had developed originally as part of the hunting-pack system" came to be directed toward something that was "quite new in the course of evolution," namely, the conception of a mysterious, divine dimension of reality.[53]

Other comparisons of this sort, illustrating the anticipation of religious sensitivity among animals, have been common. The Cambridge Platonist, Henry More, for example, observed that "at the sight of the sun or moon," apes and elephants displayed a "strange sense or impress," and their subsequent behavior indicated that these animals experienced "Love, Fear and Wonderment, near to that Passion which in us is called Veneration."[54] More recently, Wolfgang Kohler suggested that religious "emotions" are to be found among the great apes,[55] and Alfred North Whitehead claimed that the collective rituals and emotions of primitive tribes have their roots in the "individual habits" and "collective evolutions" of animals, such as the "flock of birds [that] perform their ritual evolutions in the sky."[56] B. F. Skinner, W. H. Morse, and Arthur J. Bachrach have all commented on the tendency of pigeons and other birds to engage in "superstitious" (i.e., "prayerful" and "propitiatory") rituals.[57] Adolf Portmann has called attention to the "symbolic actions" (e.g., infantile begging) incorporated by some birds in their mating rites.[58] And others have highlighted the social coordination and other patterns of ritualistic behavior among insects, felines, and nonhuman primates (e.g. the chimpanzee "rain dance").[59] Roy A. Rappaport has suggested that the "numinous" feelings of dependence, surrender, and love, whose ontogenetic base Erik Erikson has located in the "earliest ritualized (stereotyped, repetitive, periodic) interactions of a mother with her infant,"[60] may in fact "have not only [been] present in infants before they acquire language, but may have been present among the ancestors of men before language or a concept of the sacred evolved."[61]

To conclude from such comparisons, as some of the aforementioned thinkers might have had in mind, that animals actually engage in specifically religio-magical behavior, or that some "ancestral model" of religio-magical ritual could be found among animals, would make little sense.[62] Nor, therefore, would it make any sense to conclude therefrom that religion in general is "nothing but an archaic primate, or mammalian, or vertebrate, behavioral characteristic which survives in man by virtue of some evolutionary lag,"[63] or that religious rituals in particular are "nothing more than elablorate versions" of animal rituals.[64] As Karl Popper insisted, "an emergent form, although having evolved from a previous, less complex, form, cannot be reduced to the previous form from which it has emerged."[65] What such comparisons do allow us to conclude, however, is that ritual, defined as either solitary or social behavior of a repetitive, formalized sort, undertaken for the sake of arousing performance, reducing anxiety, or establishing relationships, has evolved as a form of behavior common to both animals and humans.[66] To that extent, it may be said that although the specific patterns of religious ritual displayed by the first humans (e.g., ceremonial burials, shamanistic dances, etc.) were not genetically determined, their capacity for or predisposition toward ritualistic behavior in general certainly was a product of biological evolution and genetic conditioning.[67] Furthermore, although those elements of religious ritual that make the latter specifically human may derive "from other neurobiological systems that had selective advantages totally separate from those of ritual behavior," and "appear to have been, as it were, grafted on the mainstream of the evolution of ritual behavior,"[68] they were nonetheless themselves already in evidence, in a rudimentary way, in the ritualistic activity of lower animals.

"What seems to differentiate human and animal ritual," Wallace notes, "is the self-consciousness of ritual action in man."[69] "As technology improved, and as causal connections were considered," he adds, "ritual required rationalization in order to inspire confidence." The "rationale" was found in the "idea of the soul and, by extension, of other supernatural beings."[70] The generalized form of ritual behavior became "invested with such characteristically and peculiarly human aspects of religion as a mythology and a pantheon of gods."[71] In other words, ritual became embedded in mythology, or, as Clifford Geertz has put it, in a "cognitive matrix" or "web of meaning."[72] As "sacred history," mythology organized the world in terms of its origin in the primordial activity of the gods,[73] thereby creating for humans what animals did not have, namely, a "totalistic" frame of reference in the context of which "problematic antinomies" or the "dyadic poles" of reality (e.g., god/man, heaven/hell, sky/earth, etc.) could be "metaphorically mapped" or "conceptualized,"[74] and the rite itself could be "rationalized" as the resolution of such polarities to the extent of affording the participants in the ritual an ecstatic experience of union with each other and the gods.[75] Suffering, or other environmental limitations, which animals could only have "passively endured," religious man could now, Bellah notes, "transcend and dominate."[76]

By thus being referred to "beliefs in mystical beings or powers," and elaborated linguistically along symbolic and conceptual lines, the aforementioned animal rituals were radically modified and adjusted to new needs of a specifically religious sort.[77] This could not have happened, however, without dramatic adaptation. For a capacity to mythologize "involves at least three critical higher cortical functions: conceptualization, abstract causal thinking, and antinomous thinking."[78] Furthermore, "although myth structure and ritual are theoretically not completely dependent on verbal language," d'Aquili and Laughlin note that it is "unlikely that any elaborated myths developed in the absence of spoken language."[79] The adaptive evolution of these basic components of self-awareness (i.e., symbolic thinking, communication, symbolic language, intelligence, and reasoning) in rudimentary manner among the lower animals may, with divine *concursus,* have been "sufficient" to account for the origin of the *humanum* in general, or religion in particular. But even if one must posit some kind of special divine intervention to explain the novelty of the religious phenomenon,[80] the adaptive evolution of the components of self-awareness will still need to be viewed as a necessary condition — as a condition, in other words, in the absence of which the phenomenon could not have occurred. To fully appreciate the "pre-history" of the religious category, therefore, it will be necessary also to take into serious account the evolution of the central nervous system,[81] and specifically the evolution of the tripartite brain (reptilian midbrain, mammalian limbic lobe, and the neocortex)[82] and the division of the brain into two hemispheres, the left with its analytical, structuring capacity, and the right with its disposition toward metaphorical, symbolic, holistic images.[83]

Victor Turner's work sets a good example in this regard. With his understanding of religious ritual as social drama, in which participants are given information about their place in the cosmos and provided opportunities to experience transcendence,[84] Turner came to see a link between his own studies of religious ritual in terms of "structure" and "antistructure" (e.g., *communitas* and liminality)[85] and the extensive work being done by neurobiologists on the evolution of the brain. After having long assumed that ritual was exclusively the result of social conditioning, he came to conclude that religion in general enjoyed a "genetic foundation"[86] and that religious ritual in particular was to some extent also the product of genetic inheritance.[87] Without trying to "reduce ritual to cerebral neurology (as if ritual is nothing but the structure and functioning of the brain writ large),"[88] he tried to show how it is through the interplay of all the brain's parts (left and right, upper and lower)[89] that religious ritual gives rise to the trance, or "flash" where the poles of structure and antistructure are resolved,[90] and new, "prophetic" revelations are brought to light.[91]

The evolution of self-awareness underlying the origin of religious ritual no doubt contributed also to the origination of a moral sense, which, by any definition of religion,[92] and especially the Kantian one entertained by Darwin,[93] must in turn be considered a precondition of the religious category. For, as Darwin himself noted, "no being could experience so complex an emotion [as] religious devotion" without having "advanced in his intellectual and moral faculties to at least a moderately high level."[94]

There is, of course, a sense in which religious ritual and morality are identical — in the sense, namely, as spelled out by Eliade, that ritual is nothing more than an attempt on the part of *homo religiosus* to do again what is known through mythology to have been the primordial activity of the gods.[95] And to the extent that such a radical embrace of "tradition" might imply a totally "blind" obedience, little room would seem to be left for the kind of foresight, choice, and responsibility that one normally associates with morality,[96] and the development of respect for authority would hardly differ from the process of imprinting that occurs among ducks and geese, and other subhuman animals.[97] It was on that account probably that nineteenth century evolutionists were inclined to conceive of the origin of the moral sense in the same way they had talked about the origin of religion, namely in epigenetic terms of a gradual development from a "savage," through an intermediate "barbarian" stage, to one more akin to our own "civilized" ethical disposition.[98] The same suspicion may have prompted the more recent attempt by Julian Jaynes to deny "consciousness" to early *homo religiosus* altogether, and to conclude that the latter was driven to do what he did by the god-like, hallucinatory "voices" originating from the right side of his then "bicameral mind."[99] But if, as claimed in our earlier discussion, ritual is primarily a "mental activity" generated by conscious reflection upon the "meaning" of the cosmos, and one in which participants are free to engage themselves or not and make the "standard" of their lives, there is no reason why a sense of morality could not also be considered compatible with the religious *a priori*. To conclude our survey of the prehistory of the soul, therefore, it will be necessary to take some notice also of the evolution of the human predisposition toward ethical behavior. Some naturalists and ethologists have suggested that the rudiments of a moral sense can be found among subhuman animals, by calling attention to the way dogs and pigs seem to have guilt feelings and bad consciences on occasion,[100] to the apparently compassionate behavior sometimes displayed by dolphins and elephants toward injured companions,[101] or to the seemingly self-sacrificing, altruistic behavior of ants, termites, and other social insects.[102] It was Darwin himself who pressed this line of thought most vigorously, using it to explain how human beings developed a sense of morality. In response to Kant's question ("Whence thy original?") about the origin of the sense of duty, Darwin identified four stages in the development of conscience. The last three (i.e., guilt, concern for the common good, and virtue),[103] he said, can be traced back to the "social instincts" that "lead an animal to take pleasure in the society of its fellows, to feel a certain amount of sympathy with them, and to perform various services for them."[104] Against the "sensationalist" views of Adam Smith and Alexander Bain, Darwin insisted that such feelings of sympathy on the animal's part were "instinctive, not learned associations."[105] And against objections from A. R. Wallace, St. George Mivart, and others to the effect that because altruistic behavior would favor the unfit and have no real adaptive value for the individual,[106] it could not be accounted for on Darwinian principles alone, Darwin came up with the notion of "community selection," according to which "natural selection sometimes acts on the individual, through the preservation of variations which are beneficial to the community."[107] "Under the aegis of community selection," Darwin then went on, according to Richards, to conclude that "men in social groups evolved sets of instinctive responses to preserve the welfare of the community."[108]

Closely resembling Darwin's views in this regard is the sociobiological theory on the origin of morality propounded in recent years by Edward O. Wilson,[109] and Robert J. Richards' "revised version" of them both.[110] After demonstrating that altruistic behavior in animals gradually evolved through natural selection into certain "epigenetic rules," Wilson concluded that through the

process of kin and community selection, the "disposition"
to help next of kin without hope of return, as well as the
"disposition" to assist nonrelatives with the expectation of
an eventual reciprocation, have become genetically inbred
in the human species also.[111] Like Ralph Burhoe, who has
argued that by inclining humans to break away from the
genetic selfishness of the primates, religion became the
"missing link" between ape and man,[112] Wilson will
occasionally identify religion as "above all the process by
which individuals are persuaded to subordinate their
immediate self-interests to the interests of the group."[113]
Richards' "revised version" of this evolutionary ethics
insists upon the superiority of "authentic altruism" over
the "reciprocal, contract altruism" favored by Wilson and
his supporters,[114] but it also asserts with Darwin and
Wilson that in the human species there has evolved "a set
of innate dispositions that in appropriate circumstances
move the individual to act in specific ways for the good
of the community."[115]

Some have challenged such a line of thought on
grounds that the "altruistic" behavior displayed by
animals, lacking as it does any "intentionality," is not the
same as human altruism.[116] However "altruistic" animal
behavior may seem, it is not, they say, really "moral," and
cannot, therefore, constitute a "bridge" to human
morality.[117] Eccles has made the same point more
concretely, by noting that the affectionate behavior of
domesticated animals is probably due to "immitation and
instruction," and that chimpanzees, lions, and other
animals in the wild actually "display no trace of
compassion."[118] The "earliest known signs of altruism," or
the "first evidence for compassionate behavior," he notes,
are to be found in the skeletons of two *Neanderthal* men
who apparently were kept alive for up to two years after
being incapacitated by severe injuries, and in floral
tributes accompanying burials at about the same time,

namely, c. 60,000 years ago.[119]   Such a decisive
evolutionary step away from the typically indifferent and
ruthlessly aggressive behavior of other animals, he
concludes, could have occurred only with the growth of
"self-consciousness" and an "enriched linguistic
communication" such as would make co-operation
between individuals possible.[120] G. S. Simpson argues
similarly that because subhuman animals lack freedom of
choice and a capacity to predict the results of their
actions, "it is nonsensical to speak of ethics in connection
with any animal other than man."[121]   On grounds that
"the capacity to know and to foresee the consequences of
one's own and of other people's actions" (as illustrated
"poetically" in the biblical account of man's coming to
"know good and evil") is "the fundamental biological
precondition for becoming an ethicizing being,"
Dobzhansky also concluded that it makes no sense "to
ascribe ethics to animals other than man."[122]

In this regard, however, it should be noted that
neither Darwin nor most other advocates of evolutionary
ethics had in mind to suggest that animals are actually
"ethical beings." The animal instinct of sympathy would
never have evolved into a moral sense, Darwin readily
admitted, except for the evolution of an intellect
"sufficient to recall instances when social instincts went
unsatisfied because of the intrusion of momentarily
stronger urges," the acquisition of language whereby
individuals in a group could be sensitized to mutual
needs and be able to "codify principles of their behavior,"
and finally the cultivation of "habits" by which altruistic
behavior would become second nature.[123] "Any animal
whatever," Darwin argued, "endowed with well-marked
social instincts, would inevitably acquire a moral sense or
conscience, as soon as its intellectual powers had become
as well developed, or nearly as well developed, as in
man."[124] But until such intelligence had actually been

acquired, the animal could not be regarded as a moral being. To enjoy real moral stature, in other words, the creature needs something more than a social instinct; it must also enjoy an "ability to reflect on its behavior, and so to reestablish a suppressed social instinct," or be capable of "comparing past and future actions or motives, and of approving or disapproving of them."[125] In his revised version of evolutionary ethics Richards draws a similar conclusion. "Though animals may act from altruistic motives," he writes, "they can neither form the intention of doing so, nor can they justify their behavior in terms of its motive. Hence they are not moral creatures."[126] As Otto had noted, therefore, human morality cannot be viewed as merely an epigenetic outgrowth of animal behavior.[127]

Denying an ethical character to animal behavior does not, however, preclude the possibility of finding in certain patterns of such behavior a basis for the evolution of human morality. Thus, after having denied that it makes any sense "to ascribe ethics to animals other than man," Dobzhansky will go on to note that "one may say without contradiction that certain kinds of behavior found in animals would be ethical or altruistic [e.g.,"the behavior of workers and soldiers among ants and termites"], and others unethical and egotistic [e.g., "the exclusion of many males of red grouse from feeding grounds by the more successful males"], if these behaviors were exhibited by men." Since such patterns of behavior are "shaped by natural selection in the evolutionary process," it is not inconceivable, he continues, "that man could have some behavior patterns and proclivities built into his genetic constitution during his evolution."[128] "Family ethics," involving "attitudes and evaluations" (e.g., maternal self-sacrifice) that "are consistent with the demands of natural selection acting on the individual level," as opposed to "group (or species) ethics," which are "products of cultural evolution" and "confer no advantage . . . to individuals who practice them," are of that sort.[129] "They are shared by man with at least some animals," and "they usually are genetically conditioned dispositions," and as such "can be envisaged as products of natural selection which promoted the genetic bases of these ethics in our ancestors as well as in other animal species."[130] This is not far, it seems to me, from what Darwin, Wilson, Richards, and other advocates of evolutionary ethics had in mind.

There are, of course, many other objections that can and have been raised against even such an interpretation of the origin of human morality. Some, like Stephen Jay Gould, have argued that there is "no direct evidence whatever . . . for genetic control of specific human social behavior."[131] Rejecting any kind of raw "environmentalism" such as would render human behavior altogether the product of "learning," Gould would nonetheless pit his own "concept of biological potentiality, with a brain capable of the full range of human behaviors and predisposed toward none," against Wilson's "idea of biological determinism, with specific genes for specific behavioral traits."[132] Wilson has responded to such objections by granting that "nongenetic learning" enjoys some role in human behavior,[133] and adding that "to postulate the existence of genes for the diagnostic human traits is not to imply that there exists one gene for spite, another for homosexuality, and so on, as one might envision the inheritance of flower color or seed texture in garden peas. The tendency to develop such behaviors, in a distinctively human form, is part of an immensely complex social repertory which is undoubtedly dependent on large numbers of genes."[134] C. H. Waddington and Dobzhansky have emphasized the same point. It is the "capacity to become an 'authority acceptor' and an 'ethicizing being,'" and "not the contents of the ethical tenets," that are established genetically as "a biological adaptation."[135] It would be futile, Dobzhansky notes, "to look for special genes for ethics or for values."[136] "The evolutionary process has not provided man with set ethical principles and values," or with a specific kind of Freudian superego.[137] What it has equipped humans with is a "capacity to acquire ethics and values," or an "inclination to absorb such principles from . . . parents, relatives, and other carriers of authority."[138] Dobzhansky adds that when understood in such a way, evolutionary ethics need not preclude environmental influences or freedom of choice. Genetic endowments, he says, may "condition one's behavior" and "bias one's choices," they "do not amount to rigid determination."[139] "They can be overcome by the exercise of man's will,"[140] and their "manifestation . . . depends on the social, economic, and educational environment in which [their] carrier is placed."[141] Richards concurs. "Though evolutionary processes may have resulted in sets of instinctual urges (e.g., to nurture children, to alleviate obvious distress, etc.) that promote the welfare of the community, is this not," he asks, "a goal at which careful ethical deliberation might also arrive?"[142] Furthermore, he adds, "an evolutionary account of why men generally act for the community good does not invalidate a logically autonomous argument that concludes this same standard is the ultimate moral standard." Nor does it eliminate the need for "rational deliberation" on how to apply the standard of community good intelligently.[143] In other words, an evolutionary ethics, at least in his own revised version, "will be informed by an evolving intelligence and cultural tradition."[144] In an especially poignant passage, Richards spells out what this can mean:

> Nature demands we protect our brother and sister, but we must learn who they are.

During human history, evolving cultural traditions may translate "commuity member" as "red Sioux," "black Mau Mau," or "white Englishman," and the "community good" as "sacrificing to the gods," "killing usurping colonials," or constructing factories. But as men become wiser and old fears and superstitions fade, they may come to see their brothers and sisters in every human being and to discover what really does foster the good of all people.[145]

In the final analysis, therefore, Richards concludes, "the evolutionary perspective indicates that external forces do not conspire to wrench moral acts from a person. Rather, man is ineluctably a moral being. Aristotle believed that men were by nature moral creatures. Darwin demonstrated it."[146]

To sum the chapter up: The religious category of the human soul may be said to have had a prehistory. This should not be taken to mean, however, that the burial, shamanistic, and other religious rites performed by human beings from the beginning of time differ only in degree from analogous patterns of behavior that had become fixed genetically among the lower animals and transmitted to man in the processs of biological evolution. The difference is rather one of kind. Resting upon an awareness of self and freedom that lower animals lack, religion is uniquely human, and cannot be reduced to a mere elaboration of animal behavior. As such, it must be recognized as something radically new in the evolutionary process, involving a break, or leap, that could only have occurred through a divine *concursus*. But "creation" of the soul and its structures (e.g.the religious category) need not be thought of as having been "out of nothing," or through some special act of divine intervention. The "rudiments" of religion — e.g., a capacity for ritualistic behavior, symbolic thought and talk, mystical union, altruism, dread, devotion, etc. — were already abuilding among the lower species, especially through the evolution of an ever more complex central nervous system. As "blind," or subject to the interplay of chance and necessity, as such a prehistory of the soul may have been, it may also, on the assumption of the reciprocal relationship of body and soul, have been "oriented" toward religion from the start, and transcended itself without any special intervention by God. What triggered the final leap in this process, and simultaneously gave expression to the new, religious way of being, may well have been the awareness of death.

Notes

1. See Infra, Chapter Five.

2. K. Rahner, *Hominisation: The Evolutionary Origin of Man as a Theological Problem* (New York: Herder and Herder, 1965), 63, 112 n.10.

3. R. Otto, *The Idea of the Holy*, 112; Eliade, *History*, xiii.

4. For a discussion of Creationist, Traducianist, Generationist, and other theories about the creation of the soul, see: *NCE* 4: 428; 14: 230; 5: 684; *ER* 13: 457, 470-71; Rahner, *Hominisation*, 93-109; R. Swinburne, *The Evolution of the Soul* (Oxford: Clarendon Press, 1986), 198-99.

5. See Raymond Nogar, "Evolution, Human," in *NCE*, 5: 684.

6. While concluding that only "a supernatural spiritual creation" can explain the origin of "unique self-conscious beings" (John C. Eccles, *Evolution of the Brain: Creation of the Self* [London and New York: Routledge, 1989], 235-38; John C. Eccles, *The Human Psyche* [Berlin: Springer International, 1980], 235-41), Eccles has devoted most of his work to explaining how "hominid evolution was uniquely dependent on the primate ancestry providing a superbly developed nervous system" (*Evolution of the Brain*, 217). "An appealing analogy," he says, "is to regard the body and brain as a superb computer built by genetic coding, which has been created by the wonderful process of biological evolution," and to regard the mysteriously originated Soul or Self as "the programmer of the computer" (Ibid., 238). See also Eccles's Gifford Lectures of 1977-78, especially Lecture 6 (J. C. Eccles, *The Human Mystery* [Berlin, Heidelberg, New York: Springer International, 1979], 98-122).

7. Swinburne notes that "there are passages in Descartes which can be interpreted as saying that the body is no part of the person and other passages which can be interpreted as saying that the body is a part, but not an essential

part, of the person (*Evolution*, 146 n.1.). For an expression of Swinburne's own dualism, see Ibid., 145-47.

8. Ibid., 145-47.

9. See Ibid., 199.

10. Ibid., 296-97. As noted elsewhere, Swinburne disagrees with Descartes's view that animals were "unconscious automata" (*Evolution*, 183), and sides with medieval thinkers who argued that animals do have "animal or sensitive souls" (Ibid.). He doubts that the brainless, reflex, stereotypical behavior of the invertebrates (crabs, spiders, ants, etc.) provide any evidence of mental life (Ibid., 181). But as the brain evolved and animals gradually became "conscious," first through the experience of pain and other sensations, and finally through the formulation of "beliefs," their "mental lives" became increasingly similar to that of humans (Ibid., 181-82). The human soul can to that extent be said to have its roots in the animal soul, and Swinburne will see the teleological thrust of human religious behavior as developing out of the capacity to formulate beliefs and to perform intentional actions which evolution gradually and mysteriously has afforded to animals (Ibid., 182, 193). He will also insist, however, that medieval thinkers were right in ascribing to humans a rational or intellectual soul, or, in other words, a "special kind of soul," with "mental capacities which went beyond those of animals" (Ibid., 183). Thus, in regard to the pursuit of goals, Swinburne will argue that for all their similarity, animal and human patterns of teleological behavior differ radically (Ibid. 296-97). The "major difference," he says, is that even the higher animals "do not have a structured language" (Ibid., 181, 203ff), with the result that "there are beliefs and thoughts, purposes and desires, which we have and they cannot have" (Ibid., 181). "What seems to have happened in the course of evolution," Swinburne notes, is that when genetic changes gave to animals beliefs and desires, they were beliefs about how to attain fairly immediate goals and desires for those goals (Ibid., 296). But then something new happened. The soul passed from being passive to being "active" and "structured by causally influential beliefs and desires" of a more "sophisticated sort" (Ibid. 297). "Gradually our ancestors began to have more sophisticated beliefs and desires which came to form a structure, so that the causal efficacy of beliefs and desires now included causing other beliefs and desires" (Ibid., 296-97). This gave the organism the "ability to plan" and the "purpose to pursue plans over a continued period of time" (Ibid., 297).

11. Claude Tresmontant has argued that while the great evolutionist thinker, Henri Bergson, had a much more positive appreciation of "creation" than did the Greeks of old, he nonetheless shared some of the dualistic proclivities of Plotinus, especially to the extent that he conceives of the "embodiment" of the soul as a negative "movement of inversion," whereby "the current (of life) passes through human generations, subdividing itself into individuals" (C. Tresmontant, *A Study of Hebrew Thought* [New York: Desclee, 1960], 96; see also: 10-15, and Appendix I: "The Neo-Platonism of Bergson," 159-67). For the context of Bergson's comments in this regard, see H. Bergson, *Creative Evolution* (New York: The Modern Library, 1944), 293-95.

12. See Tresmontant, *Hebrew Thought*, 6, 87-90, 95, 162; Friedrich Solmsen, "Plato and the Concept of the Soul (Psyche): Some Historical Perspectives," *Journal of the History of Ideas* 44 (July-September, 1983): 355-67; Jan Bremmer, "Soul, Greek and Hellenistic Concepts of," *ER* 13:434-38; Harrison, *Religion*, 44, 134.

13. See Tresmontant, *Hebrew Thought*, 161-63.

14. For an introduction to modern philosophical/theological interpretations of the soul, see *NCE* 13: 458-59, 462-64.

15. The Hebrew word for "soul", *nefesh*, etymologically means "breath," and like its New Testament Greek equivalent, *psyche*, came to signify the inner, animating element of life, life itself, the whole man, the concrete existing self — and never just a part of man. The closely related Hebrew and Greek words for "spirit," *Ruah* and *Pneuma*, also refer to "breath," and the life-principle, but are generally used to designate a creative, life-giving force that comes from God and lifts man out of the "flesh" (i.e., the natural order) into a "supernatural" realm of being. See Tresmontant, *Hebrew Thought*, 87-114; John L. McKenzie, *Dictionary of the Bible* (New York: Bruce, 1965), 836-39, 840-45; *ER* 13: 450-60; *NCE* 13: 449-50, 467, 570-72; Robert North, *Teilhard and the Creation of the Soul* (Milwaukee: Bruce, 1966), 163-203.

16. Karl Rahner and Herbert Vorgrimler, *Theological Dictionary* (New York: Herder and Herder, 1965), 443; Rahner, "Natural Science and Reasonable Faith," *Theological Investigations* (New York: Crossroad, 1988) XXI: 42.

17. Rahner, *Hominisation*, 112 n.10.

18. See Ibid., 93-109; Karl Rahner, "Evolution: Theological," *SM* 2: 290-93; Karl Rahner, "Hominisation," in *SM*, 2: 294-97.

19. See Rahner, *Hominisation*, 106; Rahner, "Natural Science and Reasonable Faith," 42-43.

20. According to Teilhard, the process of evolution is marked by "critical thresholds" or points "at which continuous injection of energy produces alteration of entirely discontinuous character," or, in other words, stages "where purely quantified additions produce of themselves a qualitative alteration" (See P. de Chardin, *The Phenomenon of Man* [New York: Harper and Brothers, 1959], 164-89; also: 78, 88, 230; North, *Teilhard* 12, 44, 100.

21. Rahner, *Hominisation* 75, 87, 91-92; Rahner, "Hominisation," 294. It is precisely within this context that Rahner will accept and build upon what natural science says about evolution as a process of change from the simple to the more complex (See "Natural Science and Reasonable Faith," 38-39).

22. According to Teilhard, every particle of matter possesses an "inner face" of dynamic spiritual energy, "a tiny within," which tends toward climactic complexity in human consciousness (Teilhard, *Phenomenon of Man*, 53-66; North, *Teilhard*, 10-34).

23. Rahner, "Evolution: Theological," 290; Rahner, *Hominisation*, 296. Rahner notes elsewhere in this regard that "materiality must be understood as the lowest stage of . . . spirit (even when this may perhaps be irrelevant to the pure natural scientist). Otherwise materiality cannot be conceived as originating from an absolute spirit, since this spirit cannot create something that is absolutely disparate from itself" ("Natural Science and Reasonable

Faith," 34–35).

24. Rahner, *Hominisation*, 57.

25. Ibid., 296.   Rahner's position here rests ultimately on his metaphysical assumption that "being intrinsically is knowing and being known, that being is being-present-to-itself" (Rahner, *Hearers of the Word* [New York: Herder and Herder, 1969], 42; K. Rahner, *Spirit in the World* [New York: Herder and Herder, 1968], 67-77). With Thomas, therefore, he concludes that "a thing which is, 'has' being in the measure in which it posseses the possibility of . . . a *reditio in seipsum* ["returning to itself"] (*Hearers*, 43). To guard against a pantheistic interpretation of such a metaphysical proposition, however, Rahner notes that "not everything which is, is a 'knowing' in the same sense and in the same measure" (Ibid., 50), and with Thomas he will locate all sub-human creatures at the lower end of the hierarchy of being precisely to the extent that they are not present-to-themselves because they are "limited to a particular sphere" and lack the "openness to being" or the "horizon of totality" whereby man discovers his own true nature (Ibid., 43, 49-50; see also "Natural Science and Reasonable Faith," 42-43; "The Unity of Spirit and Matter in the Christian Understanding of Faith," in *Theological Investigations* [London and New York: Darton, Longman and Todd, and Seabury Presses, 1974] VI: 153-77).

26. Rahner, *Hominisation*, 57.

27. Rahner, "Evolution: Theological," 290; Rahner, "Hominisation," 292, 294, 296; Rahner, *Hominisation*, esp. 75-76, 83, 88, 98-101; Rahner, "Natural Science and Reasonable Faith," 37, 39-41.   See also A. R.   Peacocke's comments about how the relation of the human mind to the human body provides a good analogy for "how a transcendent agent could be immanent in a physical process" (*Creation and the World of Science* [Oxford: Clarendon Press, 1979], 131-35).

28. Robert J. Richards has recently argued that Darwin himself subscribed to this principle, and its implication of progress (*The Meaning of Evolution* [Chicago and London: The University of Chicago Press, 1992], esp. 111-15, 165-80).

29. Rahner, *Hominisation*, 94.

30. See Theodosius Dobzhansky, *The Biology of Ultimate Concern* (New York: New American Library, 1969), 70-71.

31. See A. E. Emerson and R. W. Burhoe, "Evolutionary Aspects of Freedom, Death, and Dignity," *Zygon* 9, no. 2 (June, 1974): 168-71.

32. Dobzhansky, *Biology*, 70.

33. Ibid., 71.

34. See A. F. C. Wallace, *Religion: An Anthropological View* (New York: Random House, 1966), 217.

35. Dobzhansky, *Biology*, 76.

36. Ibid., 72, 76.

37. Ibid., 77.   One of man's special experiences of "transcendental reality," Rahner argues, occurs "when he is silently confronted with death and apparent nothingness" (Karl-Heinz Weger, *Karl Rahner: An Introduction to His Theology* [New York: Seabury Press, 1980], 49).   See also Paul Diel's comments on how the "concept of death [is] inseparably linked to the mystery of life,"

and contributed to the evolution of conscience (P. Diel, *The God Symbol: Its History and Its Significance* (San Francisco: Harper and Row, 1986), 51.

38. Dobzhansky, *Biology,* 69, 77.

39. Ibid., 69.

40. Ibid., 69, 72–73.

41. Ibid., 68.

42. Ibid., 58.

43. C. Darwin, *The Descent of Man,* in GB 49: 302–303.

44. Ibid., 303.

45. See Ibid.; A. Hardy, *The Biology of God* (London: Jonathan Cape, 1975), 154–55.

46. Von Huegel compares the obscure nature of the dog's awareness of its master to the obscurity of his own knowledge of God (Friedrich von Huegel, *Essays and Addresses on the Philosophy of Religion,* First Series [New York: E. P. Dutton and London: J. M. Dent and Sons, 1921], 102–103; as cited in John Hick, *Philosophy of Religion* [Englewood Cliffs, New Jersey: Prentice-Hall, 1983], 79).

47. Hardy, *Biology of God,* 154–78. Surprisingly, Hardy, an Oxford University Professor of Zoology, seemed unaware of Darwin's own use of this analogy in his *Descent of Man.*

48. Ibid., 170. On page 156, Hardy cites Read's *The Origin of Man and his Superstition* (Cambridge: Cambridge University Press, 1920); and on pages 164–78, Hardy cites Lorenz' *Man Meets Dog* (Harmondsworth: Penguin, 1988) and *King Solomon's Ring* (New York: Thomas Y. Crowell, 1961).

49. Hardy, *Biology of God,* 170.

50. Ibid., 168.

51. Ibid., 169.

52. Ibid., 170.

53. Ibid., 170–71.

54. As quoted in Harrison, *Religion,* 44–45. What More, and other Cambridge Platonists, like Joseph Glanvill and John Smith, who talked about "animal religion," had in mind to suggest was that "idolatry" could be attributed to "animal life," for "what the Apes and Elephants in Mauritania do, the same is done by the Idolaters of the East-Indies" (Ibid., 45.).

55. Wolfgang Kohler, *The Mentality of Apes,* as cited in Roy A. Rappaport, "The Sacred in Human Evolution," *Annual Review of Ecology and Systematics,* eds. Richard F. Johnston, Peter W. Frank, and Charles D. Michener (Palo Alto, Calif.: Annual Reviews, 1971), vol. 2: 31.

56. Alfred North Whitehead, *Religion in the Making* (New York: Macmillan, 1960), 20–21.

57. See B. F. Skinner, "Superstition in the Pigeon," Journal of *Experimental Psychology* 38 (1948): 168–72; B. F. Skinner and W. H. Morse, "A Second Type of 'Superstition' in the Pigeon," *American Journal of Psychology* 70 (1957): 308–11; Arthur J. Bachrach, "An Experimental Approach to Superstitious Behavior," *Journal of American Folklore* 75 (1962): 1–9; for discussion of same: Wallace, *Religion,* 220–21.

58. See Wallace, *Religion,* 222.

59. See Charles Laughlin, Jr., and John McManus, "Mammalian Ritual,"

in Eugene d'Aquili, *The Spectrum of Ritual* (New York: Columbia University Press, 1979), 86-107; D. T. Campbell, "The Conflict between Social and Biological Evolution and the Concept of Original Sin," *Zygon* 10, no. 3 (1975): 238, 242.

60. Erik H. Erikson, "The Development of Ritualization," in *The Religious Situation, 1968*, ed. Donald R. Cutler (Boston: Beacon Press, 1968), 713-15.

61. Rappaport, "Sacred in Human Evolution," 31.

62. Wallace, *Religion*, 217.

63. Wallace, *Religion*, 224.

64. W. John Smith, "Ritual and the Ethology of Communicating," in d'Aquili, *Spectrum*, 76.

65. D. Stanesby, *Science, Reason, and Religion* (London: Croom Helm Ltd., 1985), 53. See also W. H. Thorpe's discussion of Jacques Monod's radical "reductionism," in *Beyond Chance and Necessity*, ed. John Lewis (London: Garnstone Press, 1974), 1-5.

66. Smith, "Ritual," 51-53, 75-76, 156; Wallace, *Religion*, 223-24.

67. Smith, "Ritual," 76.

68. Eugene G. d'Aquili and Charles D. Laughlin, Jr., "The Neurobiology of Myth and Ritual," in d'Aquili, *Spectrum*, 154-55.

69. Wallace, *Religion*, 233.

70. Ibid.

71. Ibid., 218.

72. See C. Geertz, *The Interpretation of Cultures* (New York: Basic Books, 1973), 87-142; C. Geertz, "Religion as a Cultural System," in *Anthropological Approaches to the Study of Religion*, ed. by Michael Banton (London: Tavistock, 1966), 1-46, esp. 3-8; C. Geertz, "Religion: Anthropological Study of," *IESS* 12: 398-406, esp. 406.

73. See M. Eliade, *Sacred and Profane*, 68-113; d'Aquili and Laughlin, "Neurobiology," in d'Aquili, *Spectrum*, 168, 169, 171; W. John Smith, "Ritual," 53; Wallace, *Religion*, 224, 218.

74. d'Aquili and Laughlin, "Neurobiology," 161-62, 172; See also: Gregory Bateson, *Mind and Nature* (New York: E. P. Dutton, 1979), 209-13; G. and M. C. Bateson, *Angels Fear: Towards an Epistemology of the Sacred* (New York: Macmillan, 1987); *About Bateson*, ed. J. Brockman (New York:E. P. Dutton, 1977), Bateson's own "Afterword:" 235-47; Karl Peters, "Religion and an Evolutionary Theory of Knowledge," *Zygon* 17, no. 4 (1982): 389-92, 400; E. R. MacCormac, "Religious Metaphors: Mediators between Biological and Cultural Evolution that Generate Transcendent Meaning," *Zygon* 18, no. 1 (1983): 54, 65.

75. Wallace, *Religion*, 243, 224. d'Aquili writes that "the ultimate union of opposites that is the aim of all human religious ritual is the union of contingent and vulnerable man with a powerful, possibly omnipotent force" (d'Aquili and Laughlin, "Neurobiology," 162).

76. Robert N. Bellah, *Beyond Belief* (New York, Evanston, and London: Harper and Row, 1970), 25.

77. Smith, "Ritual," 53, 76: Wallace, *Religion* 218, 224.

78. d'Aquili and Laughlin, "Neurobiology," 162.

79. Ibid. 166-67. See also Darwin, *Descent of Man*, 298-302; Swinburne,

Evolution, 181, 203-19; Eccles, *Evolution of the Brain* 71-96; Dobzhansky, *Biology*, 55-60; Stanesby, *Science, Reason and Religion*, 59-65; Macdonald Critchley, *The Divine Banquet of the Brain and Other Essays* (New York: Raven Press, 1979), 13-31; Talcott Parsons, *Societies: Evolutionary and Comparative Perspectives* (Englewood Cliffs, N.J.: Prentice-Hall, 1966), 26-27; Rappaport, "Sacred in Human Evolution," 30. Bellah has noted in this regard: "It is very unlikely that language came into existence 'first' and that men then 'thought up' religion. Rather, we would suppose that religion in the sense of this paper was from the beginning a major element in the *content* of linguistic symbolization. Clearly the relations between language and religion are very important and require much more systematic investigation" (*Beyond Belief*, 47 n.13).

80. In defence of a "supernatural" origin of human intelligence, A. R. Wallace, the co-discoverer of the theory of natural selection, noted, for example, that "natural selection could only have endowed the savage with a brain a little superior to that of an ape, whereas he actually possesses one but little inferior to that of the average members of our learned societies" (As cited in Eccles, *Evolution*, 235-36). Gerd Theissen, explaining that by the capacity to make symbols is meant man's ability to make something like the sniffing around of a mouse, or its minuteness, refer to something beyond itself (e.g. man's own urge to explore, or his own insignificance against the background of the universe) (G. Theissen, *Biblical Faith: An Evolutionary Approach* [Philadelphia: Fortress Press, 1985], 143), goes on to note that this "capacity to make symbols and identify with them is not . . . an adequate condition for universal pro-social behavior" (Ibid. 144). That the capacity is "actualized as pro-social movement," he says, is a "constantly recurring 'miracle'" (Ibid.).

81. d'Aquili and Laughlin, "Neurobiology," 154-57, 165-70.

82. See Paul D. MacLean, *A Triune Concept of the Brain and Behaviour* (Toronto and Buffalo: University of Toronto, 1973); Charles Hampden-Turner, *Maps of the Mind* (New York: Macmillan, 1981), 80-83.

83. Hampden-Turner, *Maps*, 86-89, and references, 215; James B. Ashbrook, "Neurobiology: The Working Brain and the Work of Theology," *Zygon* 19, no. 3 (1984): 331-50.

84. See Robert Segal, "Victor Turner's Theory of Ritual," *Zygon* 18, no. 3 (September, 1983): 327. Among Turner's own prolific writings, see especially: Turner, *The Ritual Process* (Chicago: Aldine, 1969); V. Turner, *On the Edge of the Bush* (Tucson: University of Arizona Press, 1985); V. Turner, *Dramas, Fields, and Metaphors: Symbolic Action in Human Society* (Ithaca and London: Cornell University Press, 1974), esp. 23-59, 272-99; V. Turner, *The Forest of Symbols* (Ithaca: Cornell University Press, 1967); V. Turner, "Color Classification in Ndembu Ritual," in M. Banton, *Anthropological Approaches*, 47-84.

85. See Turner, *The Ritual Process*, esp. 94-203; Turner, *Dramas, Fields, and Metaphors*, esp. 272-99; Turner, *On the Edge* 11, 15, and the chapters on "Body, Brain, and Culture," 249-73, and on "The New Neurosociology," 275-89.

86. Turner, *On the Edge*, 11.

87. Ibid., 249.

88. Ibid., 272.

89. Ibid., 259-61, 282.

90. Ibid., 11.

91. Turner summarizes the work of d'Aquili, Laughlin, and other neurobiologists in this regard as follows: "They postulate that the rhythmic activity of ritual, aided by sonic, visual, photic, and other kinds of 'driving,' may lead in time to simultaneous maximal stimulation of both systems, causing ritual participants to experience what the authors call 'positive, ineffable affect.' They also use Freud's term 'oceanic experience,' as well as 'yogic ecstasy,' also the Christian term *unio mystica,* an experience of the union of those cognitively discriminated opposites, typically generated by binary, digital left-hemispherical ratiocination" (Ibid., 259-60). See also: Ibid., 11, 260, 261; d'Aquili and Laughlin, "Neurobiology," 162, 172, 175, 176, 178; G. Ronald Murphy, S.J., "A Ceremonial Ritual: The Mass," in d'Aquili, *Spectrum,* 319; Barbara W. Lex, "The Neurobiology of Ritual Trance," in d'Aquili, *Spectrum* 117-51; A. J. Mandell, "Toward a Psychobiology of Transcendence: God in the Brain," in *The Psychobiology of Consciousness* ed. Julian and Richard Davidson (New York: Plenum, 1980), 379-439.

92. From among many discussions of the problems involved in defining religion, see: K. Peters, "Religion and Evolutionary Theory of Knowledge," 386-89; M. E. Spiro, "Religion: Problems of Definition and Explanation," in Banton, *Anthropological Approaches,* 85-126; *Changing Perspectives in the Scientific Study of Religion,* ed. Allan W. Eister (New York: John Wiley and Sons, 1974), 163-200; David Tracy, *The Analogical Imagination* (New York: Crossroad, 1981), 167-78.

93. See Robert J. Richards, *Darwin and the Emergence of Evolutionary Theories of Mind and Behavior* (Chicago: University of Chicago Press, 1987), 207-208.

94. Darwin, *The Descent of Man,* 303.

95. See Eliade, *The Sacred and the Profane,* 95-113.

96. See T. Dobzhansky, "Ethics and Values in Biological and Cultural Evolution," *Zygon* 8, nos. 3-4 (September-December, 1973): 265.

97. See Lorenz, *King Solomon's Ring,* 5-9; C. H. Waddington, *The Ethical Animal* (Chicago: The University of Chicago Press, 1960), 152-53.

98. See P. Farb, *Man's Rise to Civilization* (NewYork: E. P. Dutton, 1968), 6-14; Sharpe, *Comparative Religion,* 52; R. Flannery, "Ethics in Primitive Societies," *NCE* 5, 582; G. O. Lang, "Culture," *NCE* 4: 528; see also Rudolf Otto's negative comments about such a conception of the evolution of morality (*Idea of the Holy,* 42-44).

99. J. Jaynes, *The Origin of Consciousness in the Breakdown of the Bicameral Mind* (Boston: Houghton Mifflin, 1976), 149-333.

100. See Lorenz, *Man Meets Dog,* 182-92; Waddington, *Ethical Animal* 151; Dobzhansky, "Ethics and Values," 265.

101. See Eccles, *Human Mystery,* 119; Dobzhansky, *Biology,* 71; Hudson Hoagland, "Ethology and Ethics — The Biology of Right and Wrong," *Zygon* 2, no. 1 (March, 1967): 49-50.

102. See Dobzhansky, "Ethics and Values," 269-72; Hoagland, "Ethology and Ethics," 50; Edward O. Wilson, *Sociobiology: The New Synthesis*

(Cambridge, Mass.: Belknap Press, 1975), 121-29; E.O. Wilson, *On Human Nature* (Cambridge, Mass: Harvard University Press, 1978), 150-52; Carol Kaesuk Yoon, "Social Castes Found to Be Not So Rare In Nature," *The New York Times* (January 16, 1993): C1, C6.

103. Darwin wrote: "Secondly, as soon as the mental faculties had become highly developed . . . that feeling of dissatisfaction . . . would arise, as often as it was perceived that the enduring and always present social instinct had yielded to some other instinct. . . .Thirdly, after the power of language had been acquired, and the wishes of the community could be expressed, the common opinion how each member ought to act for the public good. . . . Lastly . . . the social instinct, together with sympathy, is . . . greatly strengthened by habit" (Darwin, *Descent of Man*, 304-305; see also R. Richards, *Darwin*, 206-11).

104. Darwin, *Descent of Man*, 304-05.

105. See Richards, *Darwin*, 209.

106. Ibid. 213.

107. Darwin, *Descent of Man*, 285.

108. Richards, *Darwin*, 601. William James expressed similar views (Ibid., 449).

109. See Ibid., 213 n. 72, 601.

110. See Ibid., 603-27.

111. See Ibid., 602; Wilson, *Sociobiology*, 3-4, 106-20, 562-64; Wilson, *On Human Nature*, 153-54, 177; C. Lumsden and E. O. Wilson, *Genes, Mind, and Culture* (Cambridge: Harvard University Press, 1981), 370; Ruse, *Taking Darwin Seriously*, 217-35; R. Mattern, "Altruism, Ethics, and Sociobiology," in *The Sociobiology Debate*, ed. A. L. Caplan (New York: Harper and Row 1978), 463-64.

112. R. W. Burhoe,"Religion's Role in Human Evolution: The Missing Link between Ape-man's Selfish Genes and Civilized Altruism," *Zygon* 14 (1979): 153-58; R. W. Burhoe, "Five Steps in Evolution of Man's Knowledge of Good and Evil," *Zygon* 2 (1967): 77-78.

113. Wilson, *On Human Nature*, 176.

114. See Richards, *Darwin*, 605; Wilson, *Sociobiology*, 120-21.

115. Richards, *Darwin*, 108.

116. See Ibid., 608; Mattern, "Altruism," 464.

117. See Mattern, "Altruism," 464.

118. Eccles, *Human Mystery*, 118-19.

119. Ibid. See also: Denise L. Carmody and John T. Carmody, *Ways To The Center* (Belmont, Calif.: Wadsworth Publishing Company, 1981), 18.

120. Eccles, *Human Mystery*, 118-19; Ward H. Goodenough, "Right and Wrong in Human Evolution," *Zygon* 2, 1 (March, 1967): 66-69.

121. As cited in Dobzhansky, "Ethics and Values," 265. For further discussion of "prehuman" instances of "freedom of choice," see: A. E. Emerson and R. W. Burhoe, "Evolutionary Aspects of Freedom, Death, and Dignity," 157-82, esp. 157-68; Karl Schmitz-Moormann, "On the Evolution of Human Freedom," *Zygon* 22, no. 4 (December, 1987): 443-58.

122. Dobzhansky, "Ethics and Values," 265-66. For discussion of the related notion of "purpose," see: Swinburne, *Evolution*, 297; A. E. Emerson,

"Some Biological Antecedents of Human Purpose," *Zygon* 8, nos. 3-4 (September-December, 1973): 294-309; Goodenough, "Right and Wrong," 59-61.

123. See Richards, *Darwin*, 208.

124. Ibid., 210.

125. Ibid., 211.

126. Ibid., 610, 611.

127. Otto, *Idea of the Holy*, 44.

128. Dobzhansky, "Ethics and Values," 266. See also the comments of Lorenz and Hoagland about "right conduct in fighting" among animals: Lorenz, *King Solomon's Ring*, 181-99; Hoagland, "Ethology and Ethics," 51-53, 56-58.

129. Dobzhansky, "Ethics and Values," 270-71.

130. Ibid., 271.

131. Stephen Jay Gould, "Biological Potential vs. Biological Determinism," in Caplan, *The Sociobiology Debate*, 345.

132. Ibid., 349.

133. Ibid., 345.

134. E. O. Wilson, "Academic Vigilantism and the Political Significance of Sociobiology," in Caplan, *The Sociobiology Debate*, 295.

135. Dobzhansky, *Biology*, 86; Waddington, *Ethical Animal*, 100, 151.

136. Dobzhansky, "Ethics and Values," 266. See also in this regard: Richard Dawkins, *The Selfish Gene* (Oxford: Oxford University Press, 1976); R. C. Lewontin, Steven Rose, and Leon J. Kamin, *Not in Our Genes* (New York: Pantheon Books, 1984), which challenges "biological determinism" and champions instead a more "dialectical" appreciation of "a constant and active interpenetration of the organism with its environment" (p. 12).

Campbell also has argued that if man is altruistic, it is the result of social, not biological, evolution ("Conflict between Social and Biological Evolution and the Concept of Original Sin," 243; Campbell, "On the Conflicts between Biological and Social Evolution and between Psychology and Moral Tradition," *Zygon* 11, no. 3 [1976]: 178-96; D. T. Campbell, "Social Morality Norms as Evidence of Conflict Between Biological Human Nature and Social System Requirements," in *Morality as a Biological Phenomenon*, ed. G. S. Stent [Berkeley: University of California Press, 1980], 67-82).

137. Dobzhansky, *Biology*, 86.

138. Dobzhansky, "Ethics and Values," 265; Dobzhansky, *Biology*, 86. Stephen Toulmin notes in this regard that "it is entirely premature to assert that this capacity [for altruism] is directly encoded, as such, in the DNA of our cell nuclei" ("Human Adaptation," in U. J. Jensen and R. Harre, *The Philosophy of Evolution* [Brighton, Sussex: The Harvester Press, 1981], 192).

139. Dobzhansky, "Ethics and Values," 267. Michael Ruse argues that Natural Selection has taken a "middle course" between "firm genetic control" (as seen in ant behavior) and "purely rational" decision making, and endowed us with "epigenetic rules" that incline us, but do not force us, to be altruistic (*Taking Darwin Seriously*, 221).

140. Dobzhansky, "Ethics and Values," 271.

141. Ibid., 267.

142. Richards, *Darwin*, 611.

143. Ibid., 612.

144. Ibid., 605.

145. Ibid. Theissen notes that it was primarily by virtue of the "symbolic action" of "transference of the imagery of the family to a particular partner," whereby the "other person becomes a brother or sister," that "genetically rival beings" were able to "develop altruistic modes of behavior which [were] not just for the benefit of their kin" (*Biblical Faith*, 142-44).

146. Richards, *Darwin*, 612.

Chapter Three

The Process of Religious Evolution

The prehistory of the religious category is not the whole story about the evolution of religion. Religion also has a history, and this history, as Rudolf Otto has noted, not only "develops our natural disposition for knowing the holy," but also "manifests the holy."[1] Eliade has drawn a similar conclusion. "That all the major religious attitudes came into existence once and for all from the moment when man first became conscious of the position he stood in within the universe, does not mean," he wrote, "that 'history' has had no effect on religious experience in itself."[2] For although there is a sense in which the basic structures of hierophanies always remain the same,[3] it is also true that there is "no hierophany that is not from the date of its first becoming manifest 'historic'."[4]

Before trying to trace the course of this history of religion, we will need to pay some attention to the process by which it has occurred. How is such a process to be conceived? The assumption of this book is, of course, that religion has "evolved" historically. But in what sense?

When first introduced into biological literature by Albrecht von Haller and other eighteenth century physiologists to explain their "embryological theory of preformationism,"[5] the word 'evolution' was taken to mean exactly what it implied etymologically — i.e., a process of "unfolding" (as in the "unrolling" of a scroll),[6] that involved "no addition of new parts," but only a "simple expansion or unfolding" of what already existed in miniature form.[7] By the early nineteenth century, however, the term came to be associated with the

Aristotelian notion of 'epigenesis,' which — as used already in the seventeenth century by William Harvey to contest the 'preformationist' explanation of ontogenetic and phylogenetic development[8] — implied that the organs of the higher animals were thought to develop "sequentially, changing gradually from an amorphous, homogeneous condition to an articulated, heterogeneous state."[9] Conceived in such terms, evolution would be viewed as "a result of internal dynamics, independent of environmental contingencies," or, in other words, "as an orderly, progressive, goal-directed unfolding repeated in essential form time and again in widely varying circumstances."[10] And although Darwin did not himself altogether rule out the possibility of an orthogenetic element in the evolution of species (of the sort found also in the development of the embryo),[11] he and others would increasingly interpret evolution to mean the "modification of species through generations" along "such divergent lines as the divergent environments make optimal."[12]

In which of these different senses the term evolution can be applied to religious history will depend in turn upon what exactly the subject of religious evolution is conceived to be. When the latter is understood to be the religious category itself, the term evolution will be applied only in the more restricted sense of a process of gradual maturation, on the grounds presumably that, having been fixed in human consciousness from the very beginning, the religious category can no more undergo radical change than can any other "primal" category of the human mind.[13] Thus, after stating in his 1898 Gifford Lectures that by "religious development" he means the evolution not of "religious externals (e.g., doctrine, ritual, etc)," but of mankind's "religious nature,"[14] C. P. Tiele, for example, will go on to describe the evolution of religion not as a "supersession of the old by something new," but as an orthogenetic process of "growth from a germ, in which lies intent everything that afterwards springs from it:"[15]

> From the green bud the flower bursts forth as from its sheath, and reveals the wealth and brilliance of its colours. From the tiny acorn springs up the mighty oak in all its majesty. The man in the prime of his strength, the woman in the summer of her beauty, have once been helpless children, and we know that their growth began even before their birth. These are instances of what we call development. But the term is not applied to physical life alone. We use it also in speaking of mental endowments, of artistic skill, of individual character, and generally of civilization, art, science, and humanity. We therefore think that, in view of what the anthropological-historical investigation of religion has brought to light, we are fully entitled to apply the term to religion also. And for doing so we may appeal to no less an authority than Jesus Himself, who compared the kingdom of heaven to a grain of mustard-seed, which is the smallest of all seeds, but grows up into so mighty a tree that the fowls of the air lodge in the branches thereof. What else does this mean but that the seed sown by Him in the bosom of humanity was destined to develop into a mighty religious community."[16]

Both Otto and Jung[17] would use the same arborial imagery to describe the evolution of the human mind and its religious category. Our "natural disposition for knowing the Holy," Otto wrote, comes of age in much the same way that a child might attain the age of reason and develop its innate capacity for learning a language, or in the way that an oak-tree "comes to be that which it was predisposed or predetermined" to be by its own "potentiality."[18] Such a development results, he says, from "the interplay of predisposition and stimulus, which in the historical development of man's mind actualizes the potentiality in the former, and at that same time helps to determine its form," and through the actual experience of 'the Holy's' historically conditioned manifestations.[19]

As this last statement by Otto suggests, those who argue that a "primal" category like the religious *a priori* can only "mature," and not undergo any radical alteration, readily acknowledge, however, that there is also a more objective dimension to the history of religion, through which the religious predisposition is itself manifested and discovered.[20] These "manifestations" will themselves evolve through "their integration into different contexts of sociotic forms."[21] And it is "religion" in this objective sense — not "religious man" or "the structure of man's ultimate religious situation" — that more recent scholars of religion, like Robert Bellah, have in mind when they talk about the evolution of religion.[22] But here again the question arises about the sense in which the term evolution is being used. Were the history of objective religion nothing more than an unfolding of the sum of "true religion" already contained in some "primordial revelation," as suggested by some Renaissance thinkers,[23] its "evolution" could be understood also in a literal sense, and explained in terms of a merely "static" historiographical model. As will be seen, however, the history of religion has far exceeded a simple unfolding of primordial elements. For although most of the basic elements of religion may have been present, as Eliade claims, from the very start of human history, the way they have been combined from one time and place to another has varied greatly, with the result that new religions have been constantly coming and going. The history of religion, in other words, has been full of real change. And to account adequately for such "transformation," a more dynamic conception of evolution than the "preformationist" one will be needed. A "growth" model of historiography, as implied by the orthogenetic conception of evolution, might serve the purpose if the history of religion were nothing more than a gradual, cumulative growth from certain basic principles into the full bodies of religious doctrine and practice that we now associate with the various religions, independent of human interests or social pressures, and without any major interruptions or setbacks. But the history of religion has hardly ever been so smooth and insulated. Radical shifts of thought and practice have frequently occurred, and geographical, economic, psychological, and political forces of every sort have repeatedly impacted upon the course of religious history. To appreciate all of these different factors, "revolutionary," "Gestalt," and "social-psychological" historiographical models might be employed.[24] In the final analysis, however, a more "evolutionary" model of the kind applied in recent years by some epistemologists to the evolution of culture in general will be needed. Without suggesting that cultural evolution "obeys the same laws as biological evolution, or that cultural evolution is nothing but an extension of biological evolution," these thinkers have stressed the interaction and the many "parallels and analogies" that are to be found "in biological and cultural evolution."[25] Donald T. Campbell especially has been emphasizing the analogy between "natural selection in biological evolution" and a "variation and selective retention" model of the "process" of sociocultural evolution.[26] Implied thereby is the third of the aforementioned senses of evolution, namely, the conception of evolution as a process of "descent with adaptive modification," along the lines of which "developments from a common origin diverge in reflection of divergent environmental conditions."[27] This is, in fact, the way Bellah and others talk of the evolution of objective religion — as a process, namely, "of increasing differentiation and complexity of organization" whereby the various religions have become ever more capable of "adapting" to their respective "environments."[28]

Basic to such a "natural selection" historiographical model, as outlined by Campbell, would be, first of all, the "occurrence of variation."[29] No less than in the realm of biology, wherein variation among members of a species lead Darwin to his conclusion about "the survival of the fittest,"[30] variation is also, Campbell claims, the "raw material" of any cultural evolution. "Those social-environmental settings providing the greatest range of variations," he says, "are the most likely to produce cultural advances," even though "too high a mutation rate" might constitute a threat for "the preservation of an already achieved adaptive system."[31] Campbell notes in one essay that these variations can be of several kinds, in accordance with the different ways that groups organize themselves socially, or in the different ways that individuals within a group execute a common custom, or in the different ways a group attempts the solution of a collective problem from one time or place to another.[32] In another essay, Campbell highlights the variation of ideas, images, insights, and other theoretical expressions that are presupposed by and reflected in variations of a social or practical sort.[33]

How these variations come about — whether they are "deliberative," "intelligent," "blind," "haphazard," or "random" — does not really matter, he adds, "so long as the same range of variations occur."[34] Campbell argues, however, that while there may be some disadvantages to "blind"[35] variation, the advantages of conceiving of the variations as being blind are greater, in that, among other things, it brings into focus how changes can occur on a "trial and error"[36] basis "without any self-conscious planning or foresightful action,"[37] and highlights the "independence" of the variations from "the environmental conditions of the occasion of their occurrence."[38] The latter point was especially emphasized by William James, who was one of the first to employ a natural selection model to explain the origin of the varieties of religious experience.[39]   Contrary to the Spencerian view that cultural changes are the direct result of "environment, geography, ancestral conditions, [etc.]," James argued that the changes are "profoundly indirect"[40] because they are due to "the accumulated influences of individuals," of "great men," whose "great thoughts" and other influential "examples, initiatives, and decisions" are exactly like Darwin's "variations," which, while eventually subject to selection or rejection by nature, are originally "spontaneous" and "given."[41]   Other evolutionary epistemologists have made the same point by suggesting that most "novel ideas" or "new scientific discoveries" are "accidental occurrences" or "chance mutations of ideas" resulting from scientists and other pedestrian cognizers making "unrestrained conjectures" (rather than "logical, empirical inductions") about the possible solution of one or another problem they have encountered.[42]   Whether through blind and spontaneous "cultural mutations," or through a more deliberate, intelligent process of "cultural exchange,"[43] the history of religion, as will be seen in a later chapter, has seldom been wanting for an adequate supply of variations. As humans struggled with questions about the meaning of reality in general, or with more specific questions about who they are, where they come from, where they are going, what they are supposed to be doing, etc., "conjectures" of every sort began to surface. The "idea of the Holy," for example, was no doubt only one of countless nonrational responses of *Homo religiosus* to his or her experience of the mysterious dimension of reality. And as religious people everywhere tried to say exactly what it was that they had encountered and to endow this "wholly other" phenomenon with some sort of "form" so as the better to be able to relate to it and to each other,[44] they came up with an endless array of divine names, myths, rites, creeds, laws, social structures, and so on, only a relatively small remnant of which have survived into our own time.[45]

   To understand what might have caused some of these variations to have disappeared and others to have survived, attention will have to be paid to what Campbell calls the second essential ingredient of any Natural Selection process, namely, "consistent selection criteria" for eliminating, propagating, and retaining certain types of variations.[46] "Reality in itself" might be said in a very general way to meet this need by acting in something like an "editorial role of discarding misleading categories," and "rejecting, preserving, or destroying 'great men' and their 'ideas'."[47] And along such general lines, the various religions could be said to represent, as James claimed, so many "spontaneously generated sets of beliefs as had not yet been . . . rejected, and might never be rejected . . . by the winnowing hand of reality."[48] Other more specific criteria — like habit, rationality, verification, falsification, disciplinary interests, etc., by which "novel ideas" are put to the test of fitness, have been developed by evolutionary epistemologists.[49] In regard to varieties of ritualistic behavior in particular, Campbell lists at least six different selective systems that might be operative in the socio-cultural realm and account for their survival or non-survival.[50] Extending them into the realm of religion, one might conclude that a specific religious ritual, like circumcision, became dominant at a particular time and place either through the extinction of total societies lacking such a custom, or through the selective diffusion of such a custom in competition with other alternative customs, or through the pleasant memories associated with its past selection, through a process of imitation of reward-producing behavior, through the selective elevation to roles of differential influence of individuals who behave in such wise, or, finally, through a rational, deliberate, or culturally self-consious selection of such a custom on the basis of what the group knows about the environment in which it finds itself.[51] Which of these selective systems would kick in would depend largely on whether the variations whose survival is in question would be of an external sort — that is, among social units — or internal — that is, variations among persons within a social unit in the execution of a common custom or among occasions within a social unit.[52]

More will be said in chapter six about the sense in which religious variations of one sort or another might be of "adaptive" value.   Suffice it here to note that underlying all the aforementioned selective criteria is the analogy to Darwin's emphasis on the 'fitness' of any biological variation for survival in some ecological niche.[53] Applied to the realm of epistemology, this would mean, as James put it, that spontaneously generated "novel ideas" would be retained only if they were adapted to the intellectual problem-conditions to which they are applied, and scientific progress would consist, as Karl Popper wrote, "in replacing unfit theories with those that have solved more problems."[54] Applied to the realm of religion, it would mean that creative religious ideas about God, or justice, or any other moral principle, were the result of the selection of "fit" thought/feeling variations from among the multitude spontaneously generated.[55]

For the process of natural selection to work, however, it is not enough that there be variations and selective systems. There must also be, in Campbell's words again, "a mechanism for the preservation, duplication, or propagation of the positively selected variants."[56] In the biological realm such a mechanism is to be found, Campbell notes, in "the rigid duplication process of the chromosome-gene system in plants and animals."[57] "No such exquisitely rigid conservation machinery" as this genetic transmission "is recognizable for social evolution,"[58] he says. "Yet," he continues, "through social mechanisms of child socialization, reward and punishment, socially restricted learning opportunities, identification, imitation, emulation, indoctrination into tribal ideologies, language and linguistic meaning systems, conformity pressures, social authority systems, and the like . . . sufficient retention machinery exists for a social evolution of adaptive social belief systems and organizational principles to have taken place in addition to the less problematic social evolution of technological devises."[59] In any learning process, Campbell points out, it is the "memory" which functions to preserve information,[60] and with James Mark Baldwin and others, he agrees that in society at large, it is "tradition" that fulfills this function.[61] "A tradition," Baldwin wrote, consists of ideas that are "fit. . . for imitative reproduction and application."[62] "Traditions of knowledge," he concluded, "become established in a society and form the hereditary deposit for each generation, constituting thereby a platform for further determination of thought variations."[63] Without such "traditions," or "memes," as Richard Dawkins likes to call the "imitative ideas" by which cultural evolution is passed on,[64] "the entire structure of human society as we know it, would be destroyed in a single generation," Peter Medawar has noted.[65] Tradition, Alfred Russell Wallace implied, is the way natural selectivity works upon the human mind by "preserving and accumulating . . . every slight variation in [man's] mental and moral nature which should enable him better to guard against adverse circumstances."[66] By thus accumulating "knowledge and capacities which [go] far beyond the capacity of any individual," Theissen has noted, tradition affords human beings "the chance to keep in store ideas which might contain the solution for problems still unknown."[67] It was probably for this reason, he adds, that people in the past have been inclined to regard tradition as "sacred," and why some today, like C. H. Waddington, would have us believe that "there is even a human tendency (to which our genes predispose us?) to believe what we are told in childhood."[68]

Such a mechanism is readily available in the realm of religious symbolism.[69] At the primitive level the "collection" of myths and rites generated thereby is generally accepted blindly once it has solidified, with little or no thought being given to the possibility of further variation in the telling of stories or the execution of rites.[70] Thus, just as "natural selection describes a process by which stupid, blind, unforesightful processes can produce adaptive wisdom," so "in social evolution," Campbell writes, "we can contemplate a process in which adaptive belief systems, which none of the innovators, transmitters, or participants properly understood, can be accumulated — a tradition wiser than any of the persons transmitting it."[71] "We can imagine such a system operating," he says, "in ancient Egypt, India, or Mexico, among superstitious populations dominated by priests equally ignorant of the true adaptive functions of the belief systems they perpetuated."[72] Inevitably, such a retention system will include "a lot of noise, maladaptive mutations, and chaff, along with the selected kernels of wisdom," Campbell notes. But that cannot be helped.

"For a natural-selection type of sociocultural evolution to work, the retention system must be capable of perpetuating uncomprehended functional recipes." "Not being omniscient," it is "powerless to tell dross from gold." Accordingly, it must "dutifully hang on to both . . . by perpetuating everything it receives from the edited past."[73]   Sooner   or   later,   however,   as   rational schematization of original categories is allowed to occur,[74] respect   for   "tradition"   may   become   increasingly deliberate, as happened, for example, in ancient China when Confucius consciously and purposely selected variant principles (e.g., Wen, Li, etc.) from the Golden Age of Chinese history, and rejected others, as being more or less suitable for the solution of the problem of societal chaos then plaguing the Chinese people.[75] The use of canonical scriptures, creeds, dogmas, etc., by other religious groups down through the centuries was no doubt part of a similar process of deliberate tradition.[76] As Theissen has pointed out, however, it can happen that human   beings   and   cultures   will   sometimes   "find themselves powerless to transmit central values and norms to   the   next   generation."[77]   The   "inner   change"   or conversion implied by Christian faith, for example, is "impossible to preserve," he says, "in the same way as we preserve and can hand on scientific insights or technical skill."[78] It "cannot be brought about with any certainty by any method, any handbook, any training."[79] Thus, just as on the biological level, the exchange of genes and the isolation of variants must be supplemented by "blind and fortuitous repetition,"[80] so, in an analogous way, at the cultural level, and especially in religion and morality, "tradition" and "cultural identity" must be supported by "unplannable and spontaneous repetitions."[81] In other words, Theissen argues, to be preserved, "religious and ethical insights must constantly be rediscovered." "Each individual has to acquire [them] anew . . . as though he or she were the first to discover them."[82]

Given these three conditions, namely, the occurrence of variations, consistent selection criteria, and a mechanism for the preservation, duplication, or propagation of positively selected variants, Campbell concludes, not only biological, but socio-cultural evolution too becomes inevitable.[83] Whether the three conditions are actually present at the level of religious forms and customs will require ongoing investigation. But assuming that they are, "there will occur drift pressures toward increased adaptedness, and toward increased complexity, size, and integration of social organizational units, if such increases give selective advantage."[84] And it is the possibility of this profoundly adaptive value of traditional systems of religious belief that makes the renewed interest in the evolution of religion so significant. Exactly how religion is adaptive will be considered in a subsequent chapter. To conclude the present one, let us recall why the natural selection model seems to work better in the realm of the history of religions than do other historiographical models of a more "static," "revolutionary," "contextual," or "social-psychological" sort. To start with, the "static" model might seem better suited to accommodate the kind of "special" revelatory events that one associates with so-called "founded" religions. But such a model would have difficulty accounting for the obvious growth and development that has occurred in all religions, and especially in those of an "ethnic" sort. The natural selection model, however, does very easily account for such change. Furthermore, with its emphasis upon the "spontaneity" of variations, this model can, and especially when linked up with the version of "punctuated evolution" favored by S. J. Gould and others,[85] also allow for "special revelation," or in other words, for the kind of "diviners" Otto considered to be the very "woof" of religious evolution, or for the kind of "human mediators of the Real to humankind (Moses, Guatama, Jesus, Muhammad . . .)" that John Hick, paraphrasing Masao Abe's version of the Trikaya doctrine, wants to locate at some third level between the divine *personae* and the *Real an sich*.[86] At the same time, the natural selection model also avoids Spencerian environmental determinism against which James fought, but which seems to be enjoying a revival of late in the renewed emphasis by some on the direct influence of "geography" and "space" upon the shape of religion.[87]

For its part, a "revolutionary" historiographical model might seem more suitable for describing a history of global religion, which, as Karl Rahner has noted,[88] seems to be unfolding in quantum "leaps," rather than in the gradual, developmental manner imagined by earlier evolutionists. But, given the prevalence of the aforementioned version of "punctuated evolution," the Natural Selection model can also take such "leaps" into adequate account, and without yielding to the temptation of those taking the revolutionary approach to overthrow past modes of thought or behavior. To be sure, Natural Selectivity can be ruthless in its indifferent abandonment of non-adaptive cultural systems. But, on the whole, the Natural Selection model seems far more conservative, seeking out and preserving any and every "tradition" that might somehow enhance the cultural system's chances for survival.[89]

The Gestalt-contextual model might also seem preferable in certain respects, as for example, in its being flexible enough to accommodate the kaleidoscopic shifting of ideational paradigms that, as Hans Kueng has pointed out,[90] has characterized so much religious history. But if there are in fact such paradigmatic shifts in religious perception, they can also be accommodated by the Natural Selection model in conjunction with the aforementioned version of "punctuated evolution," and without all the "radical discontinuity" and "relativism" generally associated with the Gestaltist model.[91] Furthermore, it may be noted that one of the early proponents of the contextual model, namely Thomas Kuhn, has himself turned to a more evolutionary approach.[92]

Finally, in regard to the social-psychological model, it can readily be admitted that such an approach can help in describing the kind of exploitation to which religion has so often been subjected. Liberation and feminist theologians have all used it to good effect in recent years. As Richards has pointed out, however, those who use this model are vulnerable to being hoisted upon their own petard by the *tu quoque* argument.[93] Furthermore, the Natural Selection model can also accommodate the play of ideological forces at work in the history of religion, and without succumbing to the reductionist tendencies which have marked the thinking of Marx, Durkheim, and others who have earlier taken the social-psychological approach.

Notes

*Major parts of this chapter have been published earlier by the author in an article printed in the *Journal of Religion* (October, 1991: 538-557), and the author is grateful to the editors of the Journal for permission to reprint the material here in revised form.

1. Otto, *Idea of the Holy*, 176-77.
2. Ibid., 116.
3. Ibid., 177-78.
4. Eliade, *Patterns*, 463-64.
5. See Richards, *Meaning of Evolution*, xiii, 4, 5-16, 167; Thomas Henry Huxley, "Evolution," *Encyclopaedia Britannica*, 20th century edition (New York: The Werner Company, 1903), vol. VIII, 744-51; Peter Bowler, "The Changing Meaning of Evolution," *Journal of the History of Ideas* 36 (1975): 95-114; Thomas Munro, *Evolution in the Arts* (New York: Harry N. Abrams, n.d.), 215-24.
6. See Richards, *Meaning of Evolution*, 5.
7. See T. H. Huxley, "Evolution," 744, 751.

8. See Richards, *Meaning of Evolution*, 5-8.

9. Ibid., 7.

10. Campbell, "Variation and Selective Retention in Socio-Cultural Evolution," in Francisco Ayala and Theodosius Dobzhansky, *Studies in the Philosophy of Biology* (London: Macmillan, 1974), 22.

11. See Richards, *Meaning of Evolution*, 91-166. Richards notes further that Darwin himself rejected "the hypothesis of an *intrinsic cause of necessary progress* buried in the interstices of organization" (such as an epigenetic model might imply), but "in the beginning he nonetheless insisted, relying on the embryological model, that animals had an internal 'tendency to change,' which would be progressively molded by the *extrinsic* agency of the environment" (Ibid., 86). This notion, Richards continues, would eventually fade in his theory, and "be replaced by the supposition of environmental forces producing the kind of variations that could be transmuted into progressive forms during the development of species" (Ibid., 87). This represented a "compromise" on Darwin's part, in that it made progress "non-necessary, though general," and placed "the guide for advance in the external environment" (Ibid., 90). But it did not mean abandonment of "his conception of a progressive dynamic," or that the improvements created by natural selection were "merely relative to local environments" (Ibid. 87-89).

12. See Ibid., xiii, 73n; Campbell, "Variation and Selective Retention," 22. See also Ginsberg's distinction of the three senses in which evolution may be understood, namely, as "descent with modification," "progressive ascent toward greater multiplicity of parts and complexity of structure and function," and "emergence of genuinely novel characteristics" (Morris Ginsberg, "Social Evolution," in Michael Banton, *Darwinism and the Study of Society* [London: Tavistock; Chicago: Quadrangle, 1961], 97-99).

13. See Arthur Child, "On the Theory of the Categories," *Philosophy and Phenomenlogical Research* 7 (1946): 316-35, esp. 316, 330.

14. Cornelius Petrus Tiele, *Elements of the Science of Religion* (Edinburgh and London: William Blackwood and Sons, 1897), I: 32, 33-35, 37, 272; II: 24.

15. Ibid., I: 272.

16. bid., I: 29.

17. Carl G. Jung, *Man and his Symbols* (New York: Doubleday, 1964), 81-82.

18. Otto, *Idea of the Holy*, 176.

19. Ibid.

20. Ibid., 176-77; Tiele, *Elements*, I: 58-149; Jung, *Man and his Symbols*, 75-82.

21. Child, "Theory of the Categories," 330.

22. Bellah, *Beyond Belief*, 21. For further discussion of "differentiation" in societal evolution, see Parsons, *Societies*, 21-25.

23. See Eliade, *Quest*, 38-39.

24. For a discussion of all these historiographical models, as they apply to the history of science, see Richards, *Darwin*, 14-17, 559-93.

25. G. Vollmer, "Mesocosm and Objective Knowledge," in F. Wuketits, *Concepts and Approaches in Evolutionary Epistemology* (Dordrecht: D. Reidel,

1984), 85. For a discussion of the limits on any "analogy" between biological and social evolutionary processes, see: A. L. Kroeber, "The Superorganic," *American Anthropologist* 19.2 (1917), 163-213; J. Maynard Smith, "Evolution and History," in Banton, *Darwinism and the Study of Society*, 84-93; Ginsberg, "Social Evolution," in Ibid., 102-103. Dobzhansky, it should be noted, emphatically denied that social evolution occurred by a process of natural selection ("Ethics and Values," 276-79).

Michael Ruse has pointed out, along with M. Bradie, that there have been two different approaches to bringing evolutionary biology into the discussion of the development of knowledge and ethics. While the *analogical* approach only suggests that the "causes behind the growth of knowledge are like the causes behind the growth of organisms," the second approach takes the biology *literally*, and argues "that natural selection has left the human mind informed by various innate dispositions . . . and these dispositions incorporate our principles of thought and reasoning" (M. Ruse, *Philosophy of Biology Today* [Albany: State University of New York Press, 1988], 72-73; M. Bradie, "Assessing evolutionary epistemology," *Biology and Philosophy* 1: 401-59). With all our emphasis on the religious *a priori* in previous chapters, our own study obviously takes this "literal" approach to some extent. But this does not preclude using the "analogical" approach to explain subsequent stages of development of the religious "disposition" after it has been established as a structure of the human mind.

26. See Campbell, "Variation and Selective Retention in Socio-Cultural Evolution," in H. R. Barringer, *Social Change in Developing Areas* (Cambridge, Mass.: Schenkman Pub. Co., 1965), 19-49; Campbell, "Blind Variation and Selective Retention in Creative Thought as in other Knowledge Processes," *Psychological Review* 67, no. 6 (1960): 380-99; D. T. Campbell, "Evolutionary Epistemology," in *The Philosophy of Karl Popper*, ed. Paul Schlipp (Lasalle, Ill.: Open Court Press, 1974), 413-63; Campbell, "On the Conflict between Biological and Social Evolution," 167-207; R. J. Richards, "The Natural Selection Model of Conceptual Evolution," *Philosophy of Science* 44 (1977): 494-501; Richards, *Darwin*, 574-90.

Ginsberg notes, it may be added, that Darwin himself "made no extravagant claims for natural selection in the realm of social evolution," maintaining as he did that "in the formative period man had acquired his intellectual and moral faculties under the influence of natural selection," but that "in later phases the development of these faculties owed much more to training, education and tradition," and that natural selection was of only subordinate importance in dealing with civilized nations, since "such nations do not supplant and exterminate one another as do savage tribes" ("Social Evolution," 104).

27. See Campbell, "Variation and Selective Retention," 22; *supra*, n.12.

28. Bellah, *Beyond Belief*, 17.

29. See Campbell, "Variation and Selective Retention," 22, 26, 27; Campbell, "Evolutionary Epistemology," 421; Campbell, "Blind Variation and Selective Retention in Creative Thought," 381.

30. See Darwin, *Origin of the Species*, GB 49: 9-31; *Descent of Man*, 266-86; J. W. Kimball, *Biology* (Ready, Mass.: Addison-Wesley, 1983), 698-703; Steven

M. Stanley, *The New Evolutionary Timetable* (New York: Basic Books, 1981), 46; Alexander Alland, Jr., *Evolution and Human Behavior* (Garden City, N.Y.: The Natural History Press, 1967), 1-18.

31. Campbell, "Variation and Selective Retention," 28.

32. Ibid.

33. Campbell, "Blind Variation and Selective Retention in Creative Thought," 384-89.

34. Campbell, "Variation and Selective Retention," 28.

35. Campbell writes that "an essential connotation of blind is that the variations emitted be independent of the environmental conditions of the occasion of their occurrence. A second important connotation is that the occurrence of trials individually be uncorrelated with the solution, in that specific correct trials are no more likely to occur at any one point in a series of trials than another, nor than specific incorrect trials. A third essential connotation of blind is rejection of the notion that a variation subsequent to an incorrect trial is a 'correction' of the previous trial or makes use of the direction of error of the previous one" ("Evolutionary Epistemology," 422).

36. Campbell ascribes his own fascination with evolutionary theory to his "reading in 1952 of W. R. Ashby's *Design for a Brain*, in which the formal analogy between natural selection and trial-and-error learning is made clear" ("On the Conflicts between Biological and Social Evolution," 171).

37. If thought-trials are "sheer chance occurrences," James Mark Baldwin wrote, "an infinity of worthless thought variations would gush forth, making the selection of fit, that is relatively true ideas, entirely miraculous" (As cited in Richards, *Darwin*, 475). Baldwin went on to argue that idea-production must be seen as occurring "at the level of organization which the system in question has already reached" (Ibid., 476). Nicholas Rescher, while enthusiastically embracing evolutionary epistemology in general and the work of D. T. Campbell in particular, has recently argued that although both our capacity for intelligence and our use of it have an evolutionary basis, the modes of evolution are different, the one — that of our cognitive faculty being the product of biological evolution, or blind natural selection, the other — that of our cognitive methods, procedures, standards and techniques — being the product of a cultural evolution governed by "a rationally guided selection among purposefully devised mutational variations" (N. Rescher, *A Useful Inheritance, Evolutionary Aspects of the Theory of Knowledge* [Savage, Md.: Rowman and Littlefield, 1990], esp. 1-13). Rescher thinks that it is only by way of appealing to the "vitalist" tradition of "rational selectivity" that one can account adequately for the "substantial progress within a limited time span" in the realm of cultural, cognitive evolution (Ibid., 15-53, esp. 21-22). Similarly, S. Toulmin has argued that the "intellectual" environment (e.g., the discipline) that one finds oneself in can restrict the kind of ideas that one initially entertains (*Human Understanding* [Oxford: Oxford University Press, 1972], 130), and R. Richards has contended that some variations are "intelligent" and "intentional" ("The Natural Selection Model of Conceptual Evolution," 494-501). Campbell has replied by noting that while "introducing consideration of intentional problem-solving will explain constraints in the randomness of search . . . it will not obviate the wasteful

fumbling among alternatives that characterizes all discovery processes. If one is going beyond already trusted 'knowledge,' one has no choice but to explore blindly" ("Selection Theory and the Sociology of Scientific Validity," in *Evolutionary Epistemology*, ed. W. Callebaut and R. Pinxten [Dordrecht: D. Reidel Publ. Co., 1987], 146-47; see also Campbell, "Unjustified Variation and Selective Retention in Scientific Discovery," in Ayala and Dobzhansky, *Studies in the Philosophy of Biology*, 147-58).

38. Campbell, "Blind Variation and Selective Retention in Creative Thought," 381, 392-93.

39. See, in general, Richards, *Darwin*, 442, 449.

40. See Campbell, "Evolutionary Epistemology," 437; "Unjustified Variation," 155.

41. William James, "Great Men, Great Thoughts, and the Environment," *Atlantic Monthly* XLVI (October, 1880): 442, 443, 445; William James, *Principles of Psychology*, GB 53: 860-66.

42. See Richards, *Darwin*, 575, 576; C. H. Waddington, *The Ethical Animal*, 119.

43. See Theissen, *Biblical Faith*, 10-11.

44. See van der Leeuw, *Religion* 447-58.

45. Richard Dawkins has noted that "we do not know how [the idea of God] arose in the meme pool. Probably it originated many times by independent mutation. In any case, it is very old indeed" (*The Selfish Gene*, as cited in A. Hardy, *The Spiritual Nature of Man* [Oxford: Clarendon Press, 1979], 13).

46. Campbell, "Variation and Selective Retention," 27; Campbell, "Blind Variation and Selective Retention in Creative Thought," 381.

47. See Campbell, "Evolutionary Epistemology," 445; James, "Great Men," 445.

48. See Richards, *Darwin*, 442. It is worth noting that it is a "set of beliefs" that is selected or rejected, according to James. Richards notes in this regard that the proper analogue of an evolving "species" is the "conceptual system," whose "gene pool" is the individual ideas united into a genotype by logical compatibility and implication and ties of empirical relevance (Ibid., 579).

49. See Ibid., 575-76; Rescher, *A Useful Inheritance*, 15-53.

50. Campbell, "Variation and Selective Retention," 29-31.

51. Ibid., 30-31.

52. Ibid., 28, 29. See also Gerd Theissen's discussion of the variety of ways (e.g., aggression between species, rivalry within species, etc.) in which "the selection of most appropriate variants happens" (*Biblical Faith*, 11-14). See also: Alland, *Evolution*, 205-207, 222-23.

53. See Richards, *Darwin*, 175-76.

54. See Ibid., 436, 449, 475, 575.

55. See Dawkins' remarks concerning the survival of the idea of God (Hardy, *The Spiritual Nature of Man*, 13); also: Bianchi, "History of Religions," *ER* 6: 405-406. See Whitehead's comments about the origin of the idea of justice (*Religion in the Making*, 40-41).

56. Campbell, "Variation and Selective Retention," 27.

57. Ibid.; elsewhere Campbell writes: "What are required are mechanisms for loyally reproducing the selected variations. For biological evolution, today we have an impressive if incomplete understanding of the intricate, integrated rigidities of the genetic code, of nucleic acid templates for protein types, of the double-helix machinery for loyal gene duplication, of the elaborate maypole spindle dance of the chromosomes in meiotic and mitotic cell division" ("On the Conflicts between Biological and Social Evolution," 173). See also: Waddington, *The Ethical Animal* 111-15, and Theissen's discussion of how the preservation of variations by the exchange of genes is further enhanced at the biological level by "isolation" and "blind and fortuitous repetition" (*Biblical Faith*, 15).

58. Campbell, "On the Conflict between Biological and Social Evolution and between Psychology and Moral Tradition," 173.

59. Ibid., 173-74.

60. Campbell, "Variation and Selective Retention," 27.

61. As cited in Richards, *Darwin*, 476. For Campbell's own comments about the preservative role of tradition, see "Variation and Selective Retention," 34-35.

62. Richards, *Darwin*, 476.

63. Ibid. Among recent "hermeneutic" philosophers, Hans-Georg Gadamer especially has emphasized the need to seek the true meaning of a text in the "tradition of interpretation" which it has spawned (See Randy L. Maddox, "Hermeneutic Philosophy and Theological Studies," *Religious Studies* 21 [1985]: 523-27).

64. See Hardy, *The Spiritual Nature of Man*, 13.

65. See Hardy, *The Biology of God.*, 60-61.

66. Ibid., 63.

67. Theissen, *Biblical Faith*, 16.

68. Ibid. See also Theissen's comments about how the "equilibrium" achieved by various cultures through their "isolation" contributes to the preservation of cultural variants (Ibid.). See also Campbell's remarks about Waddington's suggestion in this regard: "On the Conflict between Biological and Social Evolution," 174.

69. See C. Geertz, "Religion as a Cultural System," 6-8.

70. See Huston Smith, *The Religions of Man* (New York: Harper and Row, 1958), 168.

71. Campbell, "On the Conflict between Biological and Social Evolution and between Psychology and Moral Tradition," 174.

72. Ibid.

73. Ibid.

74. See Reeder, "Relation of the Moral and the Numinous," 267-79.

75. H. Smith, *Religions of Man*, 165-66, 176-89. Campbell, it may be noted, also admits the possibility of such "rational" or "culturally self-conscious selective processes" ("Variation and Selective Retention," 31), but cautions that while "such selective systems undoubtedly cut down on the waste involved in the selective elimination of social systems, their efficacy is obviously limited by the state of knowledge" (Ibid.). He adds further that

"just because certain social institutions may seem to be 'rational' solutions to complex problems is no indication that rational selection or planning was involved in their development" (Ibid.).

76. For a discussion of how this occurred in early Christianity, see: Oscar Cullmann, *The Earliest Christian Confessions* (London: Butterworth Press, 1949).

77. Theissen, *Biblical Faith, 148.*

78. Ibid., 148, and 16.

79. Ibid., 149.

80. Ibid., 15.

81. Ibid., 16, 148.

82. Ibid., 148.

83. Campbell, "Variation and Selective Retention," 27.

84. Ibid.

85. See Stanley, *New Evolutionary Timetable*, 46.

86. See John Hick and Hasan Askari, eds., *The Experience of Religious Diversity* (Brookfield, Vt.: Gower Press, 1985), 19; John Hick, *An Interpretation of Religion* (New Haven, Conn.: Yale University Press, 1989), 14, 240, 264-96. Waddington notes in this connection that there must be something like natural selectivity operative in society to explain "why, for example . . . Christ and Mohammed [were] accepted as Messiahs out of all the candidates" (*The Ethical Animal*, 123).

87. See, e.g., J. Hick and P. F. Knitter, eds., *The Myth of Christian Uniqueness* (Maryknoll, N.Y.: Orbis, 1988), 98, 210-211; Beldon C. Lane, *Landscapes of the Sacred* (Mahwah, N.J.: Paulist Press, 1988).

88. See K. Rahner, "A Basic Interpretation of Vatican II," *Theological Studies* 40, no. 4 (December 1979): 716-27.

89. See Peters, "Religion and an Evolutionary Theory of Knowledge," 405-408.

90. See Kueng, *Does God Exist?*, 106-19; H. Kueng, *Theology for the Third Millennium* (New York: Doubleday, 1988), 123-285.

91. See Richards, *Darwin*, 569. Hans Kueng downplays these risks in his attempt to apply Kuhn's paradigmatic model to the development of Christianity and the world religions (see *Theology for the Third Millennium*, 153-61, 215-23).

92. See Richards, *Darwin*, 574.

93. Ibid., 13, 574.

Chapter Four

The Course of Religious Evolution: Prolegomena

As in the case of any other natural phenomenon, like the horse, for example, whose evolution has involved not only a change in specific characteristics (e.g., from multiple-toed to single-toed feet), but also speciation (e.g., from Eohippus to dozens of species, like the still extant donkeys, zebras, etc.), so with religion.[1] Its evolution has involved not only a change in religious characteristics (e.g., from *mythos* to *logos*), but also and simultaneously the origination of many different species of religion. Both of these aspects will need to be kept in view if the course of religious evolution is to be tracked adequately.

As far as the fact of religious speciation is concerned, A. F. Wallace has estimated that no less than 100,000 different species of religion have arisen during the course of human history.[2] His estimate in this regard assumes that what makes one religion distinct from another is roughly analogous to what sets one biological species off from another.[3] "One religion, as an entity, is distinct from another," he writes, "when its pantheon, its ritual, its ethical commitments, and its mythology are sufficiently different for its adherents to consider that the adherents of other religions are, in a general sense, 'unorthodox' or 'pagans' or 'nonbelievers'."[4] It also rests upon several other assumptions: first, that "religion began with the Neanderthals . . . about 100,000 years ago"; second, that "there have been at all times since the Neanderthals a thousand or more culturally distinct human communities, each with its own religions"; and finally, that "in any cultural tradition, religions change into ethnographically distinct entities at least every thousand years."[5] All of these assumptions could be debated. But there can hardly be any doubt that down through the millennia many different species of religion have in fact surfaced. One could even argue, as did Heinrich Frick, under the influence of Friedrich Schleiermacher, that "religion actually exists only in religions,"[6] or, as Albert E. Hayden and his successor at the University of Chicago, Joachim Wach, suggested, that it is the "evolution of religions," and not the "evolution of religion," which primarily concerns the historian of religion.[7]   One way of trying to track this "evolution of religions" would be to classify all the different religions in such wise as to elucidate their evolutionary origins and relationships, as well as their ever-changing, specific properties. Many attempts at doing this have been made in the past. Some were of a "normative" sort. This was obviously the case with the "theological and dogmatic" distinctions between "true" and "false" religions, between "natural" and "revealed" religions, or between "heathen" and "Christian" religions, drawn by early Christian apologists, medieval theologians, or Protestant reformers and missionaries.[8] Less obviously, the philosophical and evolutionist theories propounded by Hegel, Tylor, Frazer, and others also rested to some extent upon normative assumptions."Chronology was given valuative meaning," and "earlier" came to mean "lower and inferior," while "later" meant "higher and superior."[9]   C. P. Tiele's distinction between "natural" and "ethical" religions[10] should probably be counted in this category too, to the extent that it "confuses description and evaluation,"[11] and reflects prejudices against primitive peoples because of their supposed lack of "morality."[12] As Roger Schmidt has pointed out, "rejection of the credo of evolutionary progress in which moderns are seen as superior to earlier peoples . . . does not force us to espouse a relativism that maintains that there are no grounds for a comparative evaluation of religious beliefs and practices . . . on moral and epistemological grounds, their relative adequacy in illuminating human existence, and their contribution to the creation and maintenance of life-enhancing and environmentally sustainable societies."[13] But of whatever use such normative judgments might be in the philosophy of religion, it is "impossible," Wach argued, "to use them [as classifications] in the history of religion today."[14]

Closely related to these normative classifications, and equally "of little use," Wach argued, is the distinction between religions that "have arisen" (i.e., "ethnic" religions) and those that have been "founded."[15] Ugo Bianchi claims that such a distinction provides "the general framework for a genuinely historical typology," and tries to refine it by identifying further "subtypes" of ethnic religions (i.e., "scriptural" and "national" religions), as well as of the founded religions (i.e., "universal" and "cosmopolitan").[16] But according to Wach, "we can never be sufficiently certain about a religion's rise to apply this distinction, mainly because we always have a distorted view of the role of the founder."[17]

Others have attempted to classify the different religions along geographical lines, or, in other words, "according to geographical, anthropological, ethnological, and genealogical points of view: by continents, countries, races, peoples, and tribes."[18] Max Mueller's classification of religion along racial-genetic lines (Aryan, Semitic, Turanian) was an early example of this approach.[19] And although his version is no longer accepted, other geographical models still prevail in most textbooks of comparative religion. Wach felt that this approach in general had some merit to the extent of highlighting the way "spiritual phenomena and the physical environment are interconnected," or, in other words, "the influence of climate and landscape on religions, their rise, and their development."[20] But Partin thinks that it is highly problematic (e.g., grouping vastly different religions under the classifications of "Eastern" or "Western"), and in the final analysis rather arbitrary and trivial, since "the significance of geographical considerations, especially on a large scale, is minimal for the understanding of particular religions and groups of religions."[21]

Still other attempts at classification of the various religions have been of a philosophical sort. Hegel, for example, tried to trace the dialectical progress in the unfolding of Absolute Spirit from its manifestation in what he called the "natural religion" of the Orient, through the "artistic religion" of ancient Greece and Rome, to the "revealed or spiritual religion of Christianity."[22]   Most notable among many similar philosophical endeavors were Otto Pfleiderer's differentiation of the different religions in accordance with the way they respectively balanced poles of freedom and dependency,[23] and Eduard v. Hartmann's division of "naturalistic" (e.g. prehistoric, primitive, Greek, Roman, Teutonic, Egyptian, and Persian) and "supranaturalistic" religions (e.g., Brahmanism, Buddhism, Judaism, Islam, and Christianity), along with many subdivisions of each class, depending upon the extent to which one or another religion takes notice of natural phenomena "independent of their connection with men's welfare," and "spirit" is recognized as being "in control of the universe."[24]

Philosophical efforts of this kind to outline a "universal synthesis" of religious history have been severely criticized by Wach and others, and generally on the same grounds that Hegel himself objected to "devolutionist" hypotheses propounded by some early Christian apologists — on the grounds, namely, that they lack "historical confirmation."[25] Against them, it has been insisted that "the actual course or courses of [religious] evolution" should "not be prescribed *a priori,*" but only "after an empirical comparative study of cultural areas and types."[26] According to Wach, this would have to involve the historical study "of particular religions, or particular religious communities (churches, sects, schools), of particular objective forms (such as dogmas of one or more religions, a certain doctrine, the cult), particular personalities (such as religious heroes)," as well as of particular subjective forms of religion (e.g., piety).[27] To avoid skepticism and relativism, however, such an endeavor, Wach stated, would have to go beyond a mere compilation of historiographical material. Not only the "becoming," but also the "being" of the various religions would have to be studied. At the same time as they are studied "diachronically," they would have to be studied "synchronically." "Leading ideas and principles" which are "inherent" to the particular religions and "unfold" in their development, would have to be identified, so as to discover the "inner form" or "characteristic center" in the context of which the "particular traits" of the different religions "become comprehensible."[28] It was something like this that G. van der Leeuw, Mircea Eliade, and other phenomenologists of religion seemed to have had in mind to do when, on the basis of the "meaning" they found in certain cross-cultural religious phenomena, they classified the different religions in terms of their respective "cosmic" or "historical" orientation,[29] or, in more particular terms of "flight" (e.g.,Confucianism), "struggle" (e.g., Zoroastrianism), "strain and form" (e.g., Greek religion), "infinity and asceticism" (e.g., Hinduism), "humility' (e.g., Islam), "will and obedience" (e.g., Judaism), "love" (e.g., Christianity), etc.[30] Bianchi has written, however, that this phenomenological method "tends to focus only on the synchronic elements of religion, describing and classifying religious forms without reference to particular historical contexts," that it "aims at capturing the meaning of religious phenomena without committing itself to an analysis of the historical, cultural, social, and psychological settings of those phenomena," and that it thereby "neglects the study of the diachronic, formative processes that give a religious phenomenon its depth and endow it with the colors of real life."[31]   The objection, in other words, is that the phenomenological   approach   "is   not   sufficiently historical."[32]   The phenomenologists themselves, not surprisingly, claim to the contrary that they do in fact begin with the historical data, and seek to understand it "historically."[33]   Partin contends, however, that this is only the case at the start of their endeavor, for their "tendency is often toward abstraction, and then toward reification of these 'forms' of religious dynamic, with the result that [their] attention is drawn away from the religions in their historical particularity."[34]   Be that as it may, however, the approach of the phenomenlogists does represent an exercise in the kind of classification of religions that Wach considered the "most important," namely,   a   "descriptive"   classification,   and   might, therefore,   for   all   its   supposed   shortcomings,   be appreciated for the way it complements Wach's own efforts along such lines.

Wach distinguished four kinds of "descriptive" classification: 1) "formally objective," to which belong "such distinctions as those between mythological and dogmatic, national and global, and scriptural and oral religions"; 2) "formally subjective," among which he counted distinctions "based on the predominance of a psychological function, for example, religions of feeling and religions of will"; 3) "objective with regard to content," or classifications that "aim at the spirit of the doctrine, cult, and institutions (e.g. "describing religions as   ascetic-soteriological   or   prophetic-revealed"); 4) "subjective with regard to content," as exemplified by "a distinction among types of piety (joyful, melancholic)."[35] While admitting that these classifications frequently become "mixed," and that "none of them is better than

the others in an absolute sense," Wach went on to note
that "a truly satisfactory classification" of a "descriptive"
sort "would require not only that we understand the
historical phenomena from their centers, not only that we
penetrate as deeply as possible into their 'spirit,' but also
know more about the structure of objective religion and
its interconnections [e.g., with other cultural phenomena
like "the law, the art, and the economic order," and other
"social forces"] than we know today."[36]   Given this
deficiency of knowledge, Wach himself was reluctant to
attempt any strict classification of the evolution of
religions, and generally restricted his own discussion of
the "types" of religion to a review of the "theoretical,"
"practical," and "sociological" categories into which he
thought all expression of religious experience falls."[37] But
his conclusions in this regard, combined with the results
of other methodologies (e.g., phenomenological,
dialectical, etc.) being pursued in the history of religions
or in other fields of religious study (anthropological,
sociological, psychological, ethnological, etc.), have
certainly provided a basis for the kind of "structural"
classification of religions that comes closest to the type of
morphological taxonomy being used in the life sciences to
elucidate evolutionary origins and relationships in terms
of the acquisition of specific features.[38]   Furthermore,
although the present state of knowledge, or the sheer
vastness of the subject matter, may not now or ever allow
for much sophistication in the descriptive classification
of religions, some rudimentary distinctions, such as
Wach's own colleague, Joseph M. Kitagawa, and other
scholars, like Robert Bellah, have drawn between
"primitive," "archaic," "historic-classical," and "modern"
religions,[39] are possible and helpful.   Were such
classifications intended to be taken in a strictly
chronological sense, as, at first blush, they would seem to
be, they would, according to Wach himself, be of little

use.[40]   But that is not the case.   For, although they do
carry some rough chronological connotations, they are
meant to be understood primarily in "descriptive" terms,
and might best be seen, therefore, as being analogous to
what biologists call "grades," or, in other words, levels at
which evolving organisms acquire "novel characters and
abilities" (e.g., warm-bloodedness) and set themselves
apart thereby from other organisms.[41]   That at least is how
we will be using them in the next chapter.   Before
attempting to track the evolution of religions along such
classificatory lines, however, and to avoid the kind of
false starts made in the past, several other questions will
need to be addressed — one of a methodological sort
about the employment of ethnographical data, another
about the more general and formal characteristics of the
history of religions we will be studying.   Both questions
can best be pursued in the context of a review of what
past "evolutionists" have said about the different "stages,"
and especially the "initial" stage, of the evolution of
religions.

With their aforementioned notion about the late
invention of religion, Critias, Democritus, Euhemerus,
and other ancient Greek and Roman thinkers not
surprisingly left the impression that in its intial stage,
religion was largely an excercise in human fear, deception,
and ignorance, resulting in the apotheosis of deceased
heroes, benevolent rulers, or even inanimate objects.[42]
Early Christian apologists, like Lactantius, Augustine,
Basil, Firmicius Maternus, and Martinus of Bracara
readily admitted that such was indeed the nature of the
many pagan religions.[43]   But the "true religion," based
upon a "primordial revelation" of some sort,[44] from which
pagans had apostasized under the influence of the devil,
was, they said, originally monotheistic.[45]   Variations on
this theme surfaced repeatedly in later centuries, as, for
example, in the writings of the medieval Icelandic scholar

Snorri Sturluson, and among Renaissance and Reformation thinkers like Hugo Grotius, John Calvin, and Gerard Vossius.[46] The Cambridge Platonists, as well as Lord Herbert of Cherbury, and other eighteenth-century Deists, like John Toland and Matthew Tindal, began taking a more positive view of pagan religions, by arguing that they embodied all the essential elements of a pristine natural religion (e.g., belief in a supreme God, the worship of God, virtue, penitence, and future rewards and punishments).[47] Most of these thinkers were still convinced, however, that religion had originally been monotheistic. This lingering conviction was seriously challenged by David Hume. "If men were at first led into the belief of one Supreme Being, by reasoning from the frame of nature," Hume argued, "they could never possibly leave that belief, in order to embrace polytheism."[48] "It must appear impossible," he continued, "that theism could, from reasoning, have been the primary religion of the human race, and have afterwards, by its corruption, given birth to polytheism and to all the various superstitions of the heathen world."[49] Theism was rather the result of a later absolutization of one or another of the "several limited and imperfect deities" which the "various and contrary events of human life [storms, war, sickness]" had inclined humans to acknowledge.[50] "Polytheism or idolatry was, and necessarily must have been," Hume concluded, "the first and most ancient religion of mankind."[51]

Hume's assertion of a primordial polytheism would later be challenged by claims of Andrew Lang, Wilhelm Schmidt and others to the effect that belief in a powerful and creative High God was to be found among most primitive peoples, like the hunting tribes of Australia, the Tierra del Fuego, or Southern Africa, and might therefore be assumed to have been present at the very beginning of human history.[52] But whatever might be said of the accuracy of Hume's theory, it would prove to be exceptionally important, in that, as noted earlier, it invited others to reduce religion to one or another of its component parts, that might in turn be reduced to something other than religion itself. Nineteenth-century evolutionists readily accepted the invitation.

Relying on reports of sailors and missionaries, a contemporary of Hume, Charles de Brosses, concluded that fetishism, defined simply as the cult of animals and objects, was the primordial form of religion.[53] Auguste Comte employed the same notion to describe the nature of what he considered to be the infantile, religious, stage of man's intellectual development.[54] So, too, did Lubbock's evolutionist scheme. His aforementioned "first level" of atheism was followed, and subsequent levels of totemism, shamanism, polytheism, monotheism, and morality were preceded, he conjectured, by a fetishistic "illusion that man can compel some divine power to carry out his designs."[55] There was no evidence, however, that fetishes are found among all primitive peoples, and Lubbock himself did not clarify where the divine powers or spirits implied by the fetish were supposed to have come from.[56] Other nineteenth- century evolutionists, like E. B. Tylor, C. Darwin, and H. Spencer, would link Aristotelian and Euhemeristic notions, and argue, therefore, that the conception of the gods had derived originally from animism, or, in other words, from the belief induced by experiences of dreams, visions, and death, that there are spirits or ghosts that inhabit living creatures as well as non-living objects.[57] These "spirits," they argued, came by degrees to be venerated as "gods," until there eventually surfaced the idea of a single, universal Spirit animating all things.[58] Though very popular, and of considerable influence on the thinking of Frazer and Freud, Tylor's version of animism did not prevail in the long run. In addition to the aforementioned objections raised by Lang and Schmidt, Max Mueller, the so-called founder of comparative religion, had long argued that all god- and soul-talk was simply the result of *nomina* becoming *numina*, that is, of metaphors and symbols used to describe man's sensory experience of the infinite in nature being converted into deities.[59]   Later, R. R. Marett would argue, somewhat similarly, that there must have been some sort of animistic stage of religion, during which the belief in spirits was preceded by an experience of an awe-inspiring power (e.g., the Melanesian 'mana', or North American Indian 'wakan,' 'orenda,' or 'manitu').[60]   Still other nineteenth- and twentieth-century evolutionists, like Robertson Smith, Wilhelm Wundt, Emile Durkheim, and Freud, would refer to such 'mana' as the totemic principle, and try to explain the origin of animism, polytheism, monotheism, and other stages of religious history as a refinement of a primordial totemism, by which primitive society would solidify and apotheosize itself through communion with the totem symbol.[61] 'Souls' were said to be nothing more than individualized incarnations of the totemic principle, and 'gods' were "simply the synthesis of all the totems."[62]

As E. E. Evans-Pritchard has put it, most such theories about the evolution of religions are now as "dead as mutton."[63] This is so, because, in the first place, they were, like the "universal syntheses" attempted by Hegel and other philosophers, lacking in "historical confirmation."[64] Reports of missionaries, sea-merchants, explorers, and folklorists used to support them were all too piece-meal, second-hand, selective, and with little or no appreciation for the meaning of the information they conveyed.[65] It is also so, however, because such theories rested upon three rather dubious assumptions about the "unilinear, orthogenetic, and progressive" nature of cultural evolution: 1) "that all changes in specific cultures or societies represent progress (e.g. advances in complexity of organization, division of labor, size, and energy utilization)"; 2) "that all societies, in the course of their advance, go through the same stages"; and, therefore, 3) "that the less advanced societies in the contemporary world are similar to earlier stages of the more advanced peoples."[66]

The first assumption simply reflected, of course, the "doctrine of progress" prevailing in nineteenth-century scientific circles.[67]   But if by "progress" is understood what the nineteenth-century evolutionists meant, namely, an unswerving "advance from the simple to the complex,"[68] most biologists today would be rather reluctant to accept such a doctrine. For, whatever might be said about the overall course of evolution, one must still reckon with what Dobzhansky has called the "turmoil of particular evolution,"[69] and take into serious account the possibility of "retrogression" (or even of "extinction").[70] Campbell has noted in this regard that individual species represent "viable modes of living" in one or another ecological niche, and it is not unknown for some of these niches to have favored "reduced complexity, smaller size, etc."[71] The barnacle, "whose immediate ancestors were more complex swimming, seeing animals," was cited by Darwin as a good example of this happening.[72]   Other examples can be found in parasites, which in general have shown "degenerative" evolution, and "in recent evolutionary developments," where, as Campbell notes, "the many new viruses are very primitive forms filling ecological niches not available prior to the evolution of warm-blooded animals."[73] "Since current forms at all levels of complexity may be highly adapted to their niches," Campbell points out further, "it is hard to say that one is 'fitter' or more 'advanced' than another."[74]   Hence "the caution of biologists in pronouncing any dogma of evolution and progress."[75]

"Their sources of caution," he adds, "are quite comparable to the protests of the cultural relativists in anthropology, who emphasize the excellent adaptedness and internal coherence of simple cultures as of complex ones; who refuse to identify size with excellence or moral worth; and who recognize the provincial ethnocentrism of many social evolutionists in their assumption of their own culture's superiority."[76] "But apart from this lessened dogmatism," Campbell adds, "there remain senses in which a progressive direction is indicated by the blind-variation-and-selective-retention theory of evolution, for both organic and socio-cultural evolution."[77] He concludes in this regard:

> Over the whole course of evolution, the simpler combinations come first, and it follows that the great bulk of adjacent ecological niches are in the direction of greater complexity — 'there's always room on top' as it were. In general, the 'degenerative' ecological niches do not occur until created by the development of forms filling the 'higher' ecological niches. It also becomes very generally true of any complex form that most, if not all, of its ancestors represented forms of less complexity, and in general, of uniformly ascending complexity. It also becomes true that the mean complexity of all occupied niches steadily increases from epoch to epoch. [78]

None of this should be applied to the realm of religion in such wise as to imply that past "devolutionists," who saw nothing but "degeneration" in the course of the evolution of religions,[79] were altogether right. But it does mean that the evolutionists also were wrong in assuming that there was constant progress. For although there may have been what Bellah describes as "an increasing differentiation and complexity of organization" in the overall course of religious history, "retrogression" or "reduced complexity" (e.g., Puritanism), as well as "extinction"[80] (e.g. religions of ancient Greece and Rome), have also been factors in this evolutionary process. It will mean further that the evolutionists were also wrong in assuming as they did that modern forms of monotheistic religion were, for no other reason than their complexity, at the "higher" end of the scale of human progress than the "simpler" forms of primitive religion,[81] or that religion itself might be disposed of as an inferior product of cultural evolution to make room for Science or some "agnostic" version of naturalistic religion.[82] It should be noted that Bellah himself, around whose evolutionary scheme we will build our own discussion of the course of religious history, readily admits to the validity of both these points. "I do [not] assume," he writes, "that simpler forms cannot prosper and survive alongside more complex forms. What I mean by evolution, then, is nothing metaphysical but the simple empirical generalization that more complex forms develop from less complex forms and that the properties and possibilities of more complex forms differ from those of less complex forms."[83] As far as the comparison of different religions is concerned, Bellah, as noted earlier, is no relativist. He admits "that judgments of value can reasonably be made between religions, societies, or personalities."[84] He is quick to add, however, that "the axis of that judgment is not provided by social evolution, and if progress is used in an essentially ethical sense, then I for one will not speak of religious progress."[85] The "complex and differentiated religious symbolization," toward which he sees the overall history of religions moving, is not to be viewed, therefore, as "a better or a truer or a more beautiful one than a compact religious symbolization."[86]

The second assumption of nineteenth and twentieth-century evolutionists that "all societies, in the course of their advance, go through the same stages," or, as Spencer called them, "successive differentiations,"[87] is no less questionable than the first. It was derived from their evolutionary model of embryological development, according to which the "development from an 'indefinite incoherent homogeneity to a definite coherent heterogeneity' takes place as a result of internal dynamics, independent of environmental contingencies."[88] Although popular in the nineteenth century, such an orthogenetic conception of evolution eventually came to be replaced in both the biological and cultural realms, as we have seen, by a model of "biological species formation," according to which the process of evolution is viewed not so much as an "orderly, progressive, goal-directed unfolding, repeated in essential form time and again in widely varying circumstances," as a "meandering process almost entirely shaped by environmental contingenices." [89] Conceived according to this latter model, evolutionary progress, Campbell says, will come to be seen as being "multilinear,"[90] rather than unilinear:

> Developments from a common origin diverge in reflection of divergent environmental conditions. Parallel environmental conditions in widely differing locales would produce parallel evolutionary sequences, but parallels would only be expected under such conditions. In each of the multiple lines of speciation, there is progress or increasing adaptive adequacy, but along such divergent lines as the divergent environments make optimal."[91]

The third assumption of the past evolutionists to

the effect that "less advanced societies in the contemporary world are similar to earlier stages of the more advanced peoples," would have us believe, in other words, that elements of the religious life of modern primitives, like North American and Australian aboriginals, or the peasant folk of Europe, can be viewed as "survivals" or "living fossils" that have somehow failed to evolve under the influence of the temporal-spatial conditions of their own respective historical niches, and to that extent might be made to serve as important clues to what religion was like in primeval times.[92] Such a notion can be entertained, however, only on the basis of the aforementioned second assumption of the evolutionists about the unilinear course of evolution and the psychic unity of all mankind, which we have already seen to be without foundation. As Ninian Smart and others have noted, therefore, this third assumption of the evolutionists was, at best, "risky."[93] At worst, they say, it was racist.[94] For, implying as it did, that modern aboriginals are at "some kind of arrested stage of evolutionary development,"[95] it was to some extent spawned by, and in turn helped re-enforce racist ideologies, that conceived of such people as being "primitive," "savage," "childish, crude, prodigal, and comparable to animals and imbeciles," and therefore, "all the more suitable for enslavement and exploitation."[96] For these and other reasons, Robert Brockway has concluded that such a methodology "has been discredited beyond redemption," and concludes that the original nature of religion can only be "inferred" from "ethological and psychological investigations."[97] Other scholars are reluctant to go that far. Bruce Dickson, for example, notes that even though there are "no exact historic or modern analogues for Upper Paleolithic period society," ethnographic data can nonetheless "provide useful hypotheses about Upper Paleolithic sociocultural systems."[98]   And Mircea Eliade observes that it is still "permissible to reconstruct certain aspects of the religions of prehistory by considering the rites and beliefs typical of primitive hunters," so long at least as one takes into adequate account "all the differences that separate a prehistoric from a primitive culture," and does not "attempt to transpose the religious practices and mythologies of the 'primitives' to the men of the Old Stone Age."[99]   Both Dickson and Eliade readily admit, however, that past evolutionists often contrived evidence to match the "Paleolithic document" with ethnological analogues,[100] and made "unwarranted assumptions" about how "modern hunting and gathering peoples retain the institutions and behavior patterns of the Paleolithic period."[101]

Notes

1.   See Garret Hardin, *Biology: Its Human Implications* (San Francisco: W. H. Freeman, 1959), 415-17.

2.   Wallace, *Religion*, 3.

3.   Hardin defines a biological species as follows: "Two populations are different species if some describable difference[s] can be found between them, and if they do not interbreed in a state of nature" (*Biology*, 430-31).

4.   Wallace, *Religion*, 3.

5.   Ibid., 3-4.

6.   As cited in van der Leeuw, *Religion*, II: 591. See: F. Schleiermacher, *On Religion, Speeches to its Cultured Despisers* (New York: Harper and Row, 1958), 210-53. Otto wrote in this regard that "it may be true that the life force in its varied manifestations is one and that its unity may be recognized in the consistent scheme of its manifestations. But in the plenitude of individual manifestations it breaks into a diversity of type and character that is very real; and the same holds good in the realm of spiritual life. Historically, 'religion' is manifested as religions and these no less have their characteristic differences; as with all other functions of the human spirit their generic uniformity is inclusive, not exclusive of the specific variations in their development. As those who study the history of art are specially interested to ascertain the characteristic and individual contributions of the various individual civilizations to the general body of aesthetic achievement, so in the comparison of religions we are prompted to use an even finer discrimination in ascertaining the manner in which the common basic force, despite all apparent parallelism, takes on perfectly distinct forms in its individual

manifestations" (R. Otto, *Religious Essays* [London: Oxford University Press, 1931], 108).

7. Wach, *History of Religions*, 56; Charles H. Long, "A Look at the Chicago Tradition in the History of Religions," in *The History of Religions: Retrospect and Prospect*, ed. J. M. Kitagawa (New York and London: Macmillan, 1985), 89; J. M. Kitagawa, "The History of Religions (*Religionswissenschaft*) Then and Now," in Ibid., 121-43. Wilfred C. Smith, it may be noted, thought that in order to encourage people to think of the various religions as "on-going movements which from the start have always been in process," rather than as "fixed systems," it would be better to speak of "traditions" instead of "religions" (e.g., the "Hindu tradition" rather than "Hinduism") (W. C. Smith, "Traditions in Contact and Change: Towards a History of Religion in the Singular," in *Traditions in Contact and Change: Selected Proceedings of the XIVth Congress of the International Association for the History of Religions*, ed. by Peter Slater and Donald Wiebe (Waterloo, Ontario: Wilfrid Laurier University Press, 1983), 1-4. When Smith spoke of the need for a "history of religion in the singular" (Ibid., 11, 23), it should further be noted, he was not advocating a Hegelian-type "universal synthesis" of religious history. What he had in mind was an "overview" of the way the "evolution" or "change" endemic to all religious traditions "made possible a great deal more interchange and mutual impingement and interdependence" between the various "traditions" (Ibid., 4) and contributed to "the world's finally coherent religious history" (Ibid., 5). See also Smith's comments on how some primitive peoples have no word in their oral languages for what we call "religion" or "religions" (W. C. Smith, *Meaning and End of Religion* [New York: New American Library, 1964], 46).

8. Wach, *History of Religions*, 68; Harry B. Partin, "Classification of Religions," *ER* 3: 528.

9. Partin, "Classification," 528. Wilhelm Schmidt wrote that according to the evolutionists, "the lower, the more bestial and ugly, must also be the older; the better in each case was the higher, and therefore the later, stage of development" (W. Schmidt, *The Origin and Growth of Religion* (London: Methuen and Co., LTD., 1935), 5.

10. See Tiele, *Elements*, I: 58-149. For a summary and discussion of Tiele's scheme, see Morris Jastrow, *The Study of Religion* (London: Walter Scott, 1901), 65-70.

11. Wach, *History of Religions*, 68.

12. Partin, "Classification," 527.

13. See Roger Schmidt, *Exploring Religion* (Belmont, Calif.: Wadsworth, 1988), 44.

14. Wach, *History of Religions*, 68.

15. Ibid.

16. See U. Bianchi, "History of Religions," *ER* 6: 404-407; U. Bianchi, *The History of Religions* (Leiden: E. J. Brill, 1975), 53-56, 208, 219-20.

17. Wach, *History of Religions*, 68. See also Gustav Mensching, *Die Religion: Erscheinungsformen, Strukturtypen und Lebensgesetze* (Stuttgart: Curt E. Schwab, 1959), 108-15. Mensching discusses other classifications also (Ibid., 77-126).

18. Wach, *History of Religions*, 62-63.

19. See Jastrow, *Study of Religion*, 81-87; Partin, "Classification," 527, 528.

20. Wach, *History of Religions*, 67.

21. Partin, *Classification*, 528-29.

22. For summaries and discussions of Hegel's classification of religions, see: Howard P. Kainz, *Hegel's Phenomenology*, Part II: *The Evolution of Ethical and Religious Consciousness to the Absolute Standpoint* (Athens, Ohio: Ohio University Press, 1983), 125-71; H. Kueng, *Does God Exist*, 156-61; Jastrow, *Study of Religion*, 71-74.

23. See Partin, "Classification," 529.

24. See Jastrow, *Study of Religion*, 91-95.

25. See G. W. F. Hegel, *The Philosophy of History*, GB 46: 180. Jastrow writes that the "manifest objection" to Hegel's scheme, "which may be regarded as typical for a philosophical classification, is its unhistorical character . . . above all Hegel's classification does not accord with the actual facts as presented by the historical evolution of religion" (*Study of Religion*, 72-74). Kueng notes that Hegel was an "empiricist" too, and that his outline of religious history was no "facile, *a priori* construction" (*Does God Exist*, 151). But, as Wach has observed, it was simply impossible "to capture the wealth of phenomena within the few and often schematic categories of the great philosopher" (*History of Religions*, 55, 58, 62).

26. David Bidney, "The Ethnology of Religion and the Problem of Human Evolution," *American Anthropologist*, 56, no. 1 (February, 1954): 9.

27. Wach, *History of Religions*, 63-64.

28. Ibid., xx, 19, 55, 60, 69, 122; J. Wach, *Types of Religious Experience, Christian and Non-Christian* (Chicago: University of Chicago Press, 1951), 30.

29. See Partin, "Classification", 531. For a discussion of how according to Eliade phenomenology and history are components, not alternatives in any synthetic approach to the "morphology of the sacred," see: NCE 12, 254.

30. See Partin, "Classification", 530; van der Leeuw, *Religion*, II: 591-649.

31. Bianchi, "History of Religions," 400; see also: *History of Religions*, 10-11, 178-81, 184-91, 212-20.

32. Partin, "Classification," 530.

33. See Ibid., and van der Leeuw's own comments: *Religion*, II: 596.

34. Partin, "Classification," 530.

35. Wach, *History of Religions*, 68-69.

36. Ibid., 69, 72-79. Compare with Partin's comments about the "general requirements for a more adequate classification" ("Classification," 531), and Bianchi's emphasis upon the need for a "holistic" approach to classification that takes into account the cultural, social context ("History of Religions," 402-403; *History of Religions*, 8-12).

37. See Wach, *Types*, 34; J. Wach, *Sociology of Religion* (Chicago and London: The University of Chicago Press, 1967), 19. Bellah assumes this same division when he writes that "we should examine at each stage the kind of symbol system involved, the kind of religious action it stimulates, the kind of social organization in which this religious action occurs, and the implication for social action in general that the religious action contains" (*Beyond Belief*, 26).

38. There has been, it might be noted, anything but a consensus in the

scientific community on how best to go about classifying the estimated 3-10 million species of living organisms. For a general historical introduction, and brief discussions of some of the problems faced, see: Theodosius Dobzhansky, Francisco J. Ayala, G. Ledyard Stebbins, James W. Valentine, *Evolution* (San Francisco: W. H. Freeman, 1977), 233-313; Robert R. Sokal, Peter H. A. Sneath, *Principles of Numerical Taxonomy* (San Francisco and London: W. H. Freeman, 1963), 5-47; Lynn Margulis, Karlene V. Schwartz, *Five Kingdoms* (San Francisco: W. H. Freeman, 1982), 3-21; Peter H. Raven, George B. Johnson, *Understanding Biology* (St. Louis, Toronto, Santa Clara: Times Mirror/Mosby College Publishing, 1988), 467-81; George G. Simpson, *Principles of Animal Taxonomy* (New York: Columbia University Press, 1961).

39. See Joseph M. Kitagawa, *The History of Religions: Understanding Human Experience* (Atlanta: Scholars Press, 1987), 30. Kitagawa collapses Bellah's five stages into three (Bellah, *Beyond Belief*, 24). For further discussion of the "stages" of societal evolution in general, see Parsons, *Societies*, 26-29.

40. See Wach, *History of Religions*, 67.

41. See Dobzhansky, *Evolution*, 236. Bellah writes in this regard that his "stages" (primitive, archaic, etc.) of religious evolution are meant to be understood as "ideal types derived from a theoretical formulation of the most generally observable historical regularities; they are meant to have a temporal reference, but only in a very general sense" (Bellah, *Beyond Belief*, 24). See also the comments of Evans-Pritchard, *Theories*, 104.

42. de Vries, *Perspectives*, 7-10; Harrison, *Religion*, 15-18.

43. de Vries, *Perspectives*, 15-17; Sharpe, *Comparative Religion*, 9-10.

44. See Eliade, *Quest*, 38-39.

45. de Vries, *Perspectives*, 14-18.

46. Ibid., 21-22, 25, 26; Harrison, *Religion*, 8, 20, 144.

47. Harrison, *Religion*, 39-42, 61-98.

48. David Hume, *The Natural History of Religion*, ed. James Fieser (New York: Macmillan, 1992), 6.

49. Ibid.

50. Ibid., 9, 29-38.

51. Ibid., 4.

52. See Eliade, *Quest*, 45-48; Bianchi, *History of Religions*, 87-91. Schmidt claimed to have found evidence for his position in the worship of sky gods by the farming peoples of the Neolithic period (See Eliade, *Patterns*, 38; Maringer, *Gods*, 281-87, 189-266). Although evidence from Lower and Middle Paleolithic periods (e.g. Chou-k'ou-tien, Drachenloch) is no longer thought by most scholars to indicate belief in a supreme being, there is some evidence from the Upper Paleolithic and Mesolithic periods (Willendorf, Meiendorf, etc.) of sacrificial offerings being made to a Supreme Being or a Lord of Wild Beasts, or of depictions of the latter himself (See Eliade, *History*, I: 13-15; Maringer, *Gods*, 90-99, 271-72, 278-79). Abbé Breuil concluded, for example, that the man-animal, dancing figure he discovered at the Les Trois Frères site in France was "really the 'God' of Les Trois Frères," a conclusion that Eliade also finds somewhat plausible in the sense of a Lord of Wild Beasts (Maringer, *Gods*, Plate IX, 76; Dickson, *Dawn of Belief*, 116; Eliade, *History*, I: 18). Whether these "Lords" were perceived any more "monotheistically" than

the "Mother Goddesses," however, is impossible to say.

53. See de Vries, *Perspectives*, 32, 76; Evans-Pritchard, *Theories*, 20; Sharpe, *Comparative Religion*, 18.

54. See Kueng, *Does God Exist*, 169-71.

55. de Vries, *Perspectives*, 100.

56. Evans-Pritchard, *Theories*, 24.

57. Ibid., 23-25; de Vries, *Perspectives*, 8, 101-106; C. Darwin, *Descent of Man*, 302-303.

58. See Sharpe, *Comparative Religion*, 53; Evans-Pritchard, *Theories*, 24; *NCE*, 12: 246.

59. Evans-Pritchard, *Theories*, 20-22.

60. Ibid., 32-34; de Vries, *Perspectives*, 106-107.

61. Evans-Pritchard, *Theories*, 37-38, 42, 53-63.

62. Ibid., 60, 61.   Durkheim himself, it may be noted, based his conclusions on accounts of the Australian Aborigenes he had found in ethnographic studies by Baldwin Spencer and Frank Gillen, and it is doubtful whether he had in mind to describe thereby the "origin" of religion in any sense other than its "most basic form." But some scholars, like Evan Hadingham and Annette Laming-Emperaire, have tried to explain parietal art of the Upper Paleolithic period also as the material remains of totemic rituals, if only in the sense of constituting a kind of pictorial archive of societal relationships (See Dickson, *Dawn of Belief*, 125). But like the related theory of Arnold van Gennep, according to which the larger cluster of adolescent heel prints in the cave site of Tuc d'Audoubert in France might be interpreted as indicative of a puberty rite, and the rest of the cave art as expressions of other societal rites of passage (Ibid., 125, 126), such theories are without much empirical support.

63. Evans-Pritchard, *Theories*, 108.

64. Dickson, *Dawn of Belief*, 125-26; Evans-Pritchard, *Theories*, 52, 65-66, 101ff; Sharpe, *Comparative Religion*, 62; Eliade, *Patterns*, xiv.

65. See Wallace, *Religion*, 39-51.

66. Campbell, "Variation and Selective Retention," 21.

67. See Wallace, *Religion*, 39-51; Evans-Pritchard, *Theories*, 11; Sharpe, *Comparative Religion*, 24-26.

68. See James Waller and Mary Edwardsen, "Evolutionism," *ER* 5: 215.

69. After noting with Ian Barbour and G. G. Simpson that "viewing evolution of the living world as a whole, from the hypothetical primeval self-reproducing substance to higher plants, animals and man, one cannot avoid the recognition that progress, or advancement, or rise, or ennoblement, has occurred," Dobzhansky cautions against losing sight of the "turmoil of particular evolutions," as evidenced by the prevalence of "extinction" and "retrogression" in many lineages (Dobzhansky, "Chance and Creativity in Evolution," in Ayala and Dobzhansky, *Studies in the Philosophy of Biology*, 310-11).

70. See Dobzhansky, *Evolution*, 342-46.

71. Campbell, "Variation and Selective Retention," 39.

72. Ibid.

73. Ibid.

74. Ibid.
75. Ibid.
76. Ibid.
77. Ibid.
78. Ibid., 39–40. The "smugness" of a Comte or Frazer in this regard now strikes many scholars as being "irritating and risible" (Evans-Pritchard, *Theories*, 15).
79. See Wallace, *Religion*, 10–13.
80. Wallace writes that "for every religion which has survived and been routinized, either as a small community faith or a 'great religion' such as Christianity or Islam, there are dozens of abortive efforts by untimely prophets, victims of paranoid mental disorders, or cranks which are ignored or suppressed by the community" (*Religion*, 4)
81. See R. Schmidt, *Exploring Religion*, 39.
82. See Evans-Pritchard, *Theories*, 15; Waller and Edwardsen, "Evolutionism," *ER* 5: 215.
83. Bellah, *Beyond Belief*, 21.
84. Ibid., 22.
85. Ibid.
86. Ibid. While noting that "Darwinism is the epitome of non-progressionism," and that "there is no lower, better or worse, truer or falser" in biological evolution, since "evolving organisms are simply not going anywhere," Michael Ruse nonetheless recognizes that in science as a whole "there is a passage towards the goal of complete understanding or (not to mince words) of truth" (*Taking Darwin Seriously*, p. 149). Thus, according to Ruse, even if the evolution of the "epigenetic rules" of science are non-progressive, science itself may be progressive as it transcends its organic origins. Applied to the realm of religion, one could argue similarly that even if the evolution of the innate religious propensity was non-teleological or progressive, the product of its operation, i.e., objective religion, could still show signs of progress.
87. See Waller and Edwardsen, "Evolutionism," *ER* 5: 215.
88. Campbell, "Variation and Selective Retention," 21–22.
89. Ibid., 22.
90. Ibid.
91. Ibid. Otto, it may be noted, argued that the most important evidence in support of a universal *sensus numinis* was to be found in the "similarities" or "parallels" existing between different religions of varying times and places (R. Otto, "Parallelisms in the Development of Religion East and West," *Asiatic Society of Japan. Transactions* 40 (1912): 154; R. Otto, "Parallels and Convergences in the History of Religion," *Essays*, 96). Otto drew this conclusion after his sojourn in the East in 1910-11 (See Otto, *Idea of the Holy*, ix). He insisted, however, that the "law of parallel lines of development" was not simply an isolated case involving only several religions (e.g., Christianity and Buddhism); it was rather "a classical example of a general law, which has governed the religious development of man as a whole" (*Essays*, 95). The pattern of the development of religion from its "cruder" to its "noblest" phases, he said, can be seen to have "flourished under every clime and in

every soil with a disconcerting similarity" (Ibid., 96). Equally impressive, Otto noted, was the way the advance from mythology to theology in ancient Greek thought was "paralleled at almost exactly the same period in the very far East of civilized humanity (Pythagoras) . . . in China (Confucius and Lao-tzu) . . . in Israel (Jeremiah) . . . in India (Jina and Sakyamuni)" (*Essays*, 97–100; "Parallelisms," 154–55). Otto observed that "parallels" are also to be found in the development of certain religious concepts (e.g., Brahman/Tao/Logos; Atman/Pneuma/Logos, etc.), in the development of soteriological systems (e.g., the Brahminic *vita religiosa*/Orphism/Taoistic monasticism; Vedantic/Christian mysticism, etc.), and in the "forms of theological apparatus" (the "same kind of canonical literature, reliance upon the 'scriptures', 'tradition', concerted efforts to reconcile scripture with scripture and scripture with tradition, and to explain the relationship between revelation and reason . . . the same act of interpretation and exegesis, the scholastic-philosophic formulation of doctrine and exegesis, [etc.] . . ." (*Essays*, 101–107). "These parallels," Otto concluded, "lend overwhelming conviction to one great fact, namely the fundamental kinship of the nature and experience of mankind in general, East and West, North and South; by reason of their basic similarity, it works itself out in these parallels, manifesting similar phenomena, and in diverse territories producing similar phenomena, and in diverse territories producing similar results" (Ibid., 107). Sometimes, as in the case of the "Bhakta and Christian doctrines of salvation," these similarities become so "extreme," Otto added, that we have "to reckon with another element which we sometimes meet in biological evolutionary processes, and which is known as the 'convergence of types.' Widely different families and classes of plants or animals may go through processes of transformation in the course of which, besides those general similarities which result from the basic unity of the vital principle itself, they also reveal a growing tendency to approach one another in form and function, until they terminate in final forms startling in their congruity" (Ibid.).

92. See Sharpe, *Comparative Religion*, 49, 52, 54–55; Waller and Edwardsen, "Evolutionism," *ER* 5: 214.

93. Ninian Smart, *The World's Religions* (Englewood Clifts, N.J.: Prentice Hall, 1989), 33–34.

94. Others have noted that these theories were based on elitist assumptions about the interaction of culture and a man's biological evolution, either in the sense of supposing a genetic determination of culture (as if members of a "higher" religion would somehow be "biologically superior" to those of a more primitive one), or in the sense of implying a cultural influence on genetics (as if a religious concern for the "weak" or "unfit" might somehow jeopardize the quality of the genetic stock). See D. T. Campbell, "Variation and Selective Retention in Sociocultural Evolution," 19n.2, 23–26; and Werner Stark, "Natural and Social Selection," in Banton, *Darwinism and the Study of Society*, 49–61.

95. Smart, *World's Religions*, 34.

96. Ibid.; Evans-Pritchard, *Theories*, 8–9, 10, 100, 105–107.

97. Brockway, "Origins," 56.

98. Dickson, *Dawn of Belief*, 180–90.

99. Eliade, *History*, I: 7–8, 15, 17, 24.
100. Ibid., 17.
101. Dickson, *Dawn of Belief*, 179.

Chapter Five

The Course of Religious Evolution

The subjective and objective dimensions of religion have each been seen in an earlier chapter to enjoy an evolutionary dynamic of their own. Each also, therefore, can be expected to follow paths of evolution, which, although inextricably intertwined, are nonetheless different.

C. P. Tiele and Rudolf Otto, it will be recalled, were generally inclined to picture the evolution of the subjective dimension of religion as a process of maturation rather than epigenesis. The religious predisposition, they said, is like an acorn which, once planted, grows gradually into a mighty oak. Tiele wrote two volumes in an attempt to trace such growth, but ended up, at least in this writer's view, saying much more about the objective side of religion than about its underlying subjective aspects.[1] For his part, Otto argued that in order to track the collective course of the evolution of the religious category, we need only follow the "'fundamental biogenetic law' . . . which uses the stages and phases in the growth of the individual to throw light upon the corresponding stages in the growth of his species."[2] "In our own awakening and growth to mental and spiritual maturity," he wrote, "we trace in ourselves in some sort the evolution by which the seed develops into the tree."[3] Out of the "seed of potentiality" that was sown with the "first appearance of conscious life" has issued the "predisposition toward religion," which "awakens when aroused by divers excitations."[4] This "predisposition, which the human reason brought with it when the species Man entered history, became long ago, not merely for individuals but for the species as a whole, a *religious impulsion*, to which incitements from without and pressure from within the mind both contributed."[5] Beginning in "undirected, groping emotion, a seeking and shaping of representations," the "process by which religion comes into being in history," continues "by a continual onward striving, to generate ideas, till its nature is self-illumined and made clear by an explication of the obscure *a priori* foundation of thought itself, out of which it originated."[6] In this "emotion, this searching, this generation and explication of ideas," we have "the warp of the fabric of religious evolution," Otto concluded.[7] The "woof," he added later, is to be found in the development of the faculty of receptivity for *a priori* cognitions enjoyed by everyone, the endowment of certain individuals, like prophets, with a capacity for divination, and, at a still qualitatively higher level, as in the case of Jesus, "the capacity to reveal the very being of God."[8]

While rejecting Otto's innatist proclivities, Jean Piaget, it will be recalled, also accepted the notion that "ontogeny recapitulates phylogeny." And if such a notion has any validity, much of what Piaget himself and other social scientists have reported in recent times about the development, not only of human intelligence and language in general, but of moral, aesthetic, and religious attitudes or predispositions in particular, could also be very useful in tracking the evolutionary course of the subjective side of mankind's religion.[9] At least a few of these studies acknowledge that children have a "leaning toward a God experience from the time their consciousness awakens,"[10] and to that extent would be quite compatible with Otto's own, rather obscure, line of discussion. Given the preliminary nature of such a line of enquiry, however, it will not be pursued here at any greater length. Our primary concern in the remainder of this chapter will rather be to trace the evolutionary course taken by religion historically as the religious category

manifested itself down through the millennia in a myriad
of concrete, objective forms. It all began, as Gregory
Bateson might have put it, with mankind's attempt to
map the world metaphorically.

At all times and places, human beings have, as F.
Creuzer, E. Bevan, Suzanne Langer, and a host of other
scholars have documented, turned to the material world
around them, and the conditions of their conscious lives,
to find phenomena of one sort or another (e.g., celestial
bodies, plants, animals, spatial directions, natural forces,
etc.) for expressing the "spiritual reality" they have
experienced.[11] All stages or types of religious expression,
therefore, have rightly been said to have had their
"matrix" or "motherlode" in the "symbol,"[12] to such an
extent that religion can best be defined, perhaps, as "a set
of symbolic forms and acts that relate man to the ultimate
condition of his existence," and sets him apart from
animals who "could only 'passively endure' suffering or
other limitations imposed by the conditions of their
existence."[13] Symbols, like the Japanese *shintai,* the
Buddhist wheel, or the Christian cross, convey a "meaning
. . . which may be conceptually explained . . . acted upon
. . . and serve as an integrating factor in creating religious
fellowship."[14] Providing, as they do, a "wide scope for
interpretation and re-interpretation," these symbols
themselves can, as Eliade has explained, have a long and
involved history, first, in the sense that symbols often
depend on "precise historical situations" (e.g., dependence
of assimilation of spade to phallus on discovery of
agriculture) or become "attached to particular
socio-political and local situations" and "take form at a
precise historical moment" (e.g., symbols of royalty and
matriarchy), and secondly, in the sense that such symbols
were subject, along with other cultural elements and
ideologies, to "diffusion" from "precise cultural centers,"
thereby allowing for an historical "enrichment" of the

original symbol by way of accretion of new "meanings" (e.g. the "*renovatio*" symbolized by the Cosmic Tree being enriched by the Christian Cross).[15] In the process, there has no doubt occurred, as Erich Voegelin and Robert Bellah have noted, a certain "development from compact to differentiated symbolization."[16] In what follows we will be trying to trace this development by way of taking notice of how at each stage or level of religious experience this symbolization has found theoretical, practical, and sociological expression.

At the "primitive" level, as exemplified by the prehistoric religions of Paleolithic, Mesolithic, and Neolithic times, and the religions of non-literate peoples living in historical times (e.g. Bushmen and pygmies of Africa, Shoshones of western United States, Yoruba and Ibo of Nigeria, Zuni of New Mexico, and Hopi of Arizona),[17] the "first form of intellectual explanation of religious apprehension" is mythology,[18] or "stories" about the "primordial activity of the gods" that "explain" experiences of the sacred, mysterious dimension of reality by accounting for the creative "origin" of things, and "orientating" humans to their place and purpose in the cosmos on the basis of some primordial "paradigm."[19] Among primitive peoples, the myth remains exclusively oral, extremely "particular" in detailing the actual world, and highly "fluid" in organizing its subject matter.[20] For all its lack of sophistication, however, primitive mythology was not, contrary to Sophist and Positivist (e.g. Comtean) notions about the illusory and transitory nature of all mythology,[21] a mere alogical exercise in fiction that was left behind after passage out of some supposedly "infantile" stage of development. For, not only would mythology remain a primary source of theoretical expression at every level of religion,[22] and take on, therefore, a history of its own, but provided primitive peoples in general and the "widely separated Upper

Paleolithic peoples" in particular, "a common ideology and universal symbolic grammar for expressing it."[23]   In line with work by Leroi-Gournhan and Alexander Marschack on the "meaning" of Upper Paleolithic decorative symbols, Dickson has concluded that such an "experiential" and "complex intellectual and theological order" probably involved the generalization of "two profound natural phenomena — 1) a perceived cyclicality in the passage of time, and 2) the dialectic of human sexuality, especially the periodicity and fecundity of women — into "universal principles or 'grand analogies' that formed the basis of speculation and thought about nature, humankind, the universe, and reality" in terms of what Eliade has documented from ethnological studies as a doctrine of "eternalism," according to which religious people are in constant search of "regeneration," on the assumption that "change is illusory" and "eternal repetition" is the "nature of the cosmos."[24]

The content of this primitive mythology, as of any later forms of the theoretical expression of religion, consisted more concretely of three major themes: God, the world, and man.[25]   In regard to the first of these themes, it should be noted first of all that Wach dismissed old arguments about whether "God" was originally conceived as one or many, personal or impersonal, immanent or transcendent, with the conclusion — similarly drawn by Hartshorne and Reese in their historical survey of philosophical notions of God[26] — that in every period, and in every form of theoretical expression, "understanding of the nature of Ultimate Reality" has been "bipolar instead of monopolar." [27] And this would apply not only to the ontological typology addressed by Wach, but to the "cosmic," "social," and other typologies by which historical conceptions of God can be classified.[28]   Although it would not preclude gradual growth in the conception of God from primitive, through classical, to modern times, it does imply that whatever development there was, occurred not in a straight line from one pole to another (e.g., from primitive polytheism to classical monotheism, as Hume claimed,[29] or, as Merlin Stone and others have argued, from a primitive matriarchal conception of god to later patriarchal ones),[30] but rather along many different lines simultaneously, as various poles of ideation came to prevail at different times and places, depending upon "existential" conditions in those cultural areas.[31] Paleolithic and other primitive hunting societies, for example, may have shown some theoretical recognition of distant "sky-gods,"[32] but they conceived of the deities primarily as the "masters and mistresses" of the animals they hunted.[33] Planting cultures, on the other hand, while acknowledging "animal forms of gods," more often than not imagined maternal "earth gods of fertility."[34] Pastoral peoples tended to fashion "sky and atmospheric gods" (e.g. Heavenly Father), but entertained other ideas of god too.[35]

How the Ultimate Reality was conceived greatly influenced mythological, theological, and dogmatic theory about the second major theme of religious history, namely, the origin, structure, and destiny of the universe.[36] This was so precisely because, as Eliade has noted, for *homo religiosus* "the world becomes apprehensible as world, as cosmos, in the measure in which it reveals itself as a sacred world" — as a world, in other words, that is perceived as having been "founded" by some primordial divine activity whereby a "cosmic order" is established around an "axis" or "center" that opens communication between the sacred and profane realms and makes possible an eschatological *pleroma*.[37] Such a heterogeneous conception of the world would seem to imply that the latter's spatial/temporal dimensions are "real" only to the extent of being "totally other" than what they are in themselves.[38]   But if this was a seed of "world-rejection," it was slow to sprout. For, as Bellah has pointed out, primitive religions were basically "monistic" in their world view, with God, Nature, and humankind being viewed as constituting a "single cosmos."[39] "On the whole," he says, they "know nothing of a wholly different world relative to which the actual world is utterly devoid of value."[40]

Religious anthropology (the third major theme of religious history) has been profoundly affected by the way man has conceived of God and the world. In the "monistic" contest of the primitive religions, man generally envisioned himself as "a part of the gods' creation,"[41] "a part of the cosmos," [42] a "microcosm," in which the divinely-founded cosmos is reflected as a "paradigmatic image of human existence."[43] Eliade argues that Hegel was wrong to conclude from this that primitive man was "buried in nature," or that "he had not yet found himself as distinct from nature, as himself."[44]   "An existence open to the world," Eliade continues, "is not an unconscious existence 'buried in nature'."[45]   Such openness, he concludes, "added" value to the experience of primitive life, and contributed to primitive man's self-knowledge.[46]

Closely related to the theoretical expression of religious experience has been its "practical"[47] expression in symbolic acts of "devotion" (e.g., ritualistic adoration, sacrifice, prayer, divination, lustration, purification, sacrament)[48] and "service" (e.g., acts of charity, asceticism, virtue, propagation of the faith, etc.).[49]   Though universal, these "reactions" to the numinous experience were shaped differently by the various religions in accordance with their respective concepts of ultimate reality, and economic, social, and other historical factors.[50]   At the primitive level, this practical side of religion finds expression primarily through ritual. "Just

as the primitive symbol system is myth par excellence,"
Bellah writes, "so primitive religious action is ritual par
excellence."[51]   Although "highly intricate patterns of
worship" have surfaced among some primitive peoples,
the rituals at this level are generally more "immediate,
spontaneous, and inarticulate."[52] They also tend to be
"all-inclusive," embracing almost every aspect of everyday
life.[53]   As attempts to re-enact what is known through
mythology to have been the primordial activity of the
gods,[54] rites of passage, such as Arnold van Gennep
claimed to have detected in large clusters of adolescent
heel prints in the cave site of Tuc d'Audoubert in
France,[55] burial and sacrificial rites of the kind that seem
to have occurred, if not earlier, at least during the Upper
Paleolithic period,[56] or rites of any sort performed along
totemistic, animistic, fetishistic, or whatever lines, were
meant to provide participants with information about
their place in the cosmos and the opportunity to
experience transcendence by way of ecstatic identification
with the mythical beings represented.[57] Due to the close
identification between the participants and the "gods,"
such ritualistic participation remains "relatively passive"
among primitive peoples, Bellah notes, and on that
account it may not be possible to speak of any real
"worship," "sacrifice," or "morality" at this level.[58]   As
evidenced by the ritual practices of the Australian
aborigines, "the whole gamut of spiritual life" may be
anticipated, Bellah concludes, but "the symbolism is so
compact that there is almost no element of choice, will, or
responsibility."[59] It never dawns on the people ever to do
anything other than what the gods have done in the
beginning.[60]

Complementing the theoretical and practical
expressions of religious experience has been what Wach
called its "sociological aspect"[61] — not, it should be noted,
in   the   sense   of   the   Durkheimian "positivistic

misinterpretation of the object of worship as the collective self,"[62] but in the sense expressed by Evelyn Underhill, Max Scheler, and others to the effect that "each religious act is always simultaneously an individual and a social act."[63] It will be primarily in this latter sense that the social dimension of religion will be discussed here, although some notice will be taken also of what Bellah — obviously with greater appreciation for Durkheim's contribution — calls the "social implications" of religion, or, in other words, "the implications for social action in general that the religious action contains."[64]

According to Wach, there has been "no religion which has not evolved a type of religious fellowship."[65] What has distinguished such religious fellowship from all other forms of human association has been not only the cooperation of individuals over many generations in the making of myths, rites, and so forth, but also, and primarily, their "orientation" towards "that reality which is apprehended in religious experience."[66] At all levels of religious history (primitive, archaic, classical, modern), it has been this "numinous experience" that has drawn people together and shaped their fellowship.[67] While, therefore, the sociological expression of religious experience is universal, and brings with it many universal means by which the religious community can be "integrated" and "structured" (e.g. offices, roles, constitutions, etc.),[68] there has also been much variation from time to time and place to place in the way this expression and its forms have been implemented, depending again upon how the different religions conceived of the Ultimate Reality (e.g., the "agapic" nature of "the Christian brotherhood" being constituted "by apprehension of the love of God as it is revealed in the life and death of Jesus Christ"),[69] the "cosmic order" they had in mind to preserve,[70] and, as Bernard Berelson and Gary Steiner have pointed out, the degree of differentiation, specialization, and integration of societal structures and functions occurring within the overall sociocultural system.[71] Wallace has classified the types of "cultic institutions" resulting therefrom (i.e., individualistic, shamanic, communal, and ecclesiastical),[72] and his "scalar taxonomy" of them as a "nucleus for an evolutionary statement of religion"[73] roughly parallels Bellah's description of the development of "social organization" in the history of religion.[74] While rejecting "efforts to outline evolutionary stages of religion" by Tylor and other nineteenth-century evolutionists,[75] Wallace notes that their views contained at least the "germ of a valid model," to the extent of proposing "a beginning in . . . shamanic cult institutions and a culmination in ecclesiastical cult institutions."[76]

By an "individualistic" cult institution, Wallace means a human society in which "there is no categorical distinction between religious specialist and layman," and everyone enters "into a relationship with the deities and powers on occasion of need and requiring no shamanic or priestly intermediary."[77] Examples of such "nonspecialist cults" abound in primitive religions (e.g. the "vision quest" of the Plains Indians),[78] where, as Bellah has noted, "religious organization as a separate social structure" simply "does not exist."[79] But there is no evidence of the existence of an exclusively "individualistic" society. "Theoretically," Wallace says, "there should be — or should once have been — societies containing only individualistic cult institutions, but I know of no surviving examples."[80] Wallace concludes that "religion began with societies that possessed both individualistic and shamanic cults" (i.e., cults in which "an individual part-time practitioner, endowed by birth, training, or inspirational experience with a special power, intervenes for a fee with supernatural beings on behalf of human clients").[81]

Bellah thinks that although "specialized shamans or medicine men are found in some tribes," they "are not a necessary feature of primitive religion."[82]   "At the primitive level," he says, "religious organization as a separate social structure does not exist. Religious roles tend to be fused with other roles, and differentiations along lines of age, sex, and kin group are important."[83] Other scholars, however, have agreed with Wallace, and play up the shamanic character of primitive religious social organization. Combining ethnographic data with "inference from material patterns, and formal analysis,"[84] both Eliade and Dickson, for example, have concluded that prehistoric religion was generally shamanic.[85] "The existence of a certain type of shamanism during the Paleolithic period seems to be certain," Eliade wrote, because of, among other things, archeological evidence (e.g., the Les Trois Frères dancing figure, the Lascaux "Dead Man," the X-ray depiction of animal and human skeletons, etc.), and the seeming naturalness of the "trance" experience, as evidenced by the fact that "shamanism still dominates the religious ideology of hunters and pastoralists in our day."[86]   Eliade defines the shaman as "a specialist in the sacred," who, either because he is chosen by Superhuman Beings or himself seeks their favors, undertakes an "ecstatic journey" above or below, through the earth's "center" or "aperture" for the sake of meeting God and making an offering in the name of the community, seeking the soul of a sick man, guiding the soul of a dead man, or deepening his knowledge.[87]   "The virtual universal occurrence of such part-time specialists in the anthropological record of the world lends credence," Dickson notes too, "to the view that they also were a part of Upper Paleolithic religious practice."[88] Neither Dickson nor Eliade had in mind to suggest, however, that shamanism represented some kind of "initial stage" out of which all religion evolved, or that "the only cultic institutions found in the simpler sociocultural systems organized around the band or family cluster" were shamanic.[89] As Eliade has pointed out, the evidence documenting shamanic activity itself implies what Brockway, Smart, and others have argued, namely, that "it is very likely that religion was multifaceted from the beginning."[90] For, "on the one hand," Eliade wrote, the early incidence of shamanism implies "belief in a 'soul', able to leave the body and travel freely through the world." "On the other hand," he continues, it implies "the conviction that during such a journey, the soul can meet certain superhuman beings and ask them for help or a blessing." Finally, he concludes, "the shamanic ecstacy also implies the possibility of possessing, that is, entering, the bodies of human beings, and also of being possessed by the soul of a dead person or by a spirit or a god."[91]

Furthermore, as Dickson has noted, the burials and other archaeological bits of prehistoric evidence suggest the possibility of "communal cults," wherein besides the part-time shaman, hierarchical associations based on age, and corporate groups based on kinship, may also have played a role in the performance of Upper Paleolithic rituals. [92]

Van der Leeuw has observed how an element of "protest" seems endemic to all religion.[93] Bellah, however, is more inclined to side with Durkheim, and concludes that with or without shamanic or other types of social organization, religion — at least at the primitive level — has tended to "reinforce the solidarity of the society."[94] For all its "fluidity and flexibility," primitive religion reinforced the notion that life is a "one possibility thing," and that the world can only be accepted "in its manifold givenness."[95] In calling attention to all these common features of primitive religion, we are not, it should noted, trying to suggest that there ever was some monolithic "prehistoric religion in the singular."[96] It is, of course, still a very hotly debated issue about whether human culture has evolved "monogenetically" (i.e., from a single aboriginal center of population that eventually spread out to replace *homo erectus*), or "polygenetically" (i.e., from multiple centers of *Homo erectus* populations on each continent "evolving in parallel, through gradual mutation and interbreeding, into *Homo sapiens*").[97] But even if one subscribes to monogenesis, one could still, like the proponents of the *Kulturkreis* theory, grant that whatever common primitive culture there was in the beginning, it very soon thereafter gave way to a multiplicity of "primitive" cultural circles.[98] And just as thousands of Stone Age cultures that have survived into modern times have each developed their "own distinctive faith" of a primitive sort,[99] so in prehistoric times, or at least "after 30,000 B.C.E.," nonliterate cultures "in Siberia, Australia, Africa, Europe, and a little later, in the Americas," could have developed "very divergent patterns of ritual and belief."[100] Whether the diffusion of these primitive cultures, and the genetic-historical relations between cultures implied thereby, can ever be traced quite as precisely as Wilhelm Schmidt and other *Kulturkreis* theorists assumed they could, is highly doubtful.[101] Be that as it may, however, around 3500 B.C. there emerged the first great civilization in Mesopotamia, and shortly thereafter in Egypt, Crete, India, China, Greece, Rome, Mexico, Guatemala, and Peru, and with it the so-called "archaic" stage of religious history.[102]

Through the development of hieroglyphics and other literary devices, the "sacred stories" of more primitive times became, during the archaic period, "sacred writ"[103] (e.g., the Sumerian *enuma elish* and Epic of Gilgamesh;[104] the Egyptian Osiris myth;[105] the Greek myth of Prometheus,[106] Aztec, Mayan, Inca cosmologies,[107] etc.). In the process, archaic mythology, according to

Bellah, lost little of the "particularity and fluidity" that had characterized primitive myth.[108]   But given the increased unification and stratification of society, and the rise of a priestly class, "a relatively stable symbolic structure" came to be "worked out and transmitted over an extended period of time.[109] "With the development of literacy among at least "specially trained scribes,"[110] as in ancient Greece, myths came to be subjected to "critical reflection and innovative speculation."[111]   Ionian "rationalists," like Solon, Thales, Anaximander, and especially Xenophanes, for example, launched a "penetrating analysis" of that part of Greek mythology recorded by Homer and Hesiod,[112] "demystifying" it of its superficially "fictional" character, and searching out its ontological and allegorical "meanings."[113]   This "deliverance of the 'logos' from the 'mythos'," as Otto described it, was also, as Eliade has noted, a "victory of the *the book* over oral tradition, of the document . . . over a living experience," and often, in a more "damaging" way, of the literary *word* over religious *belief.*"[114]

As far as the content of archaic mythology is concerned, it may be noted, first of all, that whole pantheons, or sacred communities of gods, were envisioned mythologically in terms either of a cosmic typology, or as was especially the case with Indo-European religions, in terms of a "social" typology that defined sacred beings in relation to the functions they served (e.g., creation, protection, prosperity, therapy, etc.).[115] The "great paradigmatic figures" with whom more primitive peoples identified ritualistically, but "with whom they [did] not really interact," became, according to Bellah, "much more definitely characterized."[116] "The mythical beings," he says, became "more objectified, conceived as actively and sometimes willfully controlling the natural and human world, and as beings with whom men must deal in a definite and purposive way; in a word, they became gods"[117] (e.g., Marduk, Re, Zeus, Quetzalcoatl, etc.). There was also much speculation about the hierarchical relationships among the members of the different pantheons.[118] Rationalistic critiques of the theogonic myths, such as occurred, for example, in ancient Greece, were not necessarily "atheistic."[119] More often than not, they were made "in the name of an increasingly higher idea of God."[120] Solon, Thales, Anaxamander, and even Xenophanes were revolting against the "capricious," "unjust," and "immoral" character of the mythological gods of Homer and Hesiod,[121] in defense of the "One God," who, as Xenophanes wrote, "is the highest among gods and men," and "in neither his form nor his thought" is "like unto mortals."[122] They were trying, in other words, "to free the concept of the divinity from the anthropomorphic expression of the poets."[123]

Eternal struggles between some of these gods of archaic religion (e.g., between Marduk and Tiamat, Quetzalcoatl and Tezcatlipoca) personified the basically dualistic nature of the latter's conception of the cosmos.[124] And individual gods were assigned to rule over the various ages and areas into which the archaic cosmologies divided up time and space along cyclical and rhythmic lines.[125] On the whole, however, the worldview of the archaic religions remained, Bellah claims, much the same as it had been at the primitive level, namely, highly monistic, with God, Nature, and humankind being viewed generally as a "single cosmos."[126] It was not until the first millenium B.C., under the influence of a rationalist critique of archaic, monistic cosmology, that a theory of "world-rejection," according to which "the value of the given empirical cosmos" is "denigrated" in favor of some "transcendent" realm, would begin to take hold and establish itself as the prevalent *Weltanschauung* of the classical/historic religions.[127]

Archaic anthropology remained embedded in this prevailing cosmic monism. With the larger-scale and the more sophisticated urban stratification of archaic society,[128] the increase in literacy, and the development of more complex forms of religious action, however, mankind was afforded new opportunities for coming of age. This was especially the case with the emergence of what Bellah calls "the characteristic feature of archaic religion," namely, the practical expression of religion in the form of the "cult, in which the distinction between men as subjects and gods as objects is much more definite than in primitive religion."[129] In contrast to the primitive rituals, wherein participants are relatively passive in their identification with the gods, in the archaic rites of worship and sacrifice new lines of dialogue are opened up. "The sacrificial process," Bellah writes, "no matter how stereotyped, permits the human communicants a greater element of intentionality and entails more uncertainty relative to the divine response. Through this more differentiated form of religious action a new degree of freedom as well, perhaps, as an increased burden of anxiety enters the relations between man and the ultimate conditions of his existence."[130] Not all of the archaic religions, for example, promised eternal life. Some, like the Egyptian, Aztec, Inca, and Mayan religions, did.[131] But the Sumerian and Greek religions generally did not.[132] Furthermore, with the emphasis upon sacrificial rites, there was always the risk of humans themselves being sacrificed, or of becoming the targets of warfare engaged in for the sake of procuring a new supply of human blood to sate the thirst of an angry god (e.g. Huitzilopochtli).[133]

The increased complexity of social organization in archaic society (e.g. "autocratic political systems and hierarchical class structures")[134] carried over into the religious realm. In some of the archaic religions, where there existed "a professional clergy organized into a bureaucracy" and devotion to "a pantheon of Olympian deities" there was already taking hold what Wallace calls "ecclesiastical cult institutions."[135]   On the whole, however, it was the "communal cult institutions" that prevailed — cults, that is, in which "groups of laymen are responsible for calendrical or occasional performance of rituals of importance to various social groups . . . [or] to the whole community."[136]   These laymen were usually political and military power-figures (e.g., Egyptian pharoah, Aztec king, Shinto mikado, Chinese emperor), who claimed to be of divine descent and served as both monarch and priest.[137]   Whatever professional priestly class surfaced to service the many cult centers and shrines, it usually remained "subordinate to the political elite, which at this stage never completely divests itself of religious leadership."[138]   And the clientele of such cult centers were "essentially transient," and even with the most tightly organized priesthood, did not become organized "as a collectivity."[139]   Given its prevailing cosmic monism, archaic religion still tended to sanction social conformity. But with increased recognition of divine subjectivity resulting from the emergence of "true cult," an "element of openness" is introduced that is "less apparent at the primitive level."[140]

With the rise in historical times of the classical religions (e.g. Judaism, Hinduism, Jainism, Buddhism, Confucianism, Taoism, Zoroastrianism, Christianity, and Islam), the trend toward "theology" (as well as toward philosophy and other literary interests) intensified.[141] "Classical religion retained the language of myth," Kitagawa noted, "but speculative inquiry into causal principles and universal laws was no longer inhibited and stultified by the mythic mode of thinking."[142]   A desire for "coherence and preservation," along with other historical and sociological factors, now inclined *homo religiosus* to make ever greater use of reason to "explicate systematically and normatively" what the symbol only "implied," and the myth only "illustrated."[143] "Relative to archaic religions," Bellah notes, "historic religions represent a great 'demythologization'."[144] The "doctrine" or "theology" generated thereby itself went through various, often "conflicting," stages of development,[145] and eventually gave rise, in the form of "confessions of faith," "creeds," and "canonical scriptures" (as in the "book religions" of Christianity, Judaism, Islam, etc.), to a more "authoritative and definitive" expression of religious conviction,[146] which in turn triggered the growth of a secondary, semi-canonical literature of an interpretative, exegetical nature (e.g., Talmud, Vedanta, Sharia, etc.).[147]

The rationalist critiques helped clear the way for the more "transcendental" categories underlying Christian and other classical religious conceptions of God (e.g., Being: Hinduism/Buddhism; Power: Taoism/Judaism/Islam; Truth: Zoroastrianism; Love: Christianity, etc.).[148] The notion of an immanent divine principle, almost identical with nature, was still entertained in some of the classical religions (e.g., Taoism), but on the whole, God or the gods were viewed as being "beyond" the natural realm, and apart from natural phenomena.[149] Introduction of a formal monotheism in some of the classical religions was especially significant. As Bellah notes, "the notion of the one God who has neither court nor relative, who has no myth himself, and who is the sole creator and ruler of the universe" represented an "enormous simplification" of archaic mythology.[150] Bellah admits, however, that "elements of archaic cosmology" persisted "alongside [the] transcendental assertions" of the classical religions.[151] Typical in this regard was the survival in "camouflaged" form all throughout the medieval Christian world of many Greek gods and heroes of old, as well as of many of the dragon-slaying gods or heroes and fertility goddesses of pre-Christian Europe.[152]

The trancendental dimension of classical religion carried over especially into its view of the world. Under the influence of the rationalistic critique of the monistic cosmology of archaic religion, a new theory of "world-rejection," according to which "the value of the given empirical cosmos" is "denigrated" in favor of some "transcendent" realm, began to take hold and, according to Bellah, established itself as the prevalent *Weltanschauung* of the classical religions.[153] In one way or another, they almost all "distinguished between this world and the next or this world and other worlds."[154] Hinduism, for example, contrasted the "illusory and transitory character of this world with the eternal."[155] Wach claimed that most of the "founded" religions of the West "safeguarded" the "cosmic aspect, according to which man is assigned his place in the chain or hierarchy of being,"[156] and that, nothwithstanding a gradation in moral discernment (from a sense of pollution to an awareness of sin), in consciousness of guilt (from collective to individual), and in soteriology (from the notion of propitiation to that of redemption),[157] anthropocentrism, or the conception of man as the "center of our universe," was "practically unknown" in the religions of the Near and Far East.[158] With Reinhold Niebuhr and others, however, Wach readily admitted that "Greece seems to be the great exception."[159] The rationalist critique of religious mythology initiated by the ancient Greeks would increasingly downplay the theocentric/cosmocentric dimension of man's nature, and Judaism, Christianity, and other classical religions influenced by the Greek thinkers would reflect this philosophical interest in emancipating man from the cosmos.[160] According to Bellah, the historic religions "radically challenged . . . the identity diffusion characteristic of both the primitive and archaic religions," and this in turn led "for the first time to a clearly structured conception of the self."[161] Along with their "devaluation of the empirical world," the historic religions would also devalue "the empirical self," but this, Bellah claims, would only highlight their "conception of a responsible self, a core self, or a true self, deeper than the flux of everyday experience, facing a reality over against itself, a reality which has a consistency belied by the fluctuation of mere sensory impressions."[162]

While "religious concern focused on this life in primitive and archaic religions," now, at the classical level, Bellah claims, it tended "to focus on life in the other realm," and religious action became above all "action necessary for salvation."[163] Because of a conviction about the broader scope of man's sin than primitive and archaic religion had recognized,[164] such action came to be viewed also as involving a total conversion, expressed variously in terms of obedience, self-denial, surrender, submission, love, fidelity, etc., depending upon how Judaism, Buddhism, Taoism, Islam, Christianity, Shinto, etc., respectively conceived of the Ultimate Reality. More often than not, these ideals of behavior were thought to be realizable only through an ascetical withdrawal from the world,[165] undertaken with messianic expectations or the hope of future release altogether from the weary wheel of time.[166] As had been the case in the primitive and archaic stages of religion, the practical expression of the religious experience was often shaped at this classical level too by the course of historical events. Eliade cites the case, for example, of Zarathustra being inclined toward his revolutionary opposition to the bloody sacrifice of animals by the "economic interest of a society turning from a pastoral to an agricultural way of life."[167] Affiliation to the classical religions was still determined largely by social factors of family, country, etc. But trade and intermarriage also helped bring in outsiders. And there also emerged at this stage the first missionary efforts at ideological conversion.[168]

Changes in the social realm (e.g., the emergence of feudalistic class distinctions, the spread of literacy, etc.)[169] were also reflected in classical religious organization. "The single religio-political hierarchy of archaic society tend[ed] to split into two at least partially independent hierarchies, one political and one religious," Bellah writes.[170] "Together with the notion of a transcendent realm beyond the natural cosmos comes a new religious elite that claims direct relation to the transmundane world."[171] The clientele of this priestly class are no longer as transient as they had been at the archaic level, but form themselves rather into "differentiated religious collectivities."[172] Together with their priests, they come to constitute, in other words, what Wallace would call an "ecclesiastical cult institution" (church, sect, etc.).[173] Such a development involved the risk of conflict between the separated political and spiritual powers, but it also opened up the possibility of religion playing a "more dynamic and especially a more purposive role in social change than had previously been possible."[174]

At the modern stage of religious evolution, a majority of believers would continue thinking in traditional forms. Even in modern secular culture primitive and archaic mythology would linger on in "camouflaged" form.[175] But since at least the Protestant Reformation, and similar reform movements in other classcial traditions,[176] there has occurred, according to Bellah, a "fundamental break with traditional historic symbolization."[177] By concentrating "on the direct relation between the individual and transcendent reality,"[178] early modern religious symbolism triggered an intellectual movement that would eventually leave "no room for a hierarchic dualistic religious symbol system of the classical historic type."[179] The break would occur not only in intellectual circles (e.g., Bultmann's emphasis upon "demythologization," or Bonhoeffer's discussion of "religionless Christianity"), but also "at the level of mass religiosity," as evidenced by the unorthodox, private, elaborate and "often pseudoscientific rationalizations" by some members of established religions, as well as new religious groups (e.g. Bahai's, Justification Church, Church of Jesus Christ of Latter Day Saints, Church of Scientology, etc.), for the sake of bringing "their faith in its experienced validity into some kind of cognitive harmony with the twentieth-century world."[180] Canonical scriptures, dogmatic formulations, and creedal statements have helped keep most members of the historic religions close to their classical conceptions of God even in modern times. But in almost all of them, and especially in Christianity — thanks largely to Kant, Schleiermacher, and the rise of Liberal Protestantism[181] — radically new ways of thinking about God have surfaced, often in terms reminiscent of more primitive concepts (e.g., the *deus otiosus* theme underlying Nietzsche's "death of God"[182] and Bonhoeffer's "useless God";[183] the "mother goddess" theme of much radical feminist theology,[184] etc.), and just as often in bipolar terms (e.g., the personalist/impersonalist dimensions of Process Theology and of some ecumenically-minded "global" theology,[185] or the one/many conception of the divine nature by some radical pluralists).[186]

Early modern reform movements in Christianity and other religions would not entirely dislodge the classical "dualistic cosmology."[187] In some ways, devaluation of the world was even stronger in Protestantism, for example, than it had been in medieval Christianity.[188] Still, "by proclaiming the world as theater of God's glory and the place wherein to fulfill his command [instead of the monastery]," the Reformation,

Bellah claims, encouraged "autonomous action in the world,"[189] and thereby helped clear the way for the "worldview that has emerged from the tremendous intellectual advances of the last two centuries," in which, as noted, there is no room for classical dualism.[190] "This is not to be interpreted as a return to primitive monism," Bellah adds. "It is not that a single world has replaced a double one, but that an infinitely multiplex one has replaced the simple duplex structure."[191]

As noted, the historic religions had tried to "safeguard" the theocentric-cosmocentric dimensions of the "self" it was discovering. In early modern times, however, these safeguards came under new pressures. By tearing down the "walls" of the "mediated system of salvation" thrown up by the historic religions, and championing a more direct relation to God and a more immediate "salvation,"[192] the Protestant Reformation, and to some extent similar reform movements in other religions, "found a doctrinal basis on which to accept the self in all its empirical ambiguity."[193] In some modern circles, this may have given rise to the possibility of what Bellah has called "some ghastly religion of social sciences,"[194] (e.g., Comte's "humanistic religion," or Julian Huxley's "scientific religion"),[195] or, more generally, to the radical affirmation of human autonomy championed by the likes of Nietzsche and Oscar Wilde.[196] In the more sober religious movements of modern times, however, the replacement of the "one possibility thing" by "an infinite possibility thing"[197] has not amounted to a rejection of all limits. Rather, as Bellah concludes, "the fundamental symbolization of modern man and his situation is that of a dynamic multidimensional self capable, within limits, of continual self-transformation and capable, again within limits, of remaking the world, including the very symbolic forms with which he deals with it, even the forms that state the unalterable conditions of his own existence." [198]

No less than in the evolution of religious thought forms and patterns, the practical expression of religion in "devotion" and "service," Wach argued, has revealed "the same continuous interplay between compulsion and tradition, on the one hand, and the constant drive for individual liberty, making for the emergence of new impulses and the creative activity of *homines religiosi*,on the other."[199]   Just as "highly intricate patterns of worship" surfaced in primitive religions, so, he notes, "spontaneous, and even inarticulate" forms of cultic and moral behavior have appeared "at the highest level of cultural growth."[200]   On the whole, however, there is a clear line of development from the more spontaneous, all-inclusive, simple acts of devotion and service at the primitive level, to the more intentional, sacrificial rites of the archaic religions, the standardized, world-denying, salvation-oriented, cultic activity of the classical religions, and the highly sophisticated, this-worldly proclivities of modern religious activity.   With the downplaying of otherworldly asceticism and the relativization of traditional rites and moralistic demands,[201] religious action came to be conceived in early modern times as a "total demand in every walk of life."[202]   Whatever remained of the ascetical spirit would come to be directed in many Protestant circles, as Max Weber has pointed out, along "inner-worldly" lines,[203] so that now in modern times, it has become more impossible than ever to confine "man's search for meaning" to the church.[204]

By challenging the "hierarchical" structure of medieval Western Christendom, and emphasizing instead the priesthood of the laity, the Protestant Reformers of the sixteenth century introduced new social distinctions into the Christian community (e.g. between elect and reprobates).[205] This in turn contributed significantly to what Bellah has called the "institutionalization" of religiously-motivated social change in modern times.[206] It helped lay the groundwork, he says, for the "more open and flexible pattern of membership," and "the increasingly fluid type of organization," that have come to characterize "modern religion," and to render culture and personality "endlessly revisable."[207]

In concluding this brief sketch of the course of the evolution of religions, it may be well to note with Bellah that it has not been intended "as a procrustean bed into which the facts of history are to be forced but a theoretical construction against which historical facts may be illuminated."[208]   For, as Bellah has noted: "Particular lines of religious development cannot simply be forced into the terms of the scheme. In reality there may be compromise formations involving elements from two stages that . . . have for theoretical reasons [been] discriminated; earlier stages may . . . strikingly foreshadow later developments; and more developed may regress to less developed stages. And of course no stage is ever completely abandoned; all earlier stages continue to coexist with and often within later ones."[209]

NOTES

1.   Tiele was especially interested in showing how the religious idea found expression in morality and gave rise to the distinction between "nature" and "ethical" religions: See Tiele, *Elements*, I: 58–149.

2.   Otto, *Idea of the Holy*, 116.

3.   Ibid., 115.

4.   Ibid.

5.   Ibid., 116.

6.   Ibid.

7.   Ibid.

8.   Ibid., 177–78.

9.   See *Supra*, Chapter 1, notes 66–81.

10. Ernest Harms, "The Development of Religious Experience in Children," *American Journal of Sociology* 50(1944–45): 115.

11. See J. Wach, *The Comparative Study of Religions* (New York and London: Columbia University Press, 1966), 61–62. Eliade notes in this regard that although some symbols are connected with historically conditioned

"cultural events," "the majority of religious symbols *point to the world in its totality or one of its structures* (Night, Waters, Sky, Stars, seasons, vegetation, temporal rhythms, animal life, etc.), or *refer to situations that play a part in all human existence*, to the fact that man has sex, is mortal, and in quest of what we call today the 'ultimate reality'" (M. Eliade, *The Two and The One* [New York and Evanston: Harper and Row, 1965], 209. The "Observations on Religious Symbolism" quoted here are a modified version of Eliade's essay "Methodological Remarks on the Study of Religious Symbolism" printed in *The History of Religions: Essays in Methodology*, ed. by M. Eliade and J. M. Kitagawa [Chicago: The University of Chicago Press, 1959], 86-107).

12. Wach, *Comparative Study*, 65, 69-70; Wach, *Sociology*, 19. See also Paul Ricoeur's comments about rationality being the "tool which will unlock the enigma of the symbol" ("The Hermeneutics of Symbols and Philosophical Reflection," *International Philosophical Quarterly*, II, no. 2 [1962], 191-218, as cited and discussed in C. H. Long, "Archaism and Hermeneutics," [in J. M. Kitagawa, M. Eliade, and C. H. Long, *The History of Religions* (Chicago and London: University of Chicago Press, 1967), 84-85]). Karl Rahner made the same point in his insistence upon the priority of the "*Urwoerte*" (K. Rahner, "Priest and Poet," in *The Word: Readings in Theology*, ed. by Carney Gavin, Charles Pfeiffer, *et al.* [New York: P. J. Kenedy and Sons, 1964], 4-7).

13. Bellah, *Beyond Belief*, 21.

14. Wach, *Types*, 38. Wach provides the following example: "African Bushmen, awed by the presence of the numinous at a given place, utter a numinous sound in which they express the vivid emotion that grips them, while throwing a few grains into a hole in the hallowed ground, an act which at the same time expresses and reinforces the communion which exists between fellow worshippers" (Ibid.).

15. Eliade, *Two and the One*, 208-10; Wach, *Comparative Study*, 63. Evolutionist and diffusionist theories, it should be noted, are not mutually exclusive (See Bidney, "Religion and Human Evolution," 8).

16. Bellah, *Beyond Belief*, 21-22, 24.

17. See the discussion of the expression "primitive religion" in Kitagawa, *History of Religions*, 30-31. R. Schmidt, *Exploring Religion*, 45.

18. Wach, *Types*, 39.

19. See Wach, *Comparative Study*, 65-67; Wach, *Sociology*, 20; Wach, *Types*, 39; Kitagawa, *History of Religions*, 31-32.

20. Bellah, *Beyond Belief*, 27.

21. Wach, *Comparative Study*, 66; Wach, *Types*, 39.

22. Wach, *Comparative Study*, 67-69; Wach, *Types*, 39. C. H. Long has commented significantly in this regard: "This is not to say that primitive and archaic man expresses himself only on the symbolic level but that he is only consciously aware of the symbolic level of expression. It is clear from the work of . . . Godfrey Lienhardt . . . and Claude Lévi-Strauss, that a logical structure is present in primitive symbolism. That which is obscured in their expression is the rational. On the other hand, that which is obscured in the expression of modern man is the symbolic" (Long, "Archaism and Hermeneutics," 84).

23. Wach, *Comparative Study*, 78-84. See also: van der Leeuw, *Religion*, I:

159-87; Eliade, *Patterns*, 463.

24. Dickson, *Dawn of Belief*, 209, 215. For Eliade's own discussion of mythology among Paleolithic populations, see: Eliade, *History*, I: 26-27.

25. Wach, *Comparative Study*, 77; Wach, *Sociology*, 23; Wach, *Types*, 40, 62, 64.

26. Wach, *Comparative Study*, 78; Charles Hartshorne and William L. Reese, *Philosophers Speak of God* (Chicago and London: The University of Chicago Press, 1953), 1-15.

27. Wach, *Comparative Study*, 78-84. See also: van der Leeuw, *Religion*, I: 159-87; Eliade, *Patterns*, 463.

28. Theodore M. Ludwig, "Gods and Goddesses," *ER* 3: 61-66.

29. See *Supra*, Chapter Four.

30. Merlin Stone, *When God Was a Woman* (New York: The Dial Press, 1976), 1-5; see also Schmidt, *Exploring Religion*, 40-41.

31. See Raffaele Pettazzoni, "The Supreme Being: Phenomenological Structure and Historical Development," in Eliade and Kitagawa, *History of Religions*, 59-66.

32. Although evidence from Lower and Middle Paleolithic periods (eg., Chou-k'ou-tien, Drachenloch) is no longer thought by most scholars to indicate belief in a supreme being, as noted earlier, there is some evidence from the Upper Paleolithic and Mesolithic periods (Willendorf, Meiendorf, etc.) of sacrificial offerings being made to a Supreme Being or a Lord of Wild Beasts, or of depictions of the latter himself (See Eliade, *History*, I: 13-15; Maringer, *Gods*, 90-99, 271-72, 278-79). Abbé Breuil concluded, for example, that the man-animal, dancing figure he discovered at the Les Trois Frères site in France was "really the 'God' of Les Trois Frères," a conclusion that Eliade also finds somewhat plausible in the sense of a Lord of Wild Beasts (Eliade, *History*, I: 18; Maringer, *Gods*, Plate IX, 76; Dickson, *Dawn of Belief*, 116).

33. Ludwig, "Gods and Goddesses," 60; Maringer, *Gods*, 90-99, 271-72, 278-79; Eliade, *History*, I: 7, 13-15, 18, 26, 32.

34. Ludwig, "Gods and Goddesses," 60, 62; Eliade, *Patterns*, 239-264; Eliade, *History*, I: 40-44; Eliade, *Sacred and Profane*, 38-151; Pettazzoni, "Supreme Being," 65.

35. Ludwig, "Gods and Goddesses," 60; Eliade, *Patterns*, 38-123; Eliade, *Sacred and Profane*, 118-38; Pettazzoni, "Supreme Being," 65.

36. Wach, *Comparative Study*, 84; M. Eliade, *From Primitives to Zen* (New York and Evanston: Harper and Row, 1967), 83-118.

37. Eliade, *Sacred and the Profane*, 30-50, 54-58, 64; Wach, *Comparative Study*, 85-86, 88; van der Leeuw, *Religion*, 552; Kitagawa, *History of Religions*, 35.

38. See Wach, *Comparative Study*, 84-89; Eliade, *Sacred and the Profane*, 20-113.

39. Bellah, *Beyond Belief*, 23, 29, 30, 32; Schmidt, *Exploring Religion* (1988), 50, 51.

40. Bellah, *Beyond Belief*, 23.

41. Eliade, *Sacred and the Profane*, 165-66; Kitagawa, *History of Religions*, 36.

42. Wach, *Comparative Study*, 89.

43. Eliade, *Sacred and the Profane*, 165.

44. Ibid., 166.

45. Ibid., 167.

46. Ibid.

47. On the relation of theory and practice in the history of religions, see Wach, *Sociology*, 26; Kitagawa, *History of Religions*, 38-39.

48. See Wach, *Comparative Study*, 100-114; Wach, *Types*, 41-45; van der Leeuw, *Religion*, II: 339-458; Eliade, *Primitives to Zen*, 201-320.

49. See Wach, *Comparative Study*, 114-120; Wach, *Types*, 41-45; van der Leeuw, *Religion*, II: 459-539; Eliade, *Primitives to Zen*, 446-530; 551-83.

50. See Wach, *Comparative Study*, 97, 115; Eliade, *Patterns*, 464.

51. Bellah, *Beyond Belief*, 28.

52. See Wach, *Comparative Study*, 101; Wach, *Sociology*, 27; Kitagawa, *History of Religions*, 35; Bellah, *Beyond Belief*, 28.

53. Wach, *Comparative Study*, 102; Wach, *Types*, 41; Kitagawa, *History of Religions*, 33-34; Schmidt, *Exploring Religion*, 46.

54. Eliade, *Sacred and Profane*, 95-113.

55. See Dickson, *Dawn of Belief*, 125-26.

56. See Brockway, "Origins," 55, 520; Maringer, *Gods*, 274.

57. See *Supra*, Chapter Two, n. 84; Bellah, *Beyond Belief*, 28.

58. See Bellah, *Beyond Belief*, 28, 30; *Supra*, Chapter Two, ns. 95-99.

59. Bellah, *Beyond Belief*, 28.

60. See Schmidt, *Exploring Religion*, 48; *Supra*, Chapter Two, n. 96.

61. Wach, *Sociology*, 27.

62. Ibid., 28.

63. Ibid., 28-29; Wach, *Comparative Study*, 121-24.

64. Bellah, *Beyond Belief*, 26.

65. Wach, *Types*, 45; Wach, *Comparative Study*, 123.

66. Wach, *Types*, 45-46; Wach, *Comparative Study*, 123-24.

67. Wach, *Types*, 46.

68. Wach, *Types*, 46; Wach, *Comparative Study*, 127-43; Wach, *Sociology*, 34-389; Kitagawa, *History of Religions*, 39; van der Leeuw, *Religion*, I: 191-274; II: 650-67.

69. Wach, *Types*, 46.

70. Kitagawa, *History of Religions*, 39-40.

71. Bellah writes: "Changes in the sphere of religion, which constitute what I mean by religious evolution, are related to a variety of other dimensions of change in other social spheres that define the general process of sociocultural evolution" (*Beyond Belief*, 24). See also: Dickson, *Dawn of Belief*, 12.

72. Wallace, *Religion*, 86-87.

73. Ibid., 256.

74. Bellah, *Beyond Belief*, 28, 30-31, 34-35, 38-39, 43-44.

75. Wallace, *Religion*, 255-56.

76. Ibid., 256.

77. Ibid., 86.

78. Ibid.

79. Bellah, *Beyond Belief*, 28.

80. Wallace, *Religion*, 88.

81. Ibid., 86. Bellah concurs: "Specialized shamans or medicine men are found in some tribes but are not a necessary feature of primitive religion" (*Beyond Belief*, 28).

82. Bellah, *Beyond Belief*, 28.

83. Ibid.

84. Dickson, *Dawn of Belief*, 159, 190-96.

85. Ibid., 129-37; Eliade, *History*, I: 18-19.

86. Eliade, *History*, I: 19; Eliade, *Rites and Symbols*, 87-102; Eliade, *Primitives to Zen*, 423-43; Dickson, *Dawn of Belief*, 134; Carmody, *Oldest God*, 30.

87. Eliade, *Rites*, 95.

88. Dickson, *Dawn of Belief*, 199, 215.

89. Ibid., 12, 87, 97, 98-99.

90. Brockway, "Origins," 59; Smart, *World's Religions*, 36.

91. Eliade, *History*, I: 24-25.

92. Dickson, *Dawn of Belief*, 13, 199.

93. See van der Leeuw, *Religion*, 339-40.

94. Bellah, *Beyond Belief*, 28-29.

95. Ibid., 29, 33.

96. Smart, *World's Religions*, 34.

97. See Bidney, "Ethnology of Religion," 8-13; Herbert M. Watzman, "Question of Human Origins Debated Anew," *The Chronicle of Higher Education* (September 16, 1992): A7-A9.

98. For a summary, see *NCE* 8: 269-70.

99. Schmidt, *Exploring Religion*, 45.

100. Smart, *World's Religions*, 34.

101. See *NCE* 8: 270.

102. Kitagawa, *History of Religion*, 35; Schmidt, *Exploring Religion* 48; Eliade, *History* I: 56-301; II: 3-43, 107-209.

103. Schmidt, *Exploring Religion*, 49.

104. Eliade, *History*, I: 70-80.

105. Ibid., 97, 100.

106. Hesiod's myth of Prometheus, Eliade notes, was "extremely archaic and rooted deep in pre-History," having "undergone a long process of transformation and modification before the poet recorded [it]" (M. Eliade, *Myth and Reality* [New York and Evanston: Harper and Row, 1963] 4).

107. See Smart, *World's Religions*, 177-92.

108. Bellah, *Beyond Belief*, 30.

109. Ibid.

110. Ibid., 30, 48 n.31.

111. Ibid., 30.

112. Eliade, *Myth and Reality*, 149. Eliade notes that neither Homer nor Hesiod recorded "all the mythological themes that were in circulation in the Greek world" (Ibid.), with the result that much of the "living and popular side of Greek religion" escaped the "rationalist critique," and survived to some extent in European religious folk lore of the Christian era, while the "secularized and demythicized" Homeric and Hesiodian myths would retain,

as they had for "the Greek elites" of an earlier age, only a "high cultural value" (Ibid., 155-61). This is not to say that either the "elites" of ancient Greece or Christian intellectuals excluded mythology entirely from their religious beliefs, for just as Christian thinkers would turn to other new myths, so the Greek elites had turned to other mythologies "to justify and articulate new religious concepts" (e.g. the Eleusian, Orphico-Pythagorean "mysteries," Neo-Platonic mytholiges of the soul, solar mythologies, etc.) (Ibid., 158-59).

113. Ibid., 148, 151-57.   According to Eliade, this process of "demythicization" was "an attempt to go beyond mythology as divine history and to reach a primal source from which the real had flowed, to identify the womb of Being. It was in seeking the source, the principle, the *arche,* that philosophical speculation for a short time coincided with cosmogony; but it was no longer the cosmogonic myth, it was an ontological problem" (Ibid., 111). See also Wallace, *Religion,* 256, 257.

114. Otto, *Essays,* 97-98; Kitagawa, *History of Religions,* 35, 36; Eliade, *Myth and Reality,* 157, 158.

115. Ludwig, "Gods and Goddesses," 60, 63-66; Eliade, *History,* I: 87-94; 189-92; 247-53; II: 144-50; Eliade, *Primitives to Zen,* 52-68; Walter F. Otto, *The Homeric Gods* (New York: Pantheon, 1954), 41-124; H. R. Ellis Davidson, *Gods and Myths of Northern Europe* (London: Penguin, 1964), 28-30; 48-61.

116. Bellah, *Beyond Belief,* 29.

117. Ibid.

118. Ibid.

119. Eliade, *Myth and Reality,* 158.

120. Ibid., 148.

121. Ibid.

122. Ibid., 153.

123. Ibid.

124. See *NCE* 1: 1145; 7: 409; 9: 517-18.

125. Ibid.

126. Bellah, *Beyond Belief,* 29-30.

127. Ibid., 22-23, 32.

128. Schmidt, *Exploring Religion,* 48-49.

129. Bellah, *Beyond Belief,* 29, 30.

130. Ibid., 30.

131. Schmidt, *Exploring Religion,* 50.

132. Ibid.

133. See *NCE* 1: 1145.

134. Schmidt, *Exploring Religion,* 49.

135. Wallace, *Religion,* 87, 99, 256.

136. Ibid., 86-87.

137. Schmidt, *Exploring Religion,* 50.

138. Bellah, *Beyond Belief,* 31.

139. Ibid.

140. Ibid., 31-32.

141. See Schmidt, *Exploring Religion* (1988), 50. On the "evolution" of philosophy, and for that matter, science, from "theological speculation," see Wach, *Types,* 40, 62-63, 68-69; Wach, *Comparative Study,* 68-71, 106-107.

142. Kitagawa, *History of Religions*, 36.

143. Wach, *Comparative Study*, 68-69.

144. Bellah, *Beyond Belief*, 32.

145. Bellah, *Beyond Belief*, 32-33; Wach, *Comparative Study*, 68-72, 75-76; Wach, *Types*, 39; Wach, *Sociology*, 22. The "development of dogma" is, of course, a thorny issue in Christian circles, and, no doubt, in most other classical religions.

146. Wach, *Comparative Study*, 71-74; Wach, *Sociology*, 22.

147. Wach, *Comparative Study*, 72-73.

148. See Eliade, *History*, I: 241-46; 309-12; II: 28-33; Eliade, *Primitives to Zen*, 49-51; 74-80; 584-86; 594-606; 622-25; Bellah, *Beyond Belief*, 32-33.

149. Schmidt, *Exploring Religion*, 51.

150. Bellah, *Beyond Belief*, 32-33.

151. Ibid., 33

152. Eliade, *Myth and Reality*, 156, 171.

153. Bellah, *Beyond Belief*, 22-23, 32.

154. Schmidt, *Exploring Religion*, 51.

155. Ibid.

156. Wach, *Types*, 65.

157. Ibid., 70, 72, 73; Wach, *Comparative Study*, 93.

158. Wach, *Types*, 65-67.

159. Ibid., 65.

160. Bellah, *Beyond Belief*, 33.

161. Ibid., 33, 42.

162. Ibid., 33.

163. Ibid., 32-33.

164. Bellah writes: "Historic religion convicts man of a basic flaw far more serious than those conceived of by earlier religions" (Ibid., 33).

165. Ibid., 34.

166. See Schmidt, *Exploring Religion*, 51.

167. Eliade, *Patterns*, 464.

168. Schmidt, *Exploring Religion*, 52.

169. See Bellah, *Beyond Belief*, 34-35.

170. Ibid., 34.

171. Ibid.

172. Ibid., 31, 34.

173. Wallace, *Religion*, 87-88, 84-85.

174. Bellah, *Beyond Belief*, 36.

175. Eliade, *Sacred and the Profane*, 205; Eliade, *Myth and Reality*, 156, 162-93.

176. Bellah, *Beyond Belief*, 36-37; Schmidt, *Exploring Religion*, 54-55.

177. Bellah, *Beyond Belief*, 40.

178. Ibid., 37; C. G. Jung, *Psychology and Religion* (New Haven and London: Yale University Press, 1968), 62.

179. Bellah, *Beyond Belief*, 40.

180. Ibid., 36-42.

181. Ibid., 40-41.

182. See F. Nietzsche, *The Joyful Wisdom* (New York: Russell and Russell

), 167–69.

183. See D. Bonhoeffer, *Letters and Papers from Prison* (New York: Macmillan, 1971), 361.

184. In addition to Stone's aforementioned *When God Was a Woman*, see also: Naomi R. Goldenberg, *Changing of the Gods: Feminism and the End of Traditional Religions* (Boston: Beacon Press, 1979); *Mother Worship*, ed. James Preston (Chapel Hill: University of North Carolina Press, 1982).

185. See John Cobb and David Griffin, *Process Theology: An Introductory Exposition* (Philadelphia: Westminster Press, 1976); Hick, *An Interpretation of Religion*, 252–96.

186. See Robert McKim, "Could God Have More Than One Nature?," *Faith and Philosophy* 5.4 (1988): 380

187. Bellah, *Beyond Belief*, 36, 37.

188. Ibid., 37.

189. Ibid.

190. Ibid., 40.

191. Ibid.

192. Ibid., 36.

193. Ibid., 42.

194. Ibid., 42.

195. On Comte, see Kueng, *Does God Exist*, 167–68. For Huxley's views, see: J. Huxley, *Religion without Revelation* (London: Max Parrish, 1957), esp. 1–31.

196. See my comments on both in: B. Verkamp, "Recovering a Sense of Sin," *America* (November 19, 1983): 306–7.

197. Bellah, *Beyond Belief*, 40.

198. Ibid., 42.

199. Wach, *Sociology*, 27.

200. Wach, *Comparative Study*, 101.

201. See B. Verkamp, *The Indifferent Mean* (Athens, Ohio, and Detroit: Ohio University and Wayne State University Presses, 1977), 1–92.

202. Bellah, *Beyond Belief*, 37.

203. Schmidt, *Exploring Religion*, 54–55.

204. Bellah, *Beyond Belief*, 43.

205. Ibid., 38; Schmidt, *Exploring Religion*, 54.

206. Bellah, *Beyond Belief*, 38–39.

207. Ibid., 44.

208. Ibid., 24–25.

209. Ibid., 25.

Chapter Six

The Adaptive Value of Religion

Like its cognates 'apt' and 'aptitude', the term 'adaptive' connotes a certain 'match' or 'fit' between an object or action and its particular situation.[1] A cultural phenomenon will be adaptive, then, to the extent that it helps the social unit of which it is a part adjust to a specific environment. That religion has played such a role was long ago asserted by William James when, in line with his pragmatic interpretation of religion,[2] he argued against "exclusive scientificism" that any nation or race deprived of its religious sentiments would "as surely go to ruin, and fall a prey to their more richly constituted neighbors, as the beasts of the field as a whole have fallen a prey to man."[3] More recently, the anthropologist Roy A. Rappaport has noted that it would be both implausible and imprudent not to assume that anything so "universal to human culture" as religion has not contributed to human survival.[4] "When we consider further," he adds, "that religious beliefs and practices have frequently been central to human concerns and when we reflect upon the amount of time, energy, emotion, and treasure that men have expended in building religious monuments, supporting priestly hierarchies, fighting holy wars, and in sacrifices to assure their well-being in the next world, we find it hard to imagine that religion, as bizarre and irrational as it may seem or even be, has not contributed positively to human evolution and adaptation."[5] To see how this has actually happened, it will be helpful to keep in mind the distinction drawn by Stephen Toulmin between the four different kinds of adaptation:

calculative, homeostatic, developmental, and populational.[6]

The adaptation will be "homeostatic," Toulmin notes, when the adapting unit responds in such wise as to maintain a condition "that will preserve its normal functioning in the face of external changes."[7] Under the influence of the French physiologist Claude Bernard, both Emile Durkheim and Talcott Parsons, among others,[8] applied such a conception of adaptation to social processes and "ended up analysing the 'normal' workings of society as depending on the operation of 'systems' that maintain 'healthy' equilibrium, in the same general way that the normal operations of the digestive system (say) maintains healthy physiological equilibrium in the human body."[9] Both also were inclined to represent religion as one of those "systems that maintain 'healthy' equilibrium" in society. In line with his general definition of religion as a "unified system of beliefs and practices relative to sacred things, which unite into one single community . . . all those who adhere to them,"[10] Durkheim described religious rites (e.g. sacrifice, mourning) as a way society has of keeping itself together by balancing centrifugal tendencies (e.g. hunting, death) with periodic, "effervescent" reassertions of social solidarity.[11] Parsons similarly counted funereal, penitentiary, and other religious rites as being among the control mechanisms by which societal "strains" and "deviant tendencies" can be "counteracted and the system brought back, in the relevant respects, to the old equilibrium state."[12] Parsons would later pay more attention to the evolutionary aspect of adaptation,[13] but his and Durkheim's earlier emphasis upon homeostasis helped give rise to more recent "structuralist" and "cybernetic" studies of how ancestor worship, animal sacrifice, and other religious practices have played a role 'n "maintaining social equilibrium."[14] Gregory Bateson's conception of the religious, metaphorical mapping of reality as a balance against society's more logical, scientific proclivities[15] belongs to that category. So, too, does Hans J. Mol's description of religion as society's attempt through "sacralization of identity" to "modify or stabilize the differentiation it has been unable to prevent."[16]

Closely related is E. O. Wilson's suggestion that religion functions to provide authority and furnish group identity. Arguing that the human mind is uniquely predisposed through its "indoctrinability" and "penchant for sacralization" to participate in a few sacralizing processes (e.g. objectification, commitment, and myth) that "generate the institutions of organized religion,"[17] Wilson concludes that religion "congeals identity:" "In the midst of the chaotic and potentially disorienting experiences each person undergoes daily, religion classifies him, provides him with unquestioned membership in a group claiming great powers, and by this means gives him a driving purpose in life compatible with his self-interest."[18] Religion, in other words, is a "process by which individuals are persuaded to subordinate their immediate self-interest to the interest of the group."[19] "Incest taboos, taboos in general, xenophobia, the dichotomization of objects into sacred and profane, nosism, hierarchical dominance systems, intense attention toward leaders, charisma, trophyism, and trance-induction," Wilson writes, "are among the elements of religious behavior," which function "to circumscribe a social group and bind its members together in unquestioning allegiance."[20] These forms of religious practice "can be seen to confer biological advantage," and genes favoring them have been "strongly selected for."[21] The conditions to which such religious practices were adaptive may now be gone, and religion itself may give way to "scientific materialism,"[22] Wilson notes, but pas

societies practicing religion "have been much more likely
to survive than those that did not."[23]

D. T. Campbell does not think that religious
altruism is genetically based, but he does share Wilson's
view of its adaptive value. "For a social system to work
best," he writes, "the participants in it should have
behavioral dispositions optimizing social system purposes
rather than individual purposes, where these differ."[24]
Because they are transient and are generally "recruited
from the most narcissistic and egocentric of the group's
membership," particular leaders cannot effectivly reify
such social purposes.[25] They need to be reified
"transcendentally" (i.e., religiously).[26] "Committing one
self to living for a transcendent Good's purposes, not
one's own" thus becomes "a commitment to optimize the
social system rather than the individual system."[27] And
"social groups effectively indoctrinating such individual
commitments," Campbell concludes, "might well have had
a social-evolutionary advantage and thus have discovered
a functional, adaptive truth."[28] "Inhibitory moral norms,"
like the ancient Aztec preachments against human
selfishness and cowardice, or ancient Judaism's Ten
Commandments and Proverbs, along with any "religious
beliefs in afterlife with compensatory rewards for
deprivation in this life," can be viewed, Campbell notes,
"as an effort to overcome, to balance out, the biological
bias in the opposite direction," or, in other words, "to
counter the biological selfishness which genetic
competition has selected continually."[29]

Rappaport is another who has emphasized the
homeostatic nature of religious adaptation. After defining
adaptation as the "processes by which organisms or
groups of organisms maintain homeostasis," or in other
words, as a "cybernetic" process, whereby "an adaptive
system initiates corrective programs . . . in response to
system-endangering changes in the states of its

components or in some aspect of the environment,"[30] he spells out exactly how religion contributes to such a process. Cybernetic processes, he says, are primarily informational: "In response to the receipt of information concerning the states of systemic components, messages — directives or the like — specifying corrective programs are transmitted."[31] "Religious activities," he adds, "are primarily part of [these] informational processes of human societies."[32] "Both the content and the occurrence of ritual may be of importance in communication,"[33] he notes. The pre-war dances among the Maring tribesmen of New Guinea, or the potlatches of the Northwest Coast Indians, for example, convey important information, on the basis of which "corrective action may be taken if necessary or possible."[34]

Performance of a puberty rite of passage can reduce the level of ambiguity about societal expectations.[35] The heightening of emotions during the performance of rituals can also affirm the sanctity of one or another proposition.[36] Such "sanctity of the ritual also constitutes a metamessage concerning social information transmitted in the ritual" by adding an element of "unquestionable truthfulness" to the kind of "unverifiable propositions" upon which the preponderance of social actions rely.[37] Furthermore, "sanctity has quite clearly had an important, even predominant, role to play in containing the self-interested pursuits of individuals and social groups and in supporting the conventions," which may be essential to the regulation of society, but which the evolution of intelligence had inclined humans to recognize as "arbitrary."[38] Religious practices have also served as the "functional equivalent of political power" among some peoples, by regulating "social, economic, and in some instances even ecological relations," through the conveyance of information, or by constituting "corrective programs" themselves (e.g. the sacrificing of pigs in some

New Guinea Highland societies).[39]   The "virtue of regulation through religious ritual," Rappaport notes, "is that the activities of large numbers of people may be governed in accordance with sanctified conventions in the absence of powerful authorities or even of discrete human authorities of any sort."[40] Thus, "it is plausible to argue," he continues, "that religious ritual played an important role in social and ecological regulation during a time in human history when the arbitrariness of social conventions was increasing but it was not yet possible for authorities, if they existed at all, to enforce compliance."[41] And although "the sacred and the numinous may be degraded in the churches of technologically developed states," they may still, Rappaport concludes, "retain a positive role in the adaptation of contemporary societies," as, for example, by facilitating the revitalistic activities of the ecological movement.[42]

In the final analysis, however, all such homeostatic theories are, as Toulmin has noted, "of stasis, not of change."[43] They may leave some room for 'novel and inventive' actions (e.g. use of fire), that will restore and protect 'steady states,'[44] but in the end they can "explain only how the existing institutions of a society adapt their operations in the face of external changes so as to defend themselves in their present forms."[45] They are "quite unsuited" for explaining how society possesses such forms in the first place, or how those forms can be modified to take better advantage of external conditions.[46]

Adaptation will be "developmental" when the adapting unit becomes a creature of the kind "that can cope [calculatively, homeostatically, or however] effectively and independently with the problems of life."[47] Hegel was inclined to view the whole history of mankind in such terms, as a development, that is, from the Oriental "age of childhood" (which knew "only that *one* is free"), through the periods of "adolescence" and "manhood" of anicent Greece and Rome (when it was recognized "that *some* are free"), to the ripe "old age" of the Germanic world (which "knows that *all* are free")[48]. Auguste Comte,[49] and the aforementioned nineteenth-century evolutionists,[50] with their epigenetic notion of social progress, were similarly inclined.   Later historicists,[51] like Oswald Spengler and to some extent Arnold Toynbee, would reject any such linear conception of the history of 'mankind',[52] but the many different "cultures"[53] or "societies"[54] that they recognized as having "awakened out of the protospirituality"[55] in response to one or another "challenge,"[56] would still be said to have passed through the "age phases" of "childhood, youth, manhood, and old age."[57]   By thus comparing the whole of human history, or at least segments of it, to the "ontogeny of the individual organism,"[58] some of these historicists, like Comte and nineteenth- century evolutionists, obviously had in mind to downplay some of the adaptive value of religion. For if, as they were wont to say, religion was nothing but an "infantile stage" of mankind's intellectual development,[59] it would clearly undermine man's capacity to adjust calculatively, homeostatically, or in any other way, to changing environmental conditions. Not all historicists, of course, relegated religion to the "age of childhood." Hegel, for one, certainly did not. For while he readily admitted that the "imaginative thought" associated with "religious consciousness"[60] had its earlier "phases,"[61] he nonetheless insisted that it can mature, and become "the highest manifestation of Absolute Spirit short of Absolute Knowledge."[62]   Toynbee, too, after first conceiving of religion as merely the "chrysalis" of civilization,[63] eventually came to view religion as one of mankind's more "ethereal" responses to life's challenges.[64] While, therefore, a pessimist like Spengler might have thought that nothing could help a culture escape the social law o

gravity,[65] both Hegel and Toynbee were of the view that
it was precisely in and through religion that Western
Civilization had one of its best chances for survival.[66] As
Toulmin has noted, it would be all too "pat, smug, and
arbitrary" to pursue such a line of thought to the point of
ascribing "maturity" to only Western Civilization or
Western Christendom.[67] Eschewing such elitist
temptations, however, one might still think of the
adaptive value of religion to some extent in terms of the
way religion helps a society come of age and respond in
a more adult manner to the more spiritual, i.e., more
"ethereal," problems of life (e.g. how to live together in
peace).[68] As with the aforementioned "homeostatic
mechanisms," however, so with these "developmental
capacities," to explain how they originated and were
modified to take better advantage of external conditions,[69]
attention will have to be paid also to what is called
"populational adaptation."

Adaptation will be "populational," Toulmin notes,
when "some novel, advantageous feature appear[s] and
spread[s] through the population concerned, viz. one that
makes its members better equipped (fitter, better
matched) to the novel conditions confronting them."[70] In
this sense of the term, Toulmin has in mind the kind of
evolutionary process of "variation and selective
perpetuation"[71] whereby, as noted earlier, various
religious phenomena have been "selected." Here the
concern will be to identify the adaptive basis of their
selection, by taking notice of what some scholars are
saying about the way specific features of different
religions have helped one or another society defend itself
against not only extinction, but also "want and need and
ignorance of other kinds."[72]

Marvin Harris, R. Rappaport, and others have
emphasized the adaptive value of the Aztec human
sacrifices,[73] the Hindu sacralization of the cow,[74] the

Maring sacrifice of pigs,[75] the Jewish and Islamic dietary laws,[76] along such lines, by noting how all of these religious practices helped "improve the access of people to the scarce resources around them in the physical world."[77] Others have focused on the way certain features of religion have contributed to the reproductive success of individuals. V. Reynolds and R. E. S. Tanner, for example, have developed a theory that "the more unpredictable the total environment is perceived to be, the more people will want to create and support ideas favouring high levels of reproduction . . . [and] conversely, the less unpredictable the environment is perceived to be, the more people will develop ideas favouring low levels of reproduction."[78] It is to be expected, therefore, that in highly unpredictable environments (i.e., in countries where energy consumption *per capita* and gross national product *per capita* are low), religious rules favouring high levels of reproductive activity will be selected, while in highly predictable environments, anti-natalist rules will be found "fit."[79] In the correlation between relatively pro-natalist rules of Islam, Hinduism, and Judaism and the highly unpredictable environment where they have thrived, or between the relatively anti-natalist rules of Buddhism, Roman Catholicism, and Protestantism and their generally predictable environments, Reynolds and Tanner claim to have found confirmation of their theory.[80] "The 'instructions' religions give to individuals [concerning "people's obligations to reproduce a lot or a little; whether or not to contracept; whether or not to practice abortion or infanticide; whether to devote massive care to those who are born throughout their lives or to be more resigned to the facts of death; whether to marry young or to postpone marriage; whether to divorce easily or regard divorce as impossible; whether to regard sex as holy or sinful; whether to equate personal hygiene with religious purity and piety, or not to connect the two"] are 'adaptive,'" they conclude, "in the sense that they are found in countries where the results they produce will tend to enhance the reproductive success of individuals following them."[81]

As has been seen in chapter three, the "variation and selective retention" process underlying such "populational adaptation" does not altogether preclude "calculation." Some of the "variations" constituting the raw material of cultural evolution may themselves have been the product of "self-conscious planning" or "foresightful action."[82] The selection and retention of any such variations might also have involved an element of calculation.[83] Yet, given the complexity of the environment and, as Toulmin has observed, "the short-term character of human foresight and calculation in the social realm, it is hard to see how any sort of conscious, deliberate, calculated human decisions could have brought effective social arrangements into existence in the first place."[84] Appeal to "hypothetical covenants" of earlier times might help explain how "social and political *change*" has resulted from a conscious selection of "best adapted options on the basis of explicit calculations," Toulmin suggests, but it cannot explain "the very origins of social and political life in these times."[85] All the more will this be the case if, as Gerd Theissen would have us believe, the "reality" to which all biological and cultural evolution is meant to be an adaptation[86] is not just "nature," but an "ultimate reality," a "mysterious other world."[87] Scientific thought can be open to this ultimate reality, Theissen admits, but the former's hypotheses cannot really discover the mysterious dimensions of the latter.[88] In other words, man on his own cannot calculate the forms of thought and practice by which to adapt best to his "total" environment. His "mind" is simply not up to the task of comprehending so vast a realm. But this would not rule out altogether for Theissen the possibility of some "calculative adaptation" — at least not as the latter was interpreted by Giambattista Vico to mean that the "responsibility for the relevant choices" could be "shifted away from human beings themselves and given . . . to Divine Providence."[89] "From this point of view," Toulmin notes, "the adaptedness of human institutions may still be the outcome of foresight; but that foresight is no longer the finite, conditional foresight of human beings, who operate largely in ignorance of the future. Now, it is the infinite unconditioned foresight of Divine Providence, which had the capacity to arrange, long in advance, for human beings to enter into 'well adapted' social institutions as soon as the historical conditions were right."[90] Theissen would seem to have some such "providential" conception of "calculative adaptation" in mind when he identifies God as "that mysterious ultimate reality towards which all our organic, intellectual and religious structures develop attempts at adaptation."[91] By "revealing" itself "within the unending story of trial and error" that is "the history of religion,"[92] the ultimate reality has itself made possible through "faith" a calculative adaptation of unlimited scope.[93] "All forms of religion — animism, polytheism, monotheism, all world religions, all confessional systems, indeed all life," Theissen argues, "are an attempt to correspond to [this] God."[94] But he claims that three of these "spiritual mutations" (biblical monotheism, Jesus Christ, and the Holy Spirit) have been especially successful adaptations to the ultimate reality. What he says about their adaptive value might add a fine "emic" touch to this otherwise predominantly "etic" study of the evolution of religion.[95]

Theissen admits along with Darwin that nature is selective of those variations best suited for survival. He recognizes that as such, nature is extremely competitive, involving much "rivalry and conflict," because "the means of life contained in a particular environmental niche are always sparse."[96] Furthermore, he grants that religion has not only helped man compete for survival in ways suggested by Wilson and others,[97] but in its polytheistic stages has even heightened the competitiveness of the struggle. "As long as people worship a multiplicity of gods," he writes, "the move from one god to another is simply a move from one 'ecological niche' to another. Each god represents a limited sector of reality. Rivalry and conflict between the gods reflect the human fight for distribution."[98] This was as true, he adds, of the "functional gods (gods who represent the spheres of sexuality, food and drink, war, law and order)," as it was of the "territorial gods."[99] "Little would have been gained, had one god gained the upper hand in this rivalry between gods — and found universal recognition as the ruler of all gods."[100] Only when the "one God" became "the only God" and embraced "all spheres of reality, all territories and sectors of life, all peoples and groups," Theissen continues, could "humanity extricate itself from the 'bond with the environment' which leads to competition with others because of limited opportunities for survival."[101] But that was precisely the "decisive step" taken when Israel of old[102] moved from polytheism to monotheism through their portrayal of God "without images"[103] and "without a family,"[104] and presented Yahweh as not just "one ecological niche alongside others, but as the central reality behind all ecological niches."[105]

By discovering this new "dimension of depth behind all environments," or this God, "whose resources can be shared out among an infinite number of people without losing their value," there was found, Theissen concludes, "the Archimedean point from which . . . the principle of selection which controls all life" could be "shifted."[106] The step toward monotheism brought to a climax, in other words, what cultural evolution had begun;[107] it challenged the principle of natural selection. Through the radical "conversion"[108] prompted by the anti-polytheistic monotheism, the age old laws of selection (e.g., war, suppression, and exploitation)[109] were deprived of their force, and afforded a "power to survive to those who [like the Israelites themselves] otherwise would have [had] no chance."[110]

Theissen's theory in this regard can be seen as a variation on the notion of "supernatural selectivity" propounded by certain late nineteenth-century thinkers in response to concerns raised by William R. Greg and others about "the Failure of 'Natural Selectivity' in the Case of Man."[111] In his notorious *Fraser's Magazine* essay, Greg had argued that moral attributes of civilized societies (e.g. "respect for life and respect for property")[112] encouraged by religion, would in fact favor the survival of the weak, i.e., the physically, intellectually, and morally inferior individuals, and that "only calculated intervention in the social process could reinstate that 'righteous and salutary law [of natural selection] which God ordained for the preservation of a worthy and improving humanity."[113] Although Darwin himself had been inclined to think that there were "inherent checks" (e.g. increased mortality rate of the impoverished)[114] against the demise of natural selectivity in civilized societies, he also shared Greg's hope for "enlightened social legislation" such as would not arrest all competition and "check the salutary work of natural selection."[115] An editor of *The Spectator* proposed, however, a different solution to the problem. "The real answer," he wrote, "is this — that directly you reach man in the ascending stages of animal life, you reach a point where the competitive principle of 'natural selection' is more or less superseded by a higher principle, of which the key-note is not 'Let the strong trample out the weak,'

but 'Let the strong sacrifice themselves for the weak.'
This is really the law of supernatural selection, as
distinguished from the law which governs the selection of
races in the lower animal world."[116] "Natural Selection,"
the writer admits, may be the "providential principle"
governing the animal world, and it may have its "place
and function . . . even amongst us."[117] But the ultimate
"plan of God," he argues, is "to ennoble the higher part of
His universe at least, *not* so much by eliminating
imperfection, as by multiplying graces and virtues."[118]
This "principle of supernatural selection" is the "law of
self-sacrifice, the law of the Cross, the law the religious
root of which lies in the teaching that One, 'being in the
form of God,' made himself of no reputation, and took
upon himself the form of a servant, to raise creatures
infinitely below Himself up to His own level, to give
them of His life, and breathe into them His spirit, is in
its very essence and conception a reversal of the law of
'natural selection,' at least so far as man dreams of
making himself in purpose and in spirit the executioner
of that law."[119] "The history of all Christian and many
other Churches," the editor concludes on a Goethean
note, "is at bottom little but the history of the growth of
human reverence for [this] law of supernatural
selection."[120]

Theissen himself develops this line of thought
further by suggesting that in Jesus the conversion called
for by prophetic monotheism became a reality. "The
activity and proclamation of Jesus should be interpreted
primarily," Theissen writes, "as one 'mutation' among
many others," and yet as "something fundamentally new
in history," a "leap in development beyond what has
happened hitherto."[121] "Whereas the prophets arrived at
the idea that a change of conduct and conversion is better
than death [i.e., extinction], Jesus," Theissen notes,
"actually embodied the change in conduct that they called

for."[122] By proclaiming God as "the gracious father, who offers and makes possible life at the very point where human beings have offended against the basic conditions of reality,"[123] by extolling sexual abstention, love of enemies, solidarity with strangers, humility, and compassion for the weak,[124] and by working miracles "against human misery and wretchedness,"[125] Jesus challenged "the principle of selection," and broke "with biological evolution."[126] The principle of selection was replaced by the "principle of solidarity."[127] The love characterizing this "new form of humanity" must be understood, Theissen notes, "as solidarity with the weak, a contradiction of the processes in nature and history which are oriented on selection."[128]   In Jesus' "unconditional trust"[129] in a God portrayed poetically as "king"[130] and "father,"[131] we see, then, a "successful adaptation to the central reality, or the environment that "radically transcend[s] the world with which human beings [have] previously [been] familiar."[132]

"What appeared in Jesus of Nazareth," Theissen goes on to say, can be "realized,"[133] through the power of the Holy Spirit, in the lives of other human beings too. Jesus's "successful adaptation" is "not an impotent dream" for the rest of mankind.[134] By being "grasped by the Holy Spirit[135] (a power coming from outside which is not only part of the natural endowment of humanity but discloses possibilities of conduct and experience transcending all natural possibilities),"[136] individual human beings can "step beyond everything that is programmed into the biological rules of life" (e.g. hedonistic egoism),[137] as well as beyond the "socially conditioned pressure towards conformity exercised by tradition,"[138] and make the "history of the protest against selection from the beginnings of Israel to Jesus of Nazareth . . . their own activity."[139]

Whether a social institution like the Church can

also disentangle itself from "the struggle over distribution of goods and opportunities" is not immediately obvious, according to Theissen.[140]   Modern criticism of ideology, he says, might be right in claiming that institutionalized religion is just a "refined instrument in the fight over social distribution . . . [with] the objective function of legitimating privileges and offering consolation over opportunities withheld."[141]   As such, it would be "part of the selection process, not against it."[142]   Biblical religion itself, Theissen admits, may have provided its followers with "a strategy for survival at the expense of others" (through membership in the family and clan), and legitimated rule by divine right.[143]   But for all that, it does still show constant signs of going against selection by providing the possibility of survival for weak groups, and by challenging its own people's sense of security.[144]

Christianity can institutionalize such an "anti-selectionist motivation," Theissen notes, only "with many compromises."[145]   But this need not mean adaptation to everything that "contradicts the spirit of biblical religion."[146]   Blatant violations of human rights, or crude policies of distribution (e.g. apartheid), cannot be embraced without a loss of ecclesial identity.[147]   Nor can a church retain its identity if it constantly blocks "the way of the working of the Spirit in individuals and small groups."[148]   Rather, "it must allow some people . . . to live and act in the spirit of Jesus, free from the compromises of the institutional Church."[149]

A final question remains, Theissen notes, about whether the "form of life" generated by "the Spirit of the monotheistic revolution," and "the Spirit of Jesus of Nazareth" is really a "successful adaptation."[150]   Is it "an adequate structure of adaptation to the ultimate reality?"[151]   Eschewing the traditional teleological belief in pre-existing, external goals,[152] Theissen admits that "no one knows where [evolution] is leading," and concludes that if some "inner goal" of "harmony with the ultimate reality" is to be found in the process of evolution, it must be sought in the "interplay of chance and necessity."[153] The world-process of which we are a part may very well have systemic "properties," Theissen notes, which "are still hidden from us," with the result that, just as there is reason to expect that a "six" will sooner or later be rolled in dice that are not loaded, so there is a basis for hoping that what happened in the life of Jesus will be repeated in the "whole" of the future.[154] Jesus may be like the "black moth," whose adaptive success became apparent only when the environment changed (i.e., the English birchwoods turned gray and black).[155] Although "Jesus's love of his enemies may have been an impracticable dream in world history so far, the time could come — indeed is already here," Theissen suggests, "when our survival depends on how far we are successful in reducing aggression between human beings and changing our ways of reacting to enemies."[156] Our trust in this regard, he says, is not altogether blind.[157] Although evolution may have "no purpose," some evolutionary tendencies — "the tendency of smaller units to combine, the tendency towards greater independence and the tendency towards a deeper capacity for suffering" — may be seen to have been "positively reinforced," and to that extent to have "corresponded with the basic conditions of reality."[158] Evidence of these tendencies deepen our hope that the adaptations of Israel and Jesus, which they reflect,[159] may prevail in the end. The Christian doctrine of justification of sinners can also strengthen our hope that in the end God will take "the questionable attempts of human beings to adapt as being successful," regardless of how near to the "inner goal" of evolution they might be, and afford to each a "participation in something eternal."[160]

Notes

1. See Toulmin, "Human Adaptation," in Jensen, *The Philosophy of Evolution*, 177-79.

2. It will be recalled that according to James religion is "true" because it "works" (See James, *Varieties of Religious Experience*, 33-34).

3. W. James, "Reflex Action and Theism," in James, *The Will to Believe* (New York: Dover Publications, 1956), 132; see also Richards, *Darwin*, 442-43.

4. Roy A. Rappaport, "The Sacred in Human Evolution," 23.

5. Ibid.

6. Toulmin, "Human Adaptation," 179.

7. Ibid., 180. Toulmin cites the following biological analogue: "When the weather heats up in summer, our bodies respond adaptively to the higher temperatures: the vaso-motor system enlarges our pores and more perspiration evaporates, so carrying heat away and maintaining the body at its normal temperature of 98.6 [degrees] F" (Ibid.). This example involves the triggering of a reflex, physiological mobilization of energy to restore the optimal steady state, but psychologists and sociologists also speak of more complex, learned, and voluntary patterns of corrective behavior (e.g., taking a swim on a hot day) (See Ross Stagner, "Homeostasis," *IESS* 6: 499-500).

8. See Stagner, "Homeostasis," 502.

9. Toulmin, "Human Adaptation," 185.

10. E. Durkheim, *The Elementary Forms of the Religious Life* (New York: The Free Press, 1965), 62.

11. See Ibid., 388-92, 44-49.

12. See T. Parsons, *The Social System* (New York: The Free Press, 1951), 298; also: 163-67, 304-308, 315-17, 321, 525-35.

13. Toulmin, "Human Adaptation," 176; Parsons, *Societies*, 21-30; T. Parsons, "On Building Social System Theory," *Daedalus* 99, no. 4 (Fall 1970): 851-53.

14. See Clifford Geertz, "Religion: Anthropological Study," *IESS* 13: 403; Robert N. Bellah, "Religion: The Sociology of Religion," *IESS* 13: 409-11.

15. See Bateson, *Mind and Nature*, 209-13; J. Brockman, *About Bateson*, 235-47; reviews of Bateson's work by Stephen Toulmin ("The Charm of the Scout," *New York Review of Books* 27 [April 3, 1980]: 38-42), John Pfeiffer, ("Nature the Radical Conservative," *New York Times Book Review* [April 29, 1979]: 9, 52), and David L. Miller, ("I Do Not Believe in Ghosts," *New York Times Book Review* [November 15 1987]: 48). Bateson, it may be noted, thought of the mind as being something like an old-fashioned steam locomotive, the operation of whose governor resulted in a homeostatic, "self-correcting system of mutual restraints" to keep the train at a constant speed (See Hampden-Turner, *Maps of the Mind*, 166).

16. H. Mol, *Identity and the Sacred* (Oxford: Basil Blackwell, 1976), 1, 3. Mol describes "sacralization" as "a sort of brake applied to unchecked infinite adaptations" (Ibid., 5).

17. See Wilson, *On Human Nature*, 188; Mary Maxwell, *Human Evolution* (New York: Columbia University Press, 1984), 206-208. See also similar

comments by Ralph Burhoe ("Religion's Role in Human Evolution," 135-62) and Karl Peters ("Religion and an Evolutionary Theory of Knowledge," 397-99).

18. Wilson, *On Human Nature*, 188.

19. Ibid., 176.

20. Ibid., 177; Wilson, *Sociobiology*, 562.

21. Wilson, *On Human Nature*, 177, 188; *Sociobiology*, 562.

22. Wilson, *On Human Nature*, 205-209.

23. Ibid., 177. See also: William Austin's review of Wilson's work (*Religious Studies Review* 6, no. 2 (April, 1980): 102; W. H. Austin, "Are Religious Beliefs 'Enabling Mechanisms For Survival'"? *Zygon* 15, no. 2 (June, 1980): 197.

24. Campbell, "On the Conflicts between Biological and Social Evolution," 191.

25. Ibid.

26. Ibid., 192.

27. Ibid.

28. Ibid.

29. Ibid.,192-94, 202; Campbell, "Conflict between Social and Biological Evolution and the Concept of Original Sin," 143; Campbell, "Social Morality Norms," 67-82. In all of these articles, Campbell repeatedly protests against the "100- year-old effort of psychology to emancipate itself from the restraints of philosophy and tradition, and in particular in its teachings against cultural repression and in favor of the individualistic hedonism of the erogenous zones" (Ibid., 71). "The predominant goal of psychotherapy in both psychiatry and psychology," he claims, "is the liberation of narcissism" (Ibid.). Campbell, then, would also disagree with Wilson's suggestion that religion has lost much of its adaptive value.

30. Rappaport, "The Sacred in Human Evolution," 24.

31. Ibid., 25.

32. Ibid. See also: J. P. Vallee, "The Search for Knowledge: Science versus Religion?" *Journal of the Royal Astronomical Society of Canada* 83, no. 1 (1989): 8-25, wherein religion is also described as a "knowledge system;" David Sloan Wilson, "Species of Thought: A Comment on Evolutionary Epistemology" *Biology and Philosophy* 5 (1990): 37-62, wherein traditional conceptions of adaptation as knowledge, or knowledge as adaptive, are criticized for "failing to appreciate that mental representations can motivate behaviors that are adaptive in the real world without themselves directly corresponding to the real world" (Ibid., 37).

33. Rappaport, "The Sacred in Human Evolution," 25-26.

34. Ibid., 26.

35. Ibid., 27.

36. Ibid., 31.

37. Ibid., 29-31; Rappaport, *Ecology, Meaning, and Religion* (Richmond, Calif.: North Atlantic Books, 1979), 223-46.

38. Rappaport, "The Sacred in Human Evolution," 32-33, 36; Rappaport, *Ecology, Meaning, and Religion*, 230-33.

39. Rappaport, "The Sacred in Human Evolution," 37-38.

40. Ibid., 38.

41. Ibid.

42. Ibid., 41. For further discussion of religion as a revitalization process, see Wallace, *Religion*, 30-39, 157-66, 209-15.

43. Toulmin, "Human Adaptation," 185.

44. Stagner, "Homeostasis," 501.

45. Toulmin, "Human Adaptation," 186.

46. Ibid., 185, 186.

47. Ibid., 180. Toulmin gives the example of children becoming progressively less dependent on adults, and "better adapted to their conditions of life" through the "development of mobility, speech, and deliberation" (Ibid.).

48. See Hegel, *Philosophy of History*, 203-206.

49. See Kueng, *Does God Exist?*, 169-71.

50. See *Supra*, Chapter One.

51. "Historicist" is being used here to refer to any speculative attempt to explain the ultimate meaning or direction of human history in terms of one or another "historical law" (See *Ideas of History*, Vol. One *Speculative Approaches to History*, ed. Ronald H. Nash [New York: E. P. Dutton and Co., 1969], 265).

52. See excerpts of Spengler's *The Decline of the West* in Nash, *Ideas of History*, I: 148. Toynbee, it should be noted, returned to the linear view in the later volumes of his monumental history (Ibid., 178).

53. See Ibid., 148.

54. See Ibid., 176.

55. Ibid., 152-53.

56. Ibid., 176.

57. Ibid., 148, 153. Toynbee was early on inspired by a reading of Spengler's *Decline of the West* (See Ibid., 176), occasionally himself talked about "societies" in organic terms (See A. J. Toynbee, *A Study of History*, abridged by D. C. Somervell [New York and London: Oxford University Press, 1957], II: 82), and allowed that Spengler's conclusion that "societies are organisms, with natural transitions from youth and maturity to decay," does little harm when applied to "primitive societies or to arrested civilizations," but felt that such an analogy was "unsuited to express the relation in which growing civilizations stand to their individual members" (Ibid., I: 210-11, 576).

58. Toulmin, "Human Adaptation," 186.

59. See *Supra*, Chapter One.

60. F. Copleston, *A History of Philosophy*, Volume 7: *Modern Philosophy*, Part I: *Fichte to Hegel* (Garden City, N.Y.: Doubleday, 1965), 282.

61. See Ibid., 282-84.

62. Ibid., 284; *NCE* 6: 988.

63. Toynbee, *A Study of History*, II: 82.

64. Ibid., 87-92; Nash, *Ideas of History*, I: 177.

65. See Nash, *Ideas of History*, 153.

66. See Toynbee, *A Study of History*, II: 103-108.

67. Toulmin, "Human Adaptation," 186.

68. Bellah would seem to have an adaptation of this sort in mind when

he talks of religion as a product of evolution that has "endowed" society "with greater capacity to adapt to its environment, so that it is in some sense more autonomous relative to its environment" (*Beyond Belief*, 21).

69. Toulmin, "Human Adaptation," 186-87.

70. Ibid., 181.

71. Ibid.

72. Ibid., 192.

73. See M. Harris, *Cannibals and Kings: The Origins of Cultures* (New York: Random House, 1977); Wilson, *On Human Nature*, 93-95.

74. See Ibid., and V. Reynolds and R. Tanner, "The Effects of Religion on Human Biology," in *Darwinism and Divinity*, ed. John Durant (Oxford: Basil Blackwell, 1985), 133.

75. See R. A. Rappaport, "The Sacred in Human Evolution," 38; R. A. Rappaport, *Pigs for the Ancestors* (New Haven and London: Yale University Press, 1967).

76. See M. Harris, *Cows, Pigs, Wars, and Witches* (New York: Random House, 1974); M. Harris, "The cultural ecology of India's sacred cattle," *Current Anthropology* 7 (1966): 51-66; V. Reynolds and R.E.S. Tanner, *The Biology of Religion* (London and New York: Longman, 1983), 261-63.

77. Reynolds and Tanner, *Biology of Religion*, 8.

78. Ibid., 270.

79. See Ibid., 271-74, 291-92.

80. Ibid., 293, also: 14-15, 275-95.

81. Ibid. 293-94.

82. See *Supra*, Chapter Three, n.46.

83. See *Supra*, Chapter Three, ns.55-59.

84. Toulmin, "Human Adaptation," 183.

85. Ibid.

86. Theissen, *Biblical Faith*, 25.

87. Ibid., 19, 25, 72, 110.

88. Ibid., 20.

89. Toulmin, "Human Adaptation," 184.

90. Ibid.

91. Theissen, *Biblical Faith*, 25. Theissen has been praised for avoiding the tendency of Ralph Burhoe "to reduce God to random mutation and natural selection" (See Walter Wink's review of Theissen's *Biblical Faith* in *Zygon* 21, no. 4 [December 1986]: 543).

92. Theissen, *Biblical Faith*, 50.

93. For Theissen's discussion of the relation of faith and science, see Ibid., 1-41.

94. Ibid., 50.

95. Anthropologically speaking, the "emic" aspect of religion is its appearance to those practicing it, the "etic," the view from the outside (See Reynolds and Tanner, *The Biology of Religion*, 7).

96. Theissen, *Biblical Faith*, 72.

97. Theissen, it may be noted, sees his own views as being opposed to Wilson's sociobiological assumption that "cultural evolution is an extension of biological evolution — without any opposition to its tendencies" (Ibid., 177

n. 7), and concludes that "one could not say that faith in the one God is simply a sublime means of survival" (Ibid., 72, and 184 n. 38). I do not take this to mean, however, that Theissen would reject all that Rappaport and others have said about the survival value of religion.

98. Theissen, *Biblical Faith*, 73; see also: G. Theissen, *On Having a Critical Faith* (London: SCM Press, 1979), 14-15.

99. Theissen, *Biblical Faith*, 73.

100. Ibid. The "syncretistic", philosophical monotheism of the Greeks, Theissen says, was not "bound up with the demand for a fundamental change of character," and on that account was of a different nature than biblical monotheism (Ibid., 69).

101. Ibid., 73.

102. "The monotheism of Akhenaten, Zarathustra and Mohammed has a similar structure," Theissen notes (Ibid., 69).

103. Theissen argues that "objects of religious veneration [stones, trees, etc.] have precisely the same characteristic as the signals which trigger off a response in the specific environments of animals" (Ibid., 73-74). "Making images of gods," he says, "serves to stimulate archaic and numinous responses to reality by larger-than-life-substitutes" (Ibid., 74-75). The "prohibition of images," therefore, represented "a violent wrench away from an archaic bond to signals triggered by the environment" (Ibid., 75). The "image" was replaced by "the word," which was a "more appropriate structure of adaptation" toward the fascinating, dreadful, and stupendous "wholly other" reality (i.e., the one and only God) that is the "source" of the "appeal" of any specific object (e.g. the burning bush), and evokes the unspecific behavior (e.g. conversion) associated with monotheism (*Biblical Faith*, 75; *Critical Faith*, 16, 17).

104. Theissen contends that in addition to liberating man from the natural environment, the shift from the image to the word also represented "an even stronger bond to the first 'cultural,' linguistic environment of any human being, the family" (*Biblical Faith*, 77). "Once the gods take on the features of families, and are worshipped as mother or father or a heavenly couple, human beings are no longer controlled by the signals triggered off by relics, but by their first cultural experiences; by dealing with persons in a family relationship, with whom there is a family connnection" (Ibid., 78). "The appearance of father and mother deities was a step toward freedom from natural dependence" (Ibid.). It "trained human beings in [central] reality" (Ibid., 78-79). "It was a revolutionary step when the prophets broke through these categories of interpretation based on the family" (Ibid., 79). The "shattering of family imagery to symbolize this deity was an adaptation to objective reality . . . experienced as a unity: one god, not a divine couple" (Ibid., 80). This "step towards belief in the one God without a family, without a wife and children, without kith and kin," Theissen concludes, was "an important step beyond the bond between human beings and their first social environment" (Ibid.). It was "recognition that the reality which controls all things is not identical with nature and society," and as such gave rise to the possiblity of human beings "leaving nature and family," and striking up a harmonious adaptation to the whole of reality, "independently of all chances of survival and propagation" (Ibid., 81; W. Wink, it may be

noted, has called into question some of Theissen's conclusions in this regard: See Wink's review of Theissen's *Biblical_Faith* in *Zygon* 21, no. 4 [December 1986]: 544-45).

105. Theissen, *Biblical Faith*, 72.

106. Ibid., 73.

107. "Culture begins where human beings reduce the pressure of selection by intelligent behavior, i.e. it also makes human life possible where it would have no chance of survival without its deliberate intervention. Culture is a diminution of selection through change and differentiation in behaviour. At the same time it creates new forms of the pressure of selection: 'hard' selection is replaced by 'soft' selection" (Ibid., 13; see also: Ibid., 14, 112, 121, 141).

108. Theissen, *Biblical Faith*, 13-14, 69, 70.

109. Ibid., 70-72.

110. Ibid., 81.

111. For general discussion, see: Richards, *Darwin*, 172-76.

112. W. R. Greg, "On the Failure of 'Natural Selection' in the Case of Man," *Fraser's Magazine* 78 (1868): 353-62.

113. See Ibid.; Richards, *Darwin*, 173; "Natural and Supernatural Selection," *The Spectator* (October 3, 1868): 1154.

114. Richards, *Darwin*, 174.

115. Ibid., 174 n. 61.

116. "Natural and Supernatural Selection," 1155.

117. Ibid.

118. Ibid.

119. Ibid.

120. Ibid. According to Goethe, the religion of heathendom involved a reverence (*Ehrfurcht*) toward whatever is superior to man, philosophical religion a reverence toward that which is equal to ourselves, and the Christian religion a reverence for what is inferior to us ("*vor dem, was unter uns ist*"), i.e, for the weak and lowly (J. W. Goethe, *Wilhelm Meisters Wanderjahre*, II, 1, in *Gesammelte Werke*, hgb. Bernt von Heiseler [Guetersloh: Sigbert Mohn Verlag, 1960], 128-31; Harry Loewen, *Goethe's Response to Protestantism* [Berne and Frankfurt/M.: Herbert Lang and Co., 1972], 116-21; van der Leeuw, *Religion*, 596).

121. Theissen, *Biblical Faith*, 87, 106. The modern insistence on relativism, conditioning, and immanence can be integrated into the conception of Jesus as a "permanently valid" mutation, Theissen contends (*Biblical Faith*, 106-12). Theissen does not pay much attention to religions other than Christianity, but, as noted earlier, he does see some common ground between Jewish, Zoroastrian, and Islamic monotheism, and at another point he admits that Buddhism and primitive Christianity "are both expressions of a revolt against selection" (Ibid., 118).

122. Ibid., 87.

123. Ibid., 113.

124. Ibid., 115.

125. Ibid., 117.

126. Ibid., 87.

127. Ibid.

128. Ibid.

129. Ibid.

130. By refering to the 'central reality' as the "universal Kingdom of God," Jesus had in mind, Theissen says, to reveal the truth that "man is on the verge of passing over to a new phase of evolution" (Ibid., 119-23).   1 3 1 .

The 'father' metaphor used by Jesus, Theissen notes, was meant to "activate the emotional forces of man's childhood past — just as in a step forward evolution often goes back to previous stages of development" (Ibid., 128, 123-28).   It does not imply "regression in a negative sense," but "an actualization of neotonic possibilities in human life" (Ibid., 125).

132. Ibid., 119.

133. Ibid., 129.

134. Ibid.

135. The content of the Old and New Testament insights, Theissen says, "can only be handed on if it evokes constantly" what, as noted in a previous chapter, he calls "unplannable 'mutations' within each individual" (Ibid., 149). This, he concludes, is what "Christian tradition calls being grasped by the Holy Spirit" (Ibid.).

136. Ibid., 134.

137. Ibid., 140-47, 152.

138. Ibid., 140, 147-52.

139. Ibid., 140.

140. Ibid., 132.

141. Ibid., 152.

142. Ibid.

143. Ibid., 153-56.

144. Ibid., 158.

145. Ibid., 163.

146. Ibid.

147. Ibid.

148. Ibid.

149. Ibid.

150. Ibid., 132, 164.

151. Ibid., 132.

152. Ibid., 164-66.

153. Ibid., 164.

154. Ibid., 167.

155. Ibid., 168.

156. Ibid. It is true, of course, that religion itself sometimes generates conflict, and to that extent might jeopardize the long-term survival of the human race. But this does not preclude the possibility of religion being adaptive in more immediate and direct ways, and may just be an indication of the way religion, like science and technology, can, for better or worse, "soar beyond" its basic propensities (See Ruse's comments in this regard: *Taking Darwin Seriously*, 148).

157. Theissen, *Biblical Faith*, 168.

158. Ibid.

159. Ibid., 169–70.
160. Ibid., 171, 173.

Chapter Seven

Conclusion

The Naturalistic philosophy subscribed to nowadays by so many anthropologists, sociologists, and psychologists generally assumes that science alone is capable of delivering true knowledge, and that, given sufficient time, it will "demystify" any and every phenomenon brought under its empirical scrutiny. Thus, even while admitting that late nineteenth and early twentieth-century evolutionists failed in trying to explain scientifically where religion came from, when it got started, and how it developed, many of these same social scientists still harbor the conviction that sooner or later, science, and only science, will take the mystery out of religion by explaining its origin and evolution in exclusively empirical terms.

Whether so much confidence in the scientific method is warranted, however, is debatable. Our own study has left us with the impression that because of the complexity of religion, as well as the inherent limitations of empirical observation, there is much about the origin and evolution of religion that science will never be able to explain. To get the full picture of where religion has come from and how it has developed, therefore, we have had to complement the empirical observation of religious phenomena with some rational and intuitive speculation of a theological and metaphysical sort. In the light of such speculation, we have concluded that the ultimate roots of religion lie hidden in the depths of a human soul, whose own existence can only be explained as resulting from divine *concursus* in the evolution of the human body, that religion is autonomous and unique, and that, in the final analysis, it transcends the selective laws of nature that initially shaped it, and becomes the adaptive product of the supernatural selectivity exercised by an ultimate reality most religious people call God.

While thus avoiding the tendency of Naturalism to reduce religion to nothing more than a product of nature, our investigation has also steered clear of the opposite extreme voiced by some religious people who, relying exclusively upon their own mythologies, like to claim that religion in general, and their own religions in particular, have fallen ready-made from above. By taking seriously what anthropology, sociology, psychology, and other of the natural and social sciences have taught us in recent times, we have concluded instead that far from being created out of nothing, religion has evolved out of the ritualistic and altruistic capacities developed during man's animal past, and in conjunction with the evolution of the brain's capacity for holistic ideation and symbolic expression. We have further concluded that neither religion in general, nor the many different species of religion that have surfaced down through the millennia, were "fixed" once and forever from the very beginning of their existence. For, while granting that the subjective side of religion (i.e., the religious disposition) may to some extent have been "preformed" genetically into a structure of human consciousness that "unfolded" thereafter in an orthogenetic manner, and while also admitting that after having been anticipated in rudimentary fashion in animal behavior, all the basic ingredients of objective religion may already have been present at the very beginning of religion, we nonetheless went on to conclude that each of the specific religions represents a unique combination of the essential elements, and that these respective combinations themselves have been, in turn, not merely the end results of epigenetic growth independent of environmental factors, but, like other cultural phenomena, the products of an adaptive process analogous to natural selectivity in the biological realm, to such an extent that religion in general may be said, albeit not without some qualification, to have passed through progressive stages or grades of increasingly complex symbolization.

Having arrived at these conclusions, we are left with the question about what difference it makes whether we take an evolutionary rather than a fixistic view of the origin and development of religion. We still need to ask, in other words, what implications can be drawn from our conclusions about the evolution of religion.

In the first place, it may be noted that an evolutionary interpretation of religion such as we have proffered might serve to generate some long-needed, mutual respect between secular humanists and proponents of religion. For their part, secular humanists who take the evolution of religion seriously would have to acknowledge that religion has contributed significantly to the survival of mankind, human culture, and nature itself, and that it is at least conceivable that religion could yet prove to be one of the best ways we have for getting out of the social and ecological mess we are in as a result of our excessively egoistic and competitive pursuit of power and wealth. Even while denying the literal veridicality of religion, secular humanists could still in this sense admit its pragmatic truth. Champions of religion, on the other hand, might come to a better appreciation of the cultural environment out of which religion has sprung, and realize more fully how much its own survival depends upon the cultivation and preservation of those things — e.g., art, science, politics — that constitute that environment. Recognition of the evolutionary dimensions of religious history might help them see, in other words, that just as no biological species can long survive the destruction of its ecological niche, so no religion can long hope to survive if its cultural environment is not protected against obscurantism, indifference, or any other forces of cultural decay and neglect.   Secondly,   a   renewed appreciation of the evolution of religion might help to reduce some of the hostility that has sometimes arisen between religion and science in the past. For if religion has in fact evolved along the lines sketched above, those who want to know what religion is all about will have no choice but to respect the scientific method by which alone its earthly roots and branches can be discovered, and show some interest in the whole process of evolution of which religion is only a part. So too, if religion is indeed viewed as part of a larger evolutionary process, scientists honestly in pursuit of knowledge will have no alternative but to take into account not only the phenomenon of religion as a cultural entity, but also the "message" delivered by the various religions as they go about trying to map metaphorically the whole of reality. It was probably along such lines that Donald T. Campbell was thinking when, in his 1975 Presidential address to the American Psychological Association, he challenged his fellow social scientists to get beyond their usual "epistemic arrogance and literalism when dealing with religious claims for truth," and not lose sight of the possibility that religious words might "refer to truths for which there is no literal language."[1] In the process, scientists might also discover that the "meaning" of evolution is far more profound than their empirical studies ever allowed them to dream. And the many remaining disagreements[2] might thereby find a less polemical atmosphere for discussion.

        Thirdly,   an   acknowledgement   of   religion's evolutionary past might give theologians a new perspective on the nature of their own respective religions. For one thing, it might remind them not only that their own religions are "reformable," but also that the very survival of these religions is at stake in the extent to which they do or do not adapt to the ever-changing environment around them. This in turn should generate greater appreciation for religious freedom of such sort as would incline religious leaders not merely to tolerate limited variations of thought and practice, but even to encourage them as being essential to the adaptation of one or another religious community to its cultural niche.[3] It might further be noted in this regard, that far from being contradicted, key doctrines of one or another religious tradition might actually be re-enforced by an acknowledgement of the evolutionary side of religion. The "preferential option for the poor" being championed at the present time in some Christian circles by the so-called "liberation" theologians, for example, might be shown to be quite in line with the thrust of supernatural selectivity toward use of a naturally selected cultural entity, like the Church, for defense of the weak.

Fourthly, recognition of the evolutionary origin and history of the various religions might provide some ground for respective claims to uniqueness precisely at a time when traditional claims of this sort are being called into question.[4] For if one or another religion can be shown to have been, by virtue of its actual survival, the best adaptation to the cultural niche in which it finds itself, much more room will have been left for the claim that religions are, in Ernst Troeltsch's words, at least "relatively absolute,"[5] and that they are unique at least in the sense that each represents, as William P. Alston has put it, the best and only path to salvation for its particular adherents in their own time and place.[6]

Finally, and in close relation to the last conclusion, it may be noted that acceptance of the evolutionary nature of religion would also increase appreciation for the plurality of religions. For although variations within one or another specific religion may suffice to guarantee its own survival in its own environment, they are not necessarily sufficient to ensure the survival of religion in the almost infinitely variable environments that man is likely to encounter in the future. That there are many different religions, therefore, helps guard against the possibility of religion becoming altogether extinct as a result of some sudden shift in cultural paradigms around the world. In a still more positive sense, the plurality of religion generated by its evolution brings back into focus the point we made at the beginning of this book, namely, that in the evolution of religions we have a clear instance of the creative, kenotic process of "trans-decendence" that Buddhist and Christian mystics alike call "dazzling darkness."

Notes

1. See Campbell, "On the Conflict between Biological and Social Evolution and between Psychology and Moral Tradition," 196-97.

2. For a discussion of some of the points of disagreement between evolutionary and traditionally Christian lines of thought, see, for example, Chapter Ten of Michael Ruse's *The Darwinian Paradigm: Essays on its history, philosophy, and religious implications* (London and New York: Routledge, 1989), and the debate over it presented in *Zygon*, Vol. 29, No. 1 (March, 1994), 5-101.

3. See Raimundo Panikkar's comments about the positive value of variety in religious truth claims: R. Panikkar, "The Invisible Harmony: A Universal Theory of Religion or a Cosmic Confidence in Reality?" In *Toward a Universal Theology of Religion*, ed. Leonard Swidler (Maryknoll, N.Y.: Orbis, 1988), 144-48.

4. See John Hick's assertions in this regard ("The Non-Absoluteness of Christianity," in Hick and Knitter, *The Myth of Christian Uniqueness*, 30), and my own discussion of his position (B. Verkamp, "Hick's interpretation of religious pluralism," *The International Journal for Philosophy of Religion* 30 [1991]: 112-14).

5. See Verkamp, "Hick's interpretation," 113.

6. See W. P. Alston, "Religious Diversity and Perceptual Knowledge," *Faith and Philosophy* 5, no.4 (October, 1988), 433-48, esp. 441-46.

Appendix

The Religious Given

Andrew Lang may well have been right in claiming that the *sensus numinis*, from which the multiple dimensions of religion supposedly derive, is "mysterious" and "unanalysable." But that cannot serve as an excuse for making unsubstantiated conjectures about the ultimate source of religion. While it may be impossible in the final analysis, therefore, to come up with the kind of factual evidence strict empiricists might want for the verification or falsification of the hypothesis postulated by Lang and other modern scholars of religion like Otto and Eliade, an effort should be made at least to explain how a religious 'given' might be conceived, and whatever evidence there is for its existence. In this appendix, we will review within an historical context how Otto himself and other past and present thinkers have tried to come up with such an explanation.

One way to conceive of the religious 'given' might be to think of it as a set of religious ideas and beliefs that are imprinted upon the human mind at birth. Following the lead of Plato, and Stoic thinkers like Cicero and Epictetus,[1] René Descartes, for example, argued in the seventeenth century that when God created man, He left upon him the imprint of His work in the form of an innate idea of Himself.[2] Later in the same century, Lord Herbert of Cherbury, and a host of other English divines, would refer to a set of "common notions concerning religion [i.e., that the Sovereign Deity ought to be worshipped, that Piety is closely connected with Virtue, that humans have a need for repentance, and that there will be reward or punishment after this life],"[3] which in their view had been written by"the finger of God" onto the human soul at birth.[4] But what did these thinkers have in mind thereby? Did it mean, as one of their critics asked sarcastically, that children had such notions when they "first peep't into being? at the first opening of the souls eye? in the first *exordium* of Infancy? . . . in the Cradle? and were they rock't asleep with [them]?"[5] The answer, of course, was no, if this were to mean that infants in the womb, or new-born babes, enjoyed fully-fledged, actual ideas about the existence, nature, and will of God. That there are such "common notions," they said, can be proven by the extent to which assent to them is "universal and immediate."[6] This does not mean, however, that children (or savages and idiots)[7] consciously and reflectively apprehend them from the moment they come into he world.[8] But if children have no clear impression of the "common notions" at birth, can the latter be said in any meaningful sense to be known? John Locke thought not. "To say a notion is imprinted on the mind," he wrote, "and yet at the same time to say, that the mind is ignorant of it, and never yet took notice of it, is to make this impression nothing."[9] "No proposition," he added, "can be said to be in the mind which it never yet knew, which it was never yet conscious of."[10] To this, however, G. W. Leibniz soon replied that as a matter of fact, humans "have an infinite amount of knowledge of which we are not always conscious, not even when we need it," and that a child's lack of perception of "common notions" is no sign, therefore, of its being without such innate knowledge.[11] Leibniz's recognition of a "tacit" dimension of human knowledge has been picked up in more recent times by Michael Polanyi,[12] and identified by Alister Hardy and others as being the most likely "field" in which to discover the roots of religion.[13] By then, however, it had already become the basis for development of various theories, including Leibniz's own, about how the "common notions of religion" can be, if not "actually," at least "virtually" or "potentially" innate to the human mind.

In the most naive of such theories, propounded mainly by Lord Herbert and the aforementioned seventeenth- century English divines,[14] but possibibly even by Descartes and Leibniz,[15] the "common notions" were said to be "virtually" innate simply in the sense of being beyond the child's "immature" comprehension. In other words, they were considered distinct from the child's thinking ability, but still less than actual to the extent that the child remains too young and inexperienced to assent to them immediately. How exactly such innate knowledge might be conceived, however, is not easy to say. Is it an unconscious, Platonic "recollection" from a previous state of existence?[16] A supposedly Cartesian "memory" of forgotten thoughts in the womb?[17] A "persistent structural modification" consisting of "unconscious experiences," as some interpretors of Leibniz would suggest?[18]

Not infrequently, such innate knowledge was described as having been "engraved" on the human soul,[19] an expression that was closely linked etymologically with the word "character,"[20] which in turn was often used as a synonym for "instinct."[21] One of the better clues as to how the child's unconscious, innate knowledge was to be understood might perhaps be found, therefore, in Lord Herbert's description of the "common notions of religion" as being "manifestations" of a "natural instinct toward eternal Blessedness,"[22] of an "impulse for salvation," which appears in man as a higher form of the animal's instinct for self-preservation.[23] Such "manifestations," he says, are forms of "perception."[24] That children or "abnormal"[25] individuals are not conscious of them should not be all that surprising, he adds, since "it must be remembered that it is the nature of natural instinct to fulfil itself irrationally, that is to say, without foresight."[26] "Even the elements, minerals, and vegetables," he concludes, "give no evidence of possessing foresight or reason, and yet display knowledge peculiarly suited to their own preservation."[27]

Lord Herbert was neither the first nor the last to conceive of innate knowledge in such wise. Throughout the Middle Ages, many Aristotelian thinkers, following an interpretation by Avicenna of Aristotle's suggestion that "animals know by nature"[28] had tried to explain certain patterns of animal behavior, like the lamb's flight from the wolf, as the result of that animal's soul having been infused by God with a certain "instinct" or "estimative power," by which it could "know concretely" what was "suitable" or "harmful" to its survival.[29] Descartes too thought that much of animal behavior could only be explained by instinct. Denying as he did, however, that animals had souls, he generally conceived of such instinct as being blind, without "the least stirrings of intelligence or reason."[30] Leibniz, on the other hand, considered instinct to be a significant factor underlying the moral behavior of human beings, and although he distinguished it from the clear and distinct innate ideas toward which reason is disposed, he did say that instinct involved at least a "confused perception" of the truth.[31] Neo-Aristotelian and Cartesian thinkers of the eighteenth century, like Hermann Samuel Reimarus and Thomas Willis, would refer to the instinctive behavioral determinants as inborn "ideas" or "notions."[32] In the following century, Charles Darwin concluded that the substrate of instinct lay in certain "heritable unconscious brain determinations" that result from the "habits" of one or another generation, implying thereby that instinct was "a kind of memory, which could be established in earlier generations and biologically transmitted to succeeding generations."[33] In the present century, the social psychologist William McDougald and the ethologist

Konrad Lorenz have both highlighted the relation of instinct and knowledge, the former by suggesting that instincts are "more than innate tendencies or dispositions" to the extent of being "cognitively purposive,"[34] the latter by arguing that it is the "information stored in the genes,"[35] rather than any particular pattern of animal behavior, that is ontogenetically, if not phylogenetically, *a priori*[36] — prompting Franz Wuketits to conclude that it is the "first postulate of evolutionary epistemology" that "no individual living system is initially a 'clean slate' or *tabula rasa*."[37] Along the same line, Richard Swinburne has argued that the mutation of genes has gradually "structured" the human soul. "What I mean by claiming that the soul has a structure," Swinburne writes, "is very roughly that the determinants of change of belief [i.e., "what a man holds to be true about the world"][38] and desire [i.e., "a natural inclination to do some action"][39] are in part soul-states, not mere brain-states; and that if body and soul were separated, some character would remain in the soul."[40] According to such a "categorical" [as opposed to a "dispositional"][41] account of the continuation of beliefs and desires when man is not aware of them, in other words, the soul is "not totally soft"[42] or "passive and structureless;"[43] it is, rather, "structured and active;"[44] "it has to it some structure so that its shape in some parts is determined by its shape in other parts, and its shape to some extent determines that of the brain;"[45] it is "structured by causally influential beliefs and desires."[46] "We seem to find within ourselves attitudes to the world [i.e., beliefs] and longings to do things [i.e., desires] in it, which were not created by our awareness but were there prior to that awareness."[47] Swinburne sees Mary Midgley's *Beast and Man* as developing a similar line of thought, to the effect, namely, that human beings have a "nature" that is formed by our genes before it is given form or modified by one or another culture.[48] "All this may be an illusion," he concludes, "but the principle of credulity bids us suppose that things are as they seem to be, in the absence of counter-evidence."[49]

Swinburne, it may be noted, had in mind only to argue that the structure of the human soul is "far more complex, rigid, and lasting," but not to deny "that some sort of structure is present in the soul of the higher animals also."[50] And, with the obvious exception of Descartes,[51] much of the emphasis upon instinct by earlier thinkers was also in the interest of downplaying differences between animal and human intelligence. Already in the medieval Aristotelian discussion of the "estimative power" it was implied that "instinct" represented something of a bridge between the two, in that during at least the earliest years of human life, when reason and learning were not yet sufficient for guiding behavior, the child had to rely on the primitive cognition afforded by the estimative power.[52] Lord Herbert himself may have been thinking along this same line, when he concluded that "children recognize and seek God in their own way in the form of happiness, and acknowledge Him in the spontaneous gratitude which they accord their benefactor."[53] In later centuries, as seen in a chapter two, this downplaying of the distinction between human and animal behavior would incline Charles Darwin and some of his followers to seek the roots of religion in the animal kingdom,[54] in man's genetic inheritance,[55] or more specifically, in the kind of "epigenetic rules" that were supposedly already established among the primates, and then passed on through the genes to humans as "innate predispositions" or "propensities" toward thinking and acting "in various tried and trustworthy [i.e., adaptive] patterns."[56]

Whether such instinctive "information" is really knowledge, however, might be doubted. Otto, who had little taste for evolutionary thinking, was convinced that it was not.[57] But even if it does not qualify as knowledge in the strict sense, because, like a bird's nest-building savvy, it lacks "insight," or is altogether "compulsive," it can still be recognized as a significant component of any innate religious structure of the mind, comparable perhaps to the permanent software, or "firmware," with which every computer is endowed before leaving the factory so as to facilitate its later more "adaptive" programing.[58]

To suggest, however, that the religious 'given' might enjoy some sort of "informational" base is not to say that there is nothing more to say about it, or even that there is no better way to describe its instinctive dimension. For, as noted earlier, "instinct" can be, and frequently has been, described also as a "disposition" toward knowledge, and to that extent can best be appreciated within the context of other theories about how knowledge can be "virtually" innate.

Those championing the aforementioned "naive" theory of innate ideas had insisted that the human mind is not at birth a *tabula rasa*.[59] They had not, however, had a very strong impression of the mind's ability to generate ideas on its own.[60] And it was partly on that account that they had insisted upon the inscription of ideas from the outside. Eventually, however, those who wanted to defend the theory of innate ideas against empiricist claims that the mind is blank at birth came to see that their best chance of doing so was to associate the "innateness" of ideas with the mind's "ability" to acquire ideas prior to, but not necessarily independent of, experience.[61] In the process of explaining what they meant by such an "ability" or "faculty," they opened up a variety of other ways also for interpreting the religious 'given.'

To say that the mind is "able" to produce its ideas

prior to experience could mean nothing more than that the mind has certain inborn "capacities," in virtue of which it is able to function (e.g. process data, store information, learn languages, understand, etc.).[62] Implying as it would that all ideas are innate,[63] such an interpretation of the mind's innate "ability" would be rather "trivial" and "of little epistemological interest"[64] — something to which even the empiricists would agree.

But the mind's "ability" to acquire ideas and beliefs can be interpreted also as a "disposition" toward producing ideas or propositions out of itself. This would seem to have been already implied in the views of Plato[65] and the Stoics.[66] And it is one of the readings that can be made of Descartes' theory of innate ideas. As noted earlier, Descartes sometimes seemed to imply that the idea of God was "actually" innate. But in his *Notes Against a Programme* he disclaimed ever having concluded that innate ideas "are actual, or that they are some kind of species different from the faculty of thought."[67] What he really had meant, he went on to explain, was that "I observed the existence in me of certain thoughts which proceeded, not from extraneous objects nor from the determination of my will, but solely from the faculty of thinking which is within me . . . in the same sense we say that in some families generosity is innate, in others certain diseases like gout or gravel, not that on this account the babes of these families suffer from these diseases in their mother's womb, but because they are born with a certain disposition or propensity for contracting them."[68] In this sense, therefore, the idea of God might be said, for example, to be the result of the mind's "actualization of its own potency" — either in the Augustinian sense of activating "an inborn orientation of the finite human being to its author and creator," or in the sense of generating an idea of an infinite and perfect being through reflection upon itself.[69]

It was also along such a line of thought that the so-called Cambridge Platonists had already tried to modify the naive version of the theory of innate ideas several decades prior to Locke's first paper on the subject. In a manner reminiscent of both Augustine's "illuminationist" theory[70] and Thomas Aquinas' discussion of "synderesis" and the "active intellect,"[71] Henry More, Nathaniel Culverwel, Walter Charleton, Robert Ferguson, and Ralph Cudworth, all spoke of the "active sagacity," the "intellectual lamp," the "Power," the "Natural Sagacity," or the "innate vigour and activity of the mind itself," whereby the idea of the Deity and other "virtually innate" ideas are produced upon the occasion of external stimuli.[72] To Locke's objection that such an interpretation of the virtual innateness of ideas is either inconceivable, or insignificant (to the extent of affirming what nobody denies, namely, the capability of the mind to understand and assent firmly to certain self-evident propositions),[73] John Lowde, Thomas Becconsall, Henry Lee, and other seventeenth century English divines would later reply that the soul is not "equally indifferent" to the acceptance or recognition of all impressions or truths.[74] Toward certain "common notions" or "Catholick Truths" (like the idea of the Deity) it has a "certain genius" or "capacity" or "disposition."[75]

G. W. Leibniz's *New Essays* might also be interpreted as the classical philosophical expression of this "dispositional account" of innate ideas.[76] Just as a block of marble might be other than "wholly indifferent" to the figure of Hercules which a sculptor eventually discovers in its veins,[77] so the human mind, he claimed, enjoys a "particular relation . . . to these truths which renders the exercise of the faculty easy and natural in respect to them, and which causes them to be called innate."[78] The human mind, in other words, is not a *tabula rasa,*[79] a "naked faculty which consists in the mere

possibility of understanding [such truths]."[80] It is rather
"a disposition, an aptitude, a preformation, which
determines our soul and which makes it possible for [such
truths] to be derived from it."[81] Certain "ideas and
truths" may be said, therefore, to be innate "as
inclinations, dispositions, habits, or natural
potentialities."[82] Among many such ideas (like those we
have of being, substance, causality, etc.),[83] is the "idea of
God," which the mind has a special propensity to fashion,
not merely, as Locke himself would readily have granted,
out of the perceived relation between certain ideas derived
from sense experience,[84] but from within, by reflection
upon itself.[85]

Impressed by Leibniz's efforts in this regard,
Rudolf Otto wrote in his *Philosophy of Religion* that
Leibniz "had already almost overcome in his *Nouveaux
Essais* . . . the confusion between the theory of Immediate
Knowledge and that of Innate Ideas . . . [such as had
characterized] earlier versions of the theory of innate
ideas."[86] He goes on to say, however, that it was Kant,
and not Leibniz, who "gave the whole solution of the
problem."[87] The solution is to be found, Otto says, "in
the introductory paragraphs of *The Critique of Pure Reason*,
wherein Kant writes that "although all our knowledge
begins with experience, it does not follow that it arises
from experience; for it is quite possible that even our
empirical experience is a compound of that which we
receive through impressions and that which our own
faculty of knowledge (incited only by sensuous
impressions) supplies from itself."[88]

In making this statement, Kant had had in mind to
reject both Locke's empiricism and the naive version of
innate ideas, and to insist instead, not unlike Descartes
and Leibniz, upon the capacity of the human mind to
produce from within itself, on the occasion of one or
another experience, certain "concepts and principles."[89]

Picking up on another line of thought anticipated by Descartes,[90] Lord Herbert,[91] and Leibniz, [92] Kant described such concepts primarily in "formal" terms, namely, as "categories" or "forms of thought" by which the mind, in accordance with its own structure or forms of judgment, synthesizes the data of experience.[93] They are called "*a priori*" because, although they are "necessary" to experience, and "universal" (i.e., "pervasive to experience"), they are prior to experience.[94] That certain concepts and propositions are "necessary and universal" is in fact an indication of their being *a priori*.[95]

In *The Critique of Pure Reason* Kant listed, along with the perceptual categories of time and space, twelve such conceptual categories "as the *a priori* conditions of our theoretic knowledge."[96] In *The Critique of Practical Reason* he identified the Categorical Imperative of Duty as the ethical *a priori*, or the *a priori* condition or "constituent" of our practical knowledge of good and evil.[97] Underlying this latter endeavor was Kant's contention "that natural science does not really exhaust our verifiable knowledge of reality, because in our knowledge of good and evil we have available to us another and equally indisputable revelation of truth," namely, the "ultimate . . . genuinely self-evident . . . principles" implied by the categorical imperative (e.g. that all persons are to be treated as "ends").[98] Kant did not, however, give any indication in either of these two *Critiques*, or in the subsequent *Critique of Judgement*,[99] of recognizing any kind of unique *a priori* elements in religious experience.[100] Having championed a "twofold avenue of knowledge," his "only question with reference to religion," John Baillie has noted, "was this: Along which of these two ways does religious conviction come to a man?"[101]

Since Kant considered it the function of the categories of theoretical knowledge to synthesize the data of sense intuition, he did not consider them applicable to realities, like God, the soul, freedom, etc., which are not, and cannot be, given in sense experience.[102] He admitted that "pure reason" has a "natural tendency" to come up with such supersensible, "transcendental" ideas, as it seeks out the "unconditioned" unifying principles of thought and reality.[103] But, being inapplicable to the data of sense intuition, and lacking any "purely intellectual intuition" by which to be supplied with "corresponding objects," such "transcendental ideas" are merely "regulative"[104] — i.e., stimulating further scientific research by highlighting the limits of our present concepts, but in no way "constituting" knowable objects (i.e., phenomena).[105] They cannot, therefore, serve as the *a priori* elements, or the "categories," of religious experience.

If there is an *a priori* element in religion, then, it is only to be found, Kant concluded, along the second avenue to knowledge, namely, in the "moral law within," or the "ethical *a priori*."[106] This "categorical imperative" is the absolute condition of all our religious ideas,"constituting" for us the notions of a just God who rewards and punishes, etc.[107] Any religious ideas that go beyond, or cannot be derived from, these direct "moral" intuitions, is no longer knowledge, but faith, Kant concluded.[108]

Nothwithstanding his aforementioned assertion to the effect that Kant had given "the whole solution to the problem" of "immediate" or "innate" religious knowledge, Otto's own "Kantian" interpretation of religion relied considerably upon the thinking of other nineteenth and early twentieth-century philosophers, like Friedrich Schleiermacher, Jakob Fries, and Ernst Troeltsch.

Against the tendency of Romantic, skeptical friends to locate religion in either the mind (as a set of beliefs, to which one must assent), or in the will (as a derivative of morality), Schleiermacher argued that all religion derives ultimately from a "form of feeling," which he variously described as immediate consciousness of the finite self existing "in and through the Infinite," or as a sense of "absolute dependence" on "God" as "Absolute Causality" or the transcendent ground of all being.[109]

Whether Schleiermacher himself understood such a feeling of absolute dependency as a religious *a priori* is debatable. Noting that Schleiermacher did not himself use the latter expression, and that for him "religion" was "not the name for a faculty or category of the mind which, in distinction from scientific and ethical judgments, yields knowledge of God," Richard R. Niebuhr argued against "misreading" Schleiermacher "as one who sought to isolate in human nature a religious *a priori*," and criticized Otto for having interpreted Schleiermacher in such wise.[110] If we keep in mind, however, that Otto himself did not, as we shall see, intend to champion any kind of intuitive natural theology, his interpretation of Schleiermacher does not seem so out of line as Niebuhr suggests. In any event, Otto was certainly right in crediting Schleiermacher with the rediscovery of the *sensus numinis* as a "distintively religious mode of truth . . . and apprehension."[111] It should be noted, however, that Otto was also critical of what he supposed was Schleiermacher's failure to understand how "religious dependence" and "other feelings of dependence" differ "in kind," and not only "in degree," or to appreciate the "immediate and primary reference" of the religious experience "to an object outside the self."[112] And he eventually came to think that Fries' treatment of the religious "feeling" (*Ahnung*) was perhaps "superior" to Schleiermacher's in its "comprehensiveness, thoroughness, and solidity."[113] But Otto also went beyond Fries. The latter had been inclined to envision religious feeling ("of the Eternal in the Finite") as only "one aspect of the general *a priori* knowledge possessed by the human reason," and to link it up with the *a priori* principles of pure and practical reason (especially the aesthetic judgment).[114] Under considerable influence from Troeltsch, his associate at Göttingen, Otto would depart from Fries in this regard, and posit an independent religious *a priori*.

The essence of religion, Troeltsch wrote, consists of a "fearful shudder before that which surpasses all understanding and all imagination, the terror and silent fright before the unfathomable, the subjection of the will to something in which one believes but only partially sees, the ardent devotion to that which, advancing upon us out of the impenetrable, yet encourages and strengthens."[115] This "faith" was thought by Troeltsch "to possess the same quality of immediate compulsion upon the human mind as logical reflection, moral obligation, and aesthetic judgment."[116] And just as Kant had postulated *a priori* principles to account for the latter, so Troeltsch concluded, "a religious *a priori* is necessary to account for the element of universality and immediate necessity in religious faith."[117] Thinking that he had found a basis in Kant's later works for recognition of "an *a priori* that does not signify the synthetic unifying function of scientific comprehension,"[118] Troeltsch went on to postulate "a number of independent *a priori* categories, one to account for moral conviction, one for aesthetic judgment, and one for scientific knowledge, as well as one that is distinctly religious."[119]

Otto picked up on this same line of thought and concluded that "the Holy is a category of interpretation and valuation peculiar to the sphere of religion," just as the "category of the beautiful," is peculiar to the realm of aesthetics.[120] "Independent alike of the *a priori* categories of logical understanding and of moral and aesthetic judgement,"[121] it is nonetheless like them, and especially in that it can claim "objective validity, universality, and necessity."[122] The "criterion of all *a priori* knowledge," he argued, is "that, so soon as an assertion has been clearly expressed and understood, knowledge of its truth comes into the mind with the certitude of first-hand insight."[123] Following Luther's occasional description of faith as "a unique cognitive faculty," whereby even the most "wild and savage" of people have come to know of a creator-god,[124] and missionary reports about how "primitive" peoples "immediately assent" to "ideas of the unity and goodness of the divine nature,"[125] Otto concluded that our religious consciousness enjoys such features of universality and necessity, and to that extent has an *a priori* dimension.[126]

This category, however, by which "the religious interpretation of human experience is conditioned,"[127] is "complex," consisting as it does of both rational and non-rational components.[128] It manifests itself initially in the "numinous" feeling of "stupor," "dread," and "fascination."[129] But, eventually, as religion progresses under the stimulus of "prophetic divination"[130] from its crudest to its noblest forms, the category of the Holy becomes more and more closely associated with the rational and ethical.[131] In this sense, the "category of the Holy" is viewed by Otto as being also a "predisposition" or "propensity" of the human mind to fashion certain "ideas" that are different from the "faculty" of thinking.[132] In both its rational and non-rational elements, however, the religious category remains "purely *a priori*."[133] Rational concepts of the deity, of absoluteness, goodness, love, etc., and rational doctrines of predestination, the kingdom of God, etc., are no more derivable from experience or the other categories than is the 'idea of the Holy' itself.[134] They remain *a priori*, and serve to "schematize" the *mysterium*, the *tremendum*, and the *fascinans*.[135] Otto preferred not to call such rational elements "innate ideas," lest they be thought of as having been "supernaturally instilled."[136] Instead, he generally referred to them as "*a priori* cognitions," so as to play up the "capacity" of the mind to produce them out of itself.[137]   Furthermore, against the Rationalists, Otto would insist that these "rational elements" cannot ever exhaust the reality of the "numen,"[138] or afford us any "specifically theological propositions" out which to concoct a purely natural theology.[139]   At best, he would say, they are like the Platonic "ideograms" that give us only a mythical, symbolic, analogical impression of the "wholly other" reality.[140]   Yet, if we remember that "to know and to understand conceptually are two different things," they can, Otto concluded, be said to constitute real knowledge.[141]

Otto's interpretation of the religious 'given' along Leibnizian-Kantian lines had a considerable influence on Carl G. Jung's "instinctive-dispositional" account of the "archetypes."[142]   Unlike Freud, who conceived of the "unconscious" as the "gathering place of forgotten and repressed contents,"[143] Jung distinguished a "personal" and a "collective" unconscious, the former owing its existence to "personal experience," and consisting of contents which have disappeared from consciousness through having been forgotten or repressed, the latter deriving not from personal experience, but being "inborn,"[144] and consisting of contents ("essentially the archetypes")[145] that "have never been in consciousness, and therefore have never been individually acquired, but owe their existence exclusively to heredity."[146]   It is "a great mistake," therefore, Jung wrote, "to suppose that the psyche of a new-born child is a *tabula rasa* in the sense that there is absolutely nothing in it."[147] The "pre-conscious psyche — for example, that of a new-born infant — is not an empty vessel into which, under favorable conditions, practically anything can be poured."[148] On the contrary, "the child is born with a differentiated brain that is predetermined by heredity."[149] To that extent, "it meets sensory stimuli coming from outside not with *any* aptitudes, but with *specific* ones, and this necessarily results in a particular, individual choice and pattern of apperception."[150] These aptitudes can be shown to be "inherited instincts and preformed patterns, the latter being the *a priori* and formal conditions of apperception that are based on instinct. . . they are the archetypes."[151] That such archetypes do exist and are innate, Jung wrote, is evidenced by their universality.[152] This 'universality' can be demonstrated, however, only to the extent that the archetypes "manifest themselves."[153] The method for proving the existence of archetypes, therefore, is to study the material (i.e., myths, dreams, fantasies, delusions, etc.) in which they do express themselves.[154]

Jung compared[155] these archetypes not only to the Platonic Ideas, but also to what Lucien Levy-Bruhl called the "*representations collectives*" of primitive peoples,[156] to what the Durkheimian scholars, Henri Hubert and Marcel Mauss, labeled — with reference to the Kantian categories — the "categories of imagination,"[157] or, finally, to what the ethnologist Adolf Bastian classified as "elementary ideas."[158] Such a comparison may be valid to the extent that Jung's archetypes did share with all of these other concepts the feature of being "innate." But it is also problematic in certain respects. For Jung was not so confident about uncovering the origin of the *a priori* categories as were the the Durkheimian scholars.[159] Nor did he agree that language and other society factors "conditioned" the "primordial images" quite as much as was claimed by Hubert and Mauss.[160] Furthermore, it has been argued that according to the Durkheimians, "the human mind lacks an innate *capacity* to construct complex systems of classification such as every society possesses,"[161] and that the mind's "collective representations," therefore, are not so much "categories" as a "content" or "collection of ideas" that is imposed.[162] If this is actually the case, their thought would not be in line with Jung's. For he repeatedly insisted that he did not consider the archetypes "inherited ideas" or "definite mythological images."[163] The archetype, he claimed, is "empty and purely formal, nothing but a *facultas praeformandi*, a possibility of representation which is given *a priori*."[164] The "representations themselves are not inherited, only the forms, and in that respect they correspond in every way to the instincts."[165] They are an "instinctive trend, as marked as the impulse of birds to build nests, or ants to form organized colonies."[166] "Collective thought patterns of the human mind . . . innate and inherited," they are "not just static patterns," but "dynamic factors that manifest themselves in impulses,"[167] and "create myths, religions, and philosophies."[168] They are "forms, which are unconscious, but nonetheless active-living dispositions, ideas in the Platonic sense, that preform and continually influence our thoughts and feelings and actions."[169] They "direct all fantasy activity into its appointed paths and in this way produce, in the fantasy images of children's dreams as well as in the delusions of schizophrenia, astonishing mythological parallels such as can also be found, though in a lesser degree, in the dreams of normal persons and neurotics."[170] As such, they are "an *a priori* conditioning factor of consciousness and its contents."[171]

These archetypes "are not disseminated only by tradition, language, and migration,"[172] Jung contended. "They can re-arise spontaneously, at any time, at any place, and without any outside influence."[173] They are "present always and everywhere."[174] They "emanate . . . from the unconscious," and "independent of tradition . . . guarantee in every single individual a similarity and even a sameness of experience, and also of the way it is represented imaginatively."[175] "When a situation occurs which corresponds to a given archetype, that archetype becomes activated and a compulsiveness appears, which, like an instinctual drive, gains its way against all reason and will, or else produces a conflict of pathological dimensions, that is to say a neurosis."[176] Its "function" is "to compensate or correct . . . the inevitable one-sidedness and extravagances of the conscious mind"[177] by "uniting opposites" and "[mediating] between the unconscious substratum and the conscious mind."[178]

Such a conception of the function of religion has become a working hypothesis of much recent psychological and anthropological study of religion.[179] This has been due in part to the enormous influence of Jung himself.[180] But it has also been profoundly re-enforced from within anthropological circles by the theories of Claude Lévi-Strauss and other "structuralists."[181]

Just as Jung saw religion assisting the individual's psychological maturation through the resolution of conflicts, so Lévi-Strauss has associated religion with the "resolution of value conflicts intrinsic to the social structure of each society . . . [permitting] the society to maintain the partial advantages of its own contradictory segments by relieving in a symbolic, ritualized, mythic system of behavior the tensions it produces."[182] And just as Jung located the base of religion in the archetypal dispositions of the collective unconscious, so Lévi-Strauss, following the lead of Ferdinand Saussure and other modern linguists,[183] posits an "*esprit humaine*" or "over-consciousness,"[184] out of which arises the "socio-logic of the human mind" whereby "we, in society, 'make up' reality as we go along, resolve what are in fact unresolvable 'oppositions,' and so make our experiences adequate to our theoretical presuppositions,"[185] as, for example, in the Oedipus myth whose fundamental meaning is to be found in its resolution of the belief that mankind is autochthonous and the knowledge that humans are actually born from the union of man and woman.[186] All of human culture, including religion, is viewed, in other words, as "a projection of a structure which already exists in the [human] mind," in the sense that "human beings are innately predisposed to build up cultural constructs out of paired oppositions of a very simplistic kind, such as animate/inanimate, human/nonhuman, male/female, above/below, we/they, and symmetrical/asymmetrical."[187]

For all their talk of a religious *a priori*, neither Jung nor Lévi-Strauss, it should be noted, lend any unequivocal support to traditional religious convictions about the actual existence of a "totally other" reality. To that extent, they are perhaps being consistent with Kant's own critical idealism, which some have interpreted as being "transcendental" in only a "horizontal" sense.[188] And for a more "vertical" interpretation of the Kantian transcendental one may need to turn to metaphysics or theology. For that, no better example could be found in modern Christian circles than in the attempt by Karl Rahner to reconcile the metaphysical epistemology of Thomas Aquinas with Kant's transcendental method, by way of an analysis of the *a priori* conditions of all human knowledge.[189]

With Thomas, Rahner rejects outright any notion of human beings coming into the world with innate concepts imprinted upon their minds, and readily admits that all human knowledge occurs through reference to sense experience.[190] But he also argues that according to Thomas, "realistic convictions regarding the objective reality of . . . being, can be shown to be just as much necessary, *a priori* conditions of human knowledge as are space and time and the categories of the understanding."[191] He arrives at this conclusion by way of analysing Thomas' description of the "*conversio intellectus ad phantasma*"[192] in the light of Kant's claim that the "idea of limitation presupposes the totality to be limited,"[193]

Hegel's correlation of thinking and being through the postulation of an epistemological "absolute"that lies beyond "the purely formal thinking subject,"[194] and Heidegger's contention that "the asking of a question presupposes some sort of knowledge or awareness of the object sought."[195] It would far exceed the scope of this study to follow Rahner's whole argument in this regard, but its net result is to suggest that for Thomas the processes of "abstraction" and "illumination" by the agent intellect constitute a single, indivisible act whereby the "finiteness" of the concrete singular given in the sensible image (the phantasm) is grasped only in the light of the mind's *a priori*, "prereflective, preconscious awareness" of an "infinite horizon" or "totality" of being that metaphysicians refer to as the "*ens realissimum et infinitum*" and theologians call "God."[196] With such an interpretation of Thomas, Rahner moves beyond the "critical idealism" of Kant's *Critique of Pure Reason*, and embraces a position of "critical realism,"[197] according to which the religious *a priori* goes beyond the merely "modal and logical" to take on "existential" import.[198] Like Otto's 'idea of the holy,' however, it remains basically "formal," in that it yields no direct knowledge of God, and "can receive concrete and determinate content [of a mythological, symbolic, analogical sort] only through sense experience, that is, only through the revelation of God under the conditions of space and time in history,"[199] as, for example, in the encounter with human death, freedom, and love.[200]

Notes

1.   See *The Dialogues of Plato*, *GB* 7: 229; Cicero, *Tusculan- Disputations* (London: W. Heinemann, 1927), I.XIII, 35-37; Cicero, "On the Law," I.8, 24 in *Selected Works of Cicero* (New York: The Classics Club, 1948), 229-32; *The Discources of Epictetus*, *GB* 12: 106, 127, 150, 182; Diogenes Laertius, *Lives of*

Eminent Philosophers (London: W. Heinemann, 1965), 153, 161, 163. For further discussion of Plato and the Stoics on this matter, see: R. G. Kottich, *Die Lehre von den angeborenen Ideen* (Berlin: Verlagsbuchhandlung von R. Schoetz, 1917) 7-13, 16-22; W. Windelband, *A History of Philosophy* (New York: Macmillan, 1960), 203-5.

2.　　R. Descartes, *Meditations on First Philosophy*, GB 31: III, 81-89; F. Copleston, *A History of Philosophy* IV, *Descartes to Leibniz* (Garden City, N.Y.: Doubleday, 1963) 112.

3.　　Edward, Lord Herbert of Cherbury, *De Veritate*, trans. and introd. by M. H. Carre (Bristol: University of Bristol, 1937), 29, 31, 33, 293, 296, 298, 300; Lord Herbert of Cherbury, *De Religione Laici*, ed. and trans. by H. R. Hutcheson (New Haven: Yale University Press, 1944), 89-91; C. Guttler, *Eduard, Lord Herbert von Cherbury* (Munchen: C. H. Beck'sche Verlagsbuchhandlung, 1897), 63-69; Kottich, *Angeborenen Ideen*, 32-38.

4.　　John W. Yolton, *John Locke and the Way of Ideas* (Oxford: Clarendon Press, 1956), 29-39.

5.　　Comment by Nathaniel Culverwel, in Yolton, *Locke*, 26-29.

6.　　Lord Herbert, *De Veritate*, 139-140; Yolton, *Locke*, 33-34, 41, 52, 58.

7.　　Lord Herbert readily admitted that "persons who are out of their minds or mentally incapable" are exceptional to the rule of "immediate and universal consent" to the "common notions" *(De Veritate*, 139, 295). Contrary to Locke's contention that there were savage peoples who were atheistic (John Locke, *Essay Concerning Human Understanding*, Bk. I, Chap. III, 8: *GB* 35: 114), Lord Herbert expressed the doubt that such people could be found *(De Veritate*, 295). But even if they could be found, this would not disprove the "universality" of the common notions, but would only show, as diligent historians might demonstrate empirically, that they had not emerged as conscious beliefs because they had been resisted and corrupted under a superficial layer of superstitious rituals (See Harrison, *Religion*, 71).

8.　　See Lord Herbert, *De Veritate*, 31-32, 38, 126; Yolton, *Locke*, 27, 31, 35, 52.

9.　　Locke, *Essay* Bk.I, Chap. I, 3, *GB* 35: 96.

10.　Ibid.

11.　G.W. Leibniz, *New Essays Concerning Human Understanding*, trans. A. G. Langley (New York: Macmillan, 1896), 47,77, 100, 105-106. For a discussion of Leibniz's arguments for unconscious experience, see: C. D. Broad, *Leibniz, An Introduction* (London: Cambridge University Press, 1975), 131-40; N. Rescher, *Leibniz: An Introduction to his Philosophy* (Oxford: Basil Blackwell, 1979), 126-28.

12.　According to Polanyi, not all knowledge is explicit, or "formulated in words, maps, mathematical symbols, etc." (M. Polanyi, *The Study of Man* [Chicago and London: The University of Chicago Press, 1959], 12-13). There is also a "tacit dimension" to knowledge, that is, "unformulated knowledge, such as we have of something we are in the act of doing" (Ibid.). See also M. Polanyi, *The Tacit Dimension* (Garden City, N.Y.: Doubleday, 1966), 22-24; M. Polanyi, "The Logic of Tacit Inference," *Philosophy* 40 (1966): 369-86, and a related discussion of "unconscious inference" by Hermann von Helmholtz and Wilhelm Wundt (R. J. Richards, "Wundt's Early Theories of Unconscious

Inference and Cognitive Evolution in their Relation to Darwinian Biopsychology," in *Wundt Studies,* ed. by W. G. Bringmann and R. D. Tweney [Toronto: C. J. Hogrefe, 1980], 42-70).

13. See A. Hardy, *The Biology of God,* 50; G. and M. Bateson, *Angels Fear,* 20, 80, 84, 102-103, 146.

14. See Lord Herbert, *De Veritate,* 31-32, 38, 126; Yolton, *Locke* 27, 31, 35, 52.

15. David E. Cooper has argued that, contrary to the assumption of Noam Chomsky and Jerrold Katz that "Descartes and Leibniz did not take innate knowledge to be 'actual' but only 'dispositional'," "both of them [i.e., Descartes and Leibniz] often speak as if men literally and actually know certain truths prior to experience, the only unusual characteristic of such knowledge being that it is unconscious" (D. E. Cooper, "Innateness: Old and New," *The Philosophical Review* LXXXI [October, 1972]: 468-69). C. D. Broad provides a "dispositional" interpretation of Leibniz's theory of innate ideas, but concludes that after having reduced innate ideas to "innate dispositions to think in certain ways," Leibniz then in turn reduced the innate dispositions to "unconsicous experiences" (Broad, *Leibniz,* 138-39; Nicholas Jolley, "Leibniz and Malebranche on Innate Ideas," *The Philosophical Review* XCVII, No.1 [January, 1988]: 86-87). The idea of God, therefore, is innate for Leibniz, Broad concludes, in the sense that "all that is needed is to make conscious the unconscious" idea we have of Him (Broad, *Leibniz,* 139).

16. As an example of "unconscious knowledge," Leibniz had pointed to Plato's notion of innate ideas as the "memories" retained at birth by the human soul of its earlier vision of the ideal forms, but without himself accepting its underlying assumption of the pre-existence of the soul (See Leibniz, *New Essays,* 79-80). It is doubtful, however, whether Plato himself ever thought that we "bring any actual knowledge into the world ready-made with us" (See A. E. Taylor, *Plato: The Man and His Work* [New York: The Dial Press, 1936], 136). "One should be careful to bear in mind," Taylor notes, "that *anamnesis* does not properly mean in the theory 'remembering,' but 'being reminded of' something. Sensible experiences are always 'suggesting' to us 'ideal' standards which none of them actually exhibit" (Ibid. 138, n. 2). The same caution should be taken in interpreting remarks by Rudolf Otto to the effect that the less than fully conscious "teleological impressions of the universe" represent "in the truest sense a Platonic *anamnesis* of the Idea" (Otto, *The Idea of the Holy,* 63, 143-44, 147-48; Otto, *Philosophy of Religion* [London: Williams and Norgate, 1931], 93, 113, 135). Otto himself in fact insists that such "intuitive feelings" are not "innate ideas," and concludes that an "innate religion" simply does not exist, since "not a single actual knowledge exists in the soul prior to, and without experience" (Otto, *The Idea of the Holy,* 112-13, 177; Otto, *Philosophy of Religion,* 59-60 n.1).

17. In a reply to Gassendi, Descartes wrote: "You have a difficulty, however, you say as to whether I think the soul always thinks. But why should it not always think, when it is a thinking substance? Why is it strange that we do not remember the thoughts it has had in the womb or in a stupor, when we do not even remember most of those we have had when grown up, in good health, and awake" (as quoted in Cooper, "Innateness," 469).

18. Broad, *Leibniz,* 134-35; 138-39; Jolley, "Leibniz," 86-87.

19. See Yolton, *Locke,* 33, 34, 35; Leibniz, *New Essays,* 72, 74.

20. 'Character' derives from the Greek word *charassein* meaning "to engrave" (*ERE* III: 364). Locke's antagonist, Edward Stillingfleet, among others, often referred to the idea of God as an "indelible character" upon the mind (Yolton, *Locke,* 38).

21. On the origin of ethology as a "science of character," see John Durant, "Innate Character in Animals and Man," in *Biology, Medicine, and Society* 1840-1940, ed. Charles Webster (Cambridge University Press, 1981), 157-92. W. H. Thorpe notes that "the original Latin word [for instinct] implies 'being driven from within'" (W. H. Thorpe, *Learning and Instinct in Animals* [London: Methuen and Co., 1956], 15), and that prior to the exaggerated emphasis by modern behaviorists upon reflex and tropism, most "zoologists and comparative psychologists (e.g., Darwin) were thinking of instinct primarily as some sort of innate urge for activity directed towards ends biologically desirable yet essentially unknowable to the organism concerned" (Ibid.). According to R. J. Richards, C. Lloyd Morgan and William James also were inclined to think of instincts as "nothing but concatenations of simple reflexes" ("The Innate and Learned: The Evolution of Konrad Lorenz's Theory of Instinct," *Philosophy of the Social Sciences* 4(1974): 131 n. 20.

22. Lord Herbert, *De Veritate,* 31, 121. Matthew Hale and Walter Charleton similarly equated innate knowledge with natural instinct (See Yolton, *Locke,* 34, 43.1).

23. Lord Herbert, *De Veritate,* 31.

24. Ibid., 122.

25. Ibid., 41.

26. Ibid., 120.

27. Ibid.

28. See G. P. Klubertanz, "Estimative Power," *NCE* 5: 558.

29. See, for example, Thomas Aquinas, *The Summa Theologica* la, 78.4, *GB* 19: 411-13. See also: R. J. Richards, "Influence of Sensationalist Tradition on Early Theories of the Evolution of Behavior," *Journal of the History of Ideas* 40 (1979): 86; Richards, *Darwin,* 23n.5; *NCE* 5: 558.

30. Richards, "Influence," 86. Even Descartes, however, sometimes referred to the "images" and "ideas" of animal corporeal imagination (Richards, *Darwin,* 26; Richards, "Influence," 95).

31. See Leibniz, *New Essays,* 91-92.

32. Richards, *Darwin,* 23n.5, 26n.15; Richards, "Influence," 95.

33. Richards, *Darwin,* 98; Richards, "Influence," 98.

34. See William McDougall, *An Introduction to Social Psychology* (Boston: John W. Luce, 1926), 27-30. For a less than complimentary comparison of McDougall's views on instinct with those of Lorenz, see Richards, "The Innate and the Learned," 114-19.

35. K. Lorenz, *Evolution and Modification of Behavior* (Chicago: The University of Chicago, 1967), 40-41; Richards, *Darwin,* 528-36; Richards, "The Innate and the Learned," 111-33. W. H. Thorpe notes in this regard that "if we follow the origin of an innate behaviour pattern right back to the

gene mechanism, we have to assume that the instructions to the animal to develop in such a way — that, for instance, the song of a particular kind is produced when the bird is mature — has been coded in the D.N.A. of the gene" (*Learning and Instinct*, 16), and concludes that "we are justified in saying that the behaviour pattern is innate in the sense that the complexity which it displays arises primarily from the instructions in the germ cell and not from the instructions which are contributed by the environment" (Ibid.). For Lorenz's five observational criteria of innate drives, see Richards' *Darwin*, 530.

36. See K. Lorenz, *Behind the Mirror* (New York: Harcourt Brace Jovanovich, 1978), 189ff; Richards, *Darwin*, 285-87.

37. Wuketits, *Concepts*, 5, 6, 75.

38. Swinburne, *Evolution of the Soul*, 122.

39. Ibid., 103.

40. Ibid., 262.

41. Ibid., 109, 136, 285.

42. Ibid., 291.

43. Ibid., 297.

44. Ibid.

45. Ibid., 291.

46. Ibid., 297.

47. Ibid.

48. Ibid., 272 n.5.

49. Ibid., 285.

50. Ibid., 183, 262.

51. Ibid., 183.

52. See *NCE* 5: 558.

53. Lord Herbert, *De Veritate*, 296.

54. See C. Darwin, *The Descent of Man*, GB 49: 302-303.

55. V. Turner, *On the Edge of the Bush*, 11, 249, 259-61, 282; d'Aquili, *Spectrum*, 51-79, 80-113

56. Michael Ruse writes: "Our minds are not *tabulae rasae*. Rather, they are structured according to various innate dispositions, which have proven their worth in the past struggles of proto-humans. These dispositions do not yield fully explicit, innate ideas (of the kind attacked by John Locke, in his *Essay Concerning Human Understanding*); but, as we grow, triggered and informed by life's experiences, the dispositions incline us to think and act in various tried and trustworthy patterns. Such dispositions or propensities are known, technically, as 'epigenetic rules.' There is growing empirical evidence both as to their nature and of their widespread importance" (Ruse, *Darwinian Paradigm*, 260; Ruse, *Taking Darwin Seriously*, 143-47, 161-85, 205-206, 221-23, 230-35, 251; Ruse bases his views largely on the 1981 book by Charles Lumsden and E. O. Wilson entitled *Genes, Minds, and Culture* [Cambridge: Harvard University Press, 1981]). He sees Hume, rather than Kant, as the 'philosophical precursor' of this position, to the extent that Hume, as noted earlier (*Supra* I, n.65), recognized the existence of certain "propensities," which incline the mind to see things in certain ways (e.g., causal connections) not because (as Kant thought) of any 'necessity' in the nature of things, but

because of the adaptive value or 'utility' for preservation and propagation of the species (See Ruse, *Taking Darwin Seriously*, 184).

57. At one point in his treatise on the philosophy of religion, Otto noted how according to the modern Naturalists, "all creative impulses in animals, all the 'associations of ideas' underlying instinct, are just innate ideas, which in the course of evolution and of history are acquired to a species and then are innate in the individual member of the species as 'mneme' or 'engraph' or 'inherited memory'" (*The Philosophy of Religion*, 59n.1). So long as this "present-day resurrection of the old theory of innate ideas" is "discussing Instinct," Otto continued, it is "quite right" (Ibid.). But "for the inquiry after Knowledge it has nothing to tell us; it rests on an error in psychology" (Ibïd.). "Knowledge," Otto explained, "is not a matter of possessing peculiar ideas which we cannot abandon: it is a matter of possessing the *insight*, that something is thus or thus" (Ibid.). "Even if innate ideas were *per se* absolutely correct," they could at best be called only "teachings," but "neither knowledge nor insight," for "innate ideas are thoughts due to compulsion and are, therefore, not knowledge at all" (Ibid.). "This theory forgets," Otto concluded, that "neither God nor the Devil can implant actual knowledge" (Ibid.).

On Otto's views on evolution in general see Otto, *Goethe und Darwin: Darwinismus und Religion* (Göttingen: Vandenhoeck and Ruprecht 1909), 14–40; English translation in *The Crozer Quarterly* Vol. VIII (April, 1931): No. 2, 147–61, and in Otto, *Essays*, 121–39; R. Otto, *Naturalism and Religion* (London: Williams and Norgate, 1913), 85–225.

58. For further discussion of the analogy between instinct and computer software, see comments by Christopher Evans in *Philosophy and Contemporary Issues*, ed. John R. Burr and Milton Goldfinger (New York: Macmillan, 1984), 365.

59. Lord Herbert, *De Veritate*, 132; Yolton, *Locke*, 38, 50, 51, 58.

60. W. Windelband, *A History of Philosophy*, 203–205, 449–51.

61. See *Locke*, 39, 42, 43.

62. See Nicholas Rescher, "A New Look at the Problem of Innate Ideas,"*British Journal of Philosophy and Science* 17.2 (1966): 206.

63. See Stephen P. Stich, *Innate Ideas* (Berkeley: University of California, 1975), 2.

64. See comments by Rescher ("A New Look," 206) and by Nelson Goodman (J. R. Searle, *The Philosophy of Language* [London: Oxford University Press, 1971], 144).

65. The Platonic discussion of "recollection," A. E. Taylor noted, "is not a theory of 'innate ideas,' or 'innate knowledge,' in the popular sense of the words. We are not supposed to bring any actual knowledge into the world ready-made with us. On the contrary, we are said to 'have learned' truth but to have lost it again, and we have to recover what we have lost. The recovery requires a real and prolonged effort of steady thinking; what 'recollection,' or more accurately 'being reminded,' does for us is to provide the starting point for this effort" (*Plato*, 136).

66. The Stoic "general ideas" are "apparently antecedent to experience, in that we have a natural predisposition to form them" (F. Copleston, *A History*

of Philosophy Vol. I, *Greece and Rome,* Part II [Garden City, N.Y.: Doubleday, 1962], 131).

67. The Philosophical Works of Descartes, trans. by E. Haldane and G. R. T. Ross (Cambridge: Cambridge University Press, 1983), 442.

68. Ibid.

69. See Copleston, *Descartes to Leibniz,* 94. There is some confusion over what Descartes meant by an innate idea. Robert M. Adams has pointed out, for example, that Descartes spoke of innate ideas in two different senses, namely, as ideas that the mind has "a power to form . . . without receiving them from outside," and secondly, "in a narrower sense," as ideas for which "we need neither any particular sensory stimulation, nor simpler component ideas, in order to form them" ("Where Do Our Ideas Come From? — Descartes vs. Locke," in Stich, *Innate Ideas,* 78). In the former sense, Adams argues, Descartes claimed that all ideas, including the so-called "adventitious" ones that proceed from external objects, are innate (Ibid. 77-78). Judging from what Copleston says about the way Descartes sometimes uses the 'idea of God' as though we are capable of forming it from within, "without any reference to the external world," and prior to any "actual idea of the self," it would seem that Descartes considered this particular idea as being innate in the "narrower sense" discussed by Adams (Copleston, *Descartes to Leibniz,* 112-13).

70. Augustine relocated the Platonic Ideas in the divine intelligence as "certain archetypal forms or stable and immutable essences of things" (F. Copleston, *History,* II, *Medieval Philosophy,* Part I, *Augustine to Bonaventure,* 75), and argued further that true knowledge can be had only through the vision of these "eternal ideas" made possible by "divine illumination" (Ibid., 77). Contrary to what Malebranche and other Ontologists have thought, however, this Augustinian theory does not necessarily imply an "immediate intuition" of the divine essence (Ibid., 76). Nor does it imply the direct infusion by God of "innate ideas" (Ibid., 79)

71. While accepting Augustine's relocation of the Platonic Ideas into the divine intelligence, and recognizing the need for "illumination" of the human mind to grasp them (See R. McInerny, *St. Thomas Aquinas* [Notre Dame: University of Notre Dame Press, 1982], 115-18), Thomas rejected the "special" divine illumination postulated by Augustine (Copleston, *Augustine,* 79), and insisted instead upon a theory of "participation," according to which God does not illuminate human minds by His own light, but "by imprinting on them the natural light of the agent intellect" (See George A. Lindbeck, "The *A Priori* in St. Thomas' Theory of Knowledge," in *The Heritage of Christian Thought,* ed. by R. E. Cushman and E. Grislis [New York: Harper and Row, 1965], 56 n.48). Contrary to interpretations of Thomas' epistemology by the likes of Jacques Maritain and Etienne Gilson, Lindbeck concludes that Thomas actually left room for an "*apriorist* interpretation of knowledge" (Ibid, 42, 60). "It is by no means far-fetched," Lindbeck argues, "to suggest that . . . what [Thomas] said of the agent intellect and its intelligible light" is "in fact identical" to his description of "the role of being and of first principles in abstracting essences, in making all other things intelligible" (Ibid., 53). What this implies is that according to Thomas, "the intelligible light itself must be

either being, or else some kind of prereflective, preconscious awareness of being" (Ibid., 55), and that "the agent intellect is simply the intelligibility of *ens* present *a priori* to the mind" (Ibid., 60) as a "precondition for every act of knowledge" (Ibid. 61). Lindbeck agrees with Karl Rahner, therefore, in concluding that for Thomas, "abstraction" is not a process whereby "the universal form is first abstracted from the singular, and only afterward, in a separate act [converted to the phantasm or sense image]," but rather a "single, indivisible act of the illumination of the phantasm by the agent intellect [through its anticipatory grasp of being]" (Ibid., 62). Thomas' notion of being is not, Lindbeck adds, "the *summum genus* of the logicians . . . the widest and emptiest of all notions," but is rather "the infinite fullness of Being . . . . containing all entitative differences, all possible reality, in a confused state" (Ibid., 57, 63). For all its richness, however, the "concept" of being remains for Thomas purely "formal"; it may deliver a "powerful awareness of the unlimited intensional riches, extensional breadth, and existential depth of reality," but it is not itself an object of experience or knowledge; it yields no direct, clear, and distinct knowledge of being apart from our sense experience (Ibid., 57-59). For further discussion of the Thomistic notion of "synderesis" or the "innate habit of practical reason, by which man comes to know immediately the first principles of the moral order," see *NCE* 13, 881-83.

72. See Yolton, *Locke*, 40, 41, 43, 58; Copleston, *History*, 5, *Modern Philosophy: The British Philosophers*: Part I: Hobbes to Paley, 63-75; Robert L. Armstrong, "Cambridge Platonists and Locke on Innate Ideas," *Journal of the History of Ideas* 30 (1969): 187-92; Lydia Gysi, *Platonism and Cartesianism in the Philosophy of Ralph Cudworth* (Bern: Verlag Herbert Lang, 1966), 33-36; Harrison, *Religion*, 28-60.

73. Locke, *Essay*, Bk. I, Chap. I, 22, *GB* 35: 101-102.

74. Yolton, *Locke*, 58.

75. Ibid., 52, 58.

76. See Ibid., 58.

77. Leibniz, *New Essays*, 46, 76, 84, 85, 105.

78. Ibid., 81.

79. Ibid., 46, 105.

80. Ibid., 81.

81. Ibid.

82. Ibid., 46.

83. Ibid., 105, 111.

84. See Locke, *Essays*, Bk. I, Chap. III, 8-17, *GB* 35: 114-17.

85. Leibniz, *New Essays*, 70, 94, 104; See also: Copleston, *Descartes to Leibniz*, 322, 323.

86. R. Otto, *The Philosophy of Religion*, 59n.1; see also: Ibid., 24-26.

87. Ibid., 59n.1. It might be noted in passing, that while Kant was developing his theory, another solution to the problem of innate ideas was being propounded by Thomas Reid. Although Reid's approach seems a throwback in some ways to Lord Herbert of Cherbury's theory of "common notions" (See Lord Herbert, *De Veritate*, 43-44), he did not champion his "original and natural judgments" or "principles of Common Sense" in terms of innate ideas, since his whole philosophy of Common Sense rests upon a

rejection of the 'doctrine of ideas' (See Thomas Reid, *Philosophical Works* [Hildesheim: Georg Olms Verlagsbuchhandlung, 1967], I: xx; F. Copleston, *The British Philosophers*, 167-76). Reid spoke sometimes of these first principles being "self-evident" in the sense of humans having a natural propensity to believe them, or in the sense of enjoying common assent and being beyond doubt, but according to Copleston, he did not provide an "unambiguous explanation" in this regard (Ibid., 172-75).

88. Ibid.; see also: Otto, *The Idea of the Holy*, 112-13.

89. Copleston, *History*, 6: *Modern Philosophy* II, *Kant*, 8. Some truths, according to Kant, "are doubly a priori; not only is their truth knowable independently of experience but the concepts which they involve are similarly independent of experience" (D. W. Hamlyn, "A priori and a posteriori," *EP* I: 11).

90. Descartes sometimes spoke of the innate ideas as though they were "forms of thought" (See Copleston, *Descartes to Leibniz*, 94).

91. Lord Herbert sometimes referred to the "common notions" as being "necessary to every apprehension of particular objects," and to that extent "may [according to Meyrick Carre] be compared with the *a priori* forms of knowledge described by Kant" (*De Veritate*, 41).

92. By conceiving of the innate ideas as being "presupposed" by sense knowledge, Leibniz may be said to have "approached the position of Kant" (Copleston, *Descartes to Leibniz*, 321).

93. Copleston, *Kant*, 43-47, 25. The categories are, in other words, something like the structures of the mind to which any object must conform in order to be known; the *a priori* conditions of knowledge (Ibid., 21).

94. See Ledger Wood, "The Transcendental Method," in George T. Whitney, *The Heritage of Kant* (New York: Russell and Russell, 1962), 12.

95. See Kant, *Critique of Pure Reason*, Intro. II, *GB* 42: 14-15. Ledger Wood notes in this regard that "presumably the same criteria of apriority apply to the propositions and forms alike. . . . Kant's failure to differentiate between apriority of forms and categories on the one hand and the apriority of knowledge on the other is just one of the many confusing ambiguities of his terminology" (L. Wood, "The Transcendental Method," in George Topley Whitney, *The Heritage of Kant* [New York: Russell and Russell, 1962], 12).

96. Ibid. 45; J. Baillie, *The Interpretation of Religion* (New York: Charles Scribner's Sons, 1928), 237.

97. Baillie, *The Interpretation of Religion*, 237.

98. Ibid., 243, 245.

99. As far as the "category of the beautiful," with which others would later compare the religious *a priori*, is concerned, it should be noted that although Kant does highlight certain "universal and necessary features" of the aesthetic judgment — to the extent of arguing that one's disinterested delight in the beautiful *ought* to be shared by *all*, he does not seem to have had in mind an *a priori* category of the beautiful in the sense of a logical principle or concept such as was implied by his categories of understanding and practical reason (See Copleston, *Kant*, 150-54; W. H. Walsh, "Kant, Immanuel," *EP* IV: 319-20).

100. Baillie, *The Interpretation of Religion*, 237.

101. Ibid., 244.

102. Copleston, *Kant*, 25, 9.

103. Ibid., 25, 11, 19, 27, 72, 76, 97.

104. Ibid., 26, 77, 94-100. W. H. Urban argued that "it was one of Kant's most serious limitations that while he recognized that the knowledge of nature, in our terms its intelligibility, is conditioned, by certain forms immanent in mind, to the equally necessary forms of the interpretation of life and world, he allowed merely the character of practical postulates and regulative ideas. It escaped him entirely that reality, as we live it and know it, is likewise our reality only as the stuff of experience is formed by the categories of value. . . . Non-temporal and non-empirical forms of value are also the *a priori* of an intelligible world" (*The Intelligible World*: *Metaphysics and Value* [New York: Macmillan, 1929], 344-45). According to R. F. Davidson, it was precisely this deficiency in Kantian thought for which Otto was trying to compensate (R. F. Davidson, *Rudolf Otto's Interpretation of Religion* [Princeton: Princeton University Press, 1947], 170-71).

105. Copleston, *Kant*, 60, 76, 94, 97.

106. Baillie, *The Interpretation of Religion*, 244.

107. Ibid., 237, 241.

108. Ibid., 246. See also: Michel Despland, *Kant on History and Religion* (Montreal and London: McGill-Queen's University Press, 1973), 117-20.

109. See F. Schleiermacher, *On Religion*, 36; F. Schleiermacher, *The Christian Faith* (New York: Harper and Row, 1963), I: 5-26; Richard R. Niebuhr, *Schleiermacher on Christ and Religion* (New York: Charles Scribner's Sons, 1964), 174-96; C. W. Christian, *Friedrich Schleiermacher* (Waco, Texas: Word Books, 1979), 98-103; Richard R. Niebuhr, "Friedrich Schleiermacher," in Martin E. Marty and Dean G. Peerman, eds., *A Handbook of Christian Theologians* (Cleveland and New York: World Publishing Co., 1967), 28; John Dillenberger and Claude Welch, *Protestant Christianity* (New York: Charles Scribner's Sons, 1954), 182-89.

110. R. R. Niebuhr, *Schleiermacher*, 194; R. R. Niebuhr, "Schleiermacher," 29, 34.

111. Otto, *Idea of the Holy*, 9; Otto, *Essays*, 68-77; Bernard E. Meland, "Rudolf Otto," in Marty and Peerman, *Handbook*, 170-71.

112. Otto, *Idea of the Holy*, 9-10.

113. Otto, *Philosophy of Religion*, 15.

114. See Jakob Friedrich Fries, *Dialogues on Morality and Religion* (Totowa, N.J.: Barnes and Noble, 1982), 232, xi; Davidson, *Otto's Interpretation*, 136, 165, 171.

115. Davidson, *Otto's Interpretation*, 46.

116. Ibid.

117. Ibid.

118. Ibid., 168, 43-49.

119. Ibid., 165-66. See also: Karl Bornhausen, "Das religiöse Apriori bei Ernst Troeltsch und Rudolf Otto," *Zeitschrift fuer Philosophie und philosophische Kritik* 139 (1910), 93-206; Ernst Troeltsch, *Writings on Theology and Religion*, trans. and ed. by Robert Morgan and Michael Pye (London: Duckworth, 1977), 14-23; 82-104, 241; Philip C. Almond, *Rudolf Otto, An*

Introduction to his Philosophical Theology (Chapel Hill and London: University of North Carolina Press, 1984), 91–93; Douglas C. Macintosh, "Troeltsch's Theory of Religious Knowledge," *American Journal of Theology*, July (1919): 274–89; H. Richard Niebuhr, "The Religious Philosophy of Ernst Troeltsch" (Unpublished Ph.D. dissertation, Yale University, 1924).

120. Otto, *The Idea of the Holy*, 5, 7, 51, 134, 113, 134, 137, 160, 175; Almond, *Otto*, 41–42, 90, 157.

121. Otto, *The Idea of the Holy*, 114, 136; Davidson, *Otto's Interpretation*, 159, 166-67. See also: Soren Holm, "Apriori und Urphänomen bei Rudolf Otto," in *Rudolf Ottos Bedeutung fuer die Religionswissenschaft und die Theologie Heute*, hgb. von Ernst Benz (Leiden: E. J. Brill, 1971), 70–83; Almond, *Otto*, 34–38, 47–54, 69–70, 93–102; D. Bastow, "Otto and Numinous Experience," *Religious Studies* 12 (1976): 159–76. On the non-moral connotations of the term 'holy,' see: Otto, *The Idea of the Holy*, 5.

122. Otto, *The Idea of the Holy*, 149, 140.

123. Ibid., 137.

124. Ibid., 137–39.

125. Ibid., 139. While admitting that "everyone" is "capable of having *a priori* cognitions," Otto denies that everyone does have them spontaneously (*Ibid.*, 177). Most people, he says, have "merely a faculty of receptivity and a principle of judgement and acknowledgement, not a capacity to produce the cognitions in question for oneself independently" (Ibid.). They must be "awakened through the instrumentality of other more highly endowed natures," who, like the prophets, are "specially endowed" with the aforementioned faculty of "divination," and by those who, like Jesus, are able, at a still qualitatively higher level, "to reveal the very being of God" (Ibid., 177–78, 150).

126. Ibid., 140, 149. The best evidence of universality of the *sensus numinis*, Otto said, was to be found in the "parallels" existing between the various religions (See *Infra*, Chapter Four, n. 91).

127. Bastow, "Otto and Numinous Experience," 171.

128. Otto, *The Idea of the Holy*, 5, 45, 110, 112, 136.

129. Ibid., 8–40.

130. Bastow seems to want simply to identify the faculty of divination with the "experience of the numinous" ("Otto and Numinous Experience," 161, 170). It would seem more accurate to say with Davidson, however, that according to Otto, the "sense of the numinous" is the "source from which the persistent intuitions of historical religion spring" (*Otto's Interpretation*, 125), or, in other words, that the "immediate intuitive awareness of religious value" that accompanies the initial "feeling" of the "holy" is the "condition" of the "divination of the deity" that gives rise to the symbolic "ideograms" of a religious sort (Ibid., 129–30). So conceived, for example, the notion of "God's wrath" should be seen as "conditioned" by the prior intuition or feeling of "creaturely unworthiness" (Ibid.). This interpretation would seem to be supported by Almond's aforementioned suggestion that "divination" represents for Otto the "turning outward toward the world of appearances" of the religious *a priori* which has apprehended the *mysterium* in the depth of the

self" (*Otto*, 106-109). The "ideogram" in this sense represents a "recollection" of the pure idea grasped in the sense of the numinous (Ibid.). This interpretation is further substantiated by Otto's tendency to equate "rationalization" with "schematization." In other words, the sense of the numinous might be considered the pure 'category', while the "ideogram" its schema. Otto's discussion of the Eucharist as an *anamnesis* that "schematizes" the "numinous event" of Christ's redemptive death brings these various lines of thought together most poignantly (*Essays*, 45-67, v).

131. Otto, *The Idea of the Holy*, 6, 51-59, 75, 82, 109, 111, 114-15, 134, 136-42.

132. Ibid., 15, 114-15, 146, 177.

133. Ibid., 112.

134. Ibid., 112, 136.

135. Ibid., 140, 6, 31, 45-49, 61, 63, 134. Otto's talk of "schematization" is not without problems. Kant himself had in mind thereby the process whereby "the concrete data of sense experience are subsumed under the *a priori* categories" through an image that unites the particularity of the former with the universality of the latter. Thus, for example, the category of causality is schematized as "regular succession in time," or the category of substance as "the permanence of the real in time" (Copleston, *Kant*, 51-53). What exactly Kant meant thereby, however, is a matter of considerable controversy (See: John P. Reeder, Jr., "The Relation of the Moral and the Numinous in Otto's Notion of the Holy," in *Religion and Morality* ed. by G. Outka and J. P. Reeder, Jr. [Garden City: Anchor Press, 1973], 267-79). Otto's attempt to apply this "baffling" bit of Kantian doctrine to his own theory about religion (see Ibid., 264ff; Almond, *Otto*, 97-102) has been described by some as its "weakest point" (Wach, *Types*, 222), and by others as "ingenious nonsense" (See Davidson, *Otto's Interpretation* 188).

Perhaps the best approach would be not to get bogged down in the question of whether Otto was using the term "schema" in exactly the same sense as Kant, and to concentrate instead on the "process" Otto was trying to describe, namely, how the "non-rational" numinous feelings of stupor, dread, and fascination (the pure religious "categories," so to speak) are given "clear" historical "shape" by having their "necessary" and "essential" association with other "rational" and "ethical" feelings and ideas brought into focus, in much the same way as the verbal text of a song expresses natural feelings and thereby "schematizes" or "rationalizes" the "unique and mysterious . . . inner content" of the underlying music (Otto, *The Idea of the Holy*, 45-49).

136. Otto, *The Idea of the Holy*, 138, 177.

137. Ibid., 138, 177; see also: *supra*, note 118.

138. Ibid., 1-7, 13, 19, 24, 30, 31, 57-59, 79, 91, 95, 104, 107-08, 135, 170; Otto, *Essays*, 84-88.

139. See Davidson, *Otto's Interpretation*, 120-32, 69-70; Almond, *Otto*, 53, 67, 83; Baillie, *The Interpretation of Religion*, 246-55.

140. Otto, *The Idea of the Holy*, 90-95; 19, 24, 30, 59; on the "wholly other" dimension: Ibid., 25-30; *Essays*, 78-94.

141. Otto, *The Idea of the Holy*, 135, 147; Davidson, *Otto's Interpretation*, 109-32.

142. See Jung, *Psychology and Religion*,4-6.

143. C. G. Jung, *The Archetypes and the Collective Unconscious*, in *The Collected Works of C.G. Jung*, Volume 9, Part I, ed. William McGuire *et al.* (Princeton University Press, 1959), 3.

144. Ibid., 42, 3.

145. Ibid., 42.

146. Ibid., 42, 43, 77, 156.

147. Ibid., 66, 57.

148. Ibid., 77.

149. Ibid., 66.

150. Ibid.

151. Ibid. See for concrete examples of various archetypes: Ibid., 21ff (Shadow); Ibid., 25ff (Anima); Ibid., 37 (Wise Old Man); Ibid., 81ff (Mother); Ibid., 151ff (Child).

152. Ibid., 48, 58-59, 160; Jung, *Man and his Symbols* (New York: Doubleday, 1964), 75. Piaget has argued that "the whole weakness of the works of Jung lies in the fact that he believed that because a myth is general it corresponds to an innate archetype" (Piattelli-Palmarini, *Language and Learning*, 81).

153. Jung, *The Archetypes*, 79-80.

154. Ibid., 48-50.

155. Ibid., 5, 42-43, 67n. 25, 75, 76, 79.

156. In his 1922 *La Mentalité primitive*, Levy-Bruhl emphasized the difference between civilized and primitive peoples by arguing that the latter are of a "prelogical" (i.e., unscientific and uncritical) "mentality" (See Evans-Pritchard, *Theories*, 78-99; de Vries, *Perspectives*, 165-66). In such a raw, pristine form, his hypothesis has been generally rejected. He himself withdrew it before his death in 1937. As a description of a unique type of thought that is common to all humans, primitive or civilized, however, it still enjoys considerable respect (Evans-Pritchard, *Theories*, 82-84, 88-92, 91). In such a sense, the "primitive mind" is viewed as a certain "mystical," often tacit, "pattern or category of thought," which is collective to the extent of being "common to all, or most members of a society," and which is innate in the sense of being present prior to experience and "before the individual who acquires [it]" (see Ibid. 83-84).

157. Emile Durkheim had tried to find a way around what he perceived to be two prevailing theses about the origin of the categories: the empirical one, according to which the categories are the product of either direct or inherited individual experience, and the rationalistic one, according to which the categories are "imminent in the human mind by virtue of its inborn constitution" (Durkheim, *Elementary Forms*, 26). While the former undermines the "characteristic properties" ("universality and necessity") of the categories, and in the process reason itself, the latter, he says, neither explains nor justifies the power of the mind to transcend experience (Ibid., 26-28). The solution, he concluded, was to ascribe a "social origin to the categories," and to conceive of them as ever-changing "collective representations" which result neither from individual experience nor divine *fiat*, but from society itself (Ibid., 28). See also: E. Durkheim and M. Mauss, *Primitive Classification*,

trans. and ed. by Rodney Needham (Chicago: The University of Chicago Press, 1963), 3-9.

158. Already in 1881, in the context of the new *Voelkerpsychologie*, Bastian had posited certain "collective" or "ethnic" ideas as the only way to explain the "similar solutions" to problems evidenced by very different and separated nations (See de Vries, *Perspectives*, 86, 146). He called such ideas "elementary" to highlight his conviction that they are "inherent in the human psyche" (Ibid., 86), and express "the structure of the human mind" (Ibid., 146). De Vries notes that most ethnologists have preferred a "diffusionist" interpretation of such similarities (Ibid., 147).

159. See Jung, *The Archetypes*, 78-79.

160. Ibid., 67 n. 25.

161. Durkheim and Mauss, *Primitive Classification*, xi.

162. Ibid., xxvi, xxvii.

163. Ibid., 66; Jung, *Man and his Symbols*, 67.

164. Jung, *The Archetypes*, 79, 48.

165. Ibid., 79.

166. Jung, *Man and his Symbols*, 69.

167. Ibid., 76; Jung, *The Archetypes*, 43.

168. Jung, *Man and his Symbols*, 79.

169. Jung, *The Archetypes*, 79.

170. Ibid., 66, 155.

171. Ibid., 58, 27, 66, 77.

172. Ibid., 79.

173. Ibid.

174. Ibid., 42.

175. *The Archetypes*, 58, 66-67.

176. Ibid., 48.

177. Ibid., 162.

178. Ibid., 174.

179. See, for example, Abraham Maslow, *Religions, Values, and Peak-Experiences* (New York: The Viking Press, 1970), 65-66 (see also Ibid., 11-29, 59-68, where Maslow argues that the "peak experiences," involving a "mystical experience of a unified cosmos," are "rooted deep in human nature"); Turner, *On the Edge of the Bush*, 259-60; d'Aquili, *Spectrum*, 162, 163, 172, 175, 176, 319. Turner also expressed an affection for Wilhelm Dilthey's epistemology, which, with its emphasis upon the priority of "lived experience," left little room for any kind of *a priori*, whether of the Kantian categorical sort, or of the "historical" sort championed by R. G. Collingwood (see Turner, *On the Edge of the Bush*, 190, 211; R. G. Collingwood, *The Idea of History* [London: Oxford University Press, 1969], 248). His embrace, therefore, of Jung, or, for that matter, of Lévi-Strauss, was not altogether unqualified.

180. Turner, *On the Edge of the Bush*, 266-69, 282-89; d'Aquili, *Spectrum*, 163; Wallace, *Religion*, 21-29.

181. For a good introduction, see: Terence Hawkes, *Structuralism and Semiotics* (Berkeley and Los Angeles: University of California Press, 1977).

182. Wallace, *Religion*, 29.

183. At the heart of the "phonological revolution" developed by Saussure, Roman Jakobson, and others, was the "discovery that it is the combination of sounds, not the sounds in themselves, which provides the significant data" (C.Lévy- Strauss, *Structural Anthropology* (New York: Basic Books, 1963), Volume I: 208. "A child's first logical operation," Jakobson claimed, "is the discernment of binary opposition" (Hawkes, *Structuralism*, 24). This operation is tacit, he says, and derives from "a capacity (which is innate in all human beings) to discriminate sounds as bundles of binary oppositions" (Edmund Leach, "Structuralism," in *ER* 14: 55). According to A. J. Greimas, "these binary oppositions form the basis of a deep-lying 'actantial model' . . . from whose structure the superficial structures of individual stories derive" (Hawkes, *Structuralism*, 89). It was Lévi-Strauss' contribution to see that many of the "nonverbal elements of human culture — such as cosmologies, art styles, architectural designs, the layout of villages, rules concerning descent, residence, and the regulation of marriage," could be similarly "broken down into sets of cultural distinctive features which are recognizable as binary oppositions," and the "matrix combination" of which "determines the characteristics of a cultural feature in any particular ethnographic setting" (Leach, "Structuralism," 55-56).

For further discussion by Noam Chomsky, Dan Sperber, Michael Ruse and others about the innate structure of language, symbolism, logic, and mathematics, see: J. R. Searle, *The Philosophy of Language*, esp. 71-100, 121-30; Piattelli-Palmarini, *Language and Learning*, 35-54, 109-30, 244-55, 310-24; Dan Sperber, *Rethinking Symbolism* (London: Cambridge University Press, 1975), esp. x-xiii; Ruse, *Taking Darwin Seriously*, 160-68.

184. See Turner, *On the Edge of the Bush*, 278, 281.

185. Hawkes, *Structuralism*, 48-49; Lévi-Strauss, *Structural Anthropology*, 230. This is not to say, of course, that religion is directed toward some sort of rational synthesis of contradictory positions (See B. J. Verkamp, "Kueng's Ecumenical Dialectic," *Faith and Philosophy* 6.3 [1989]: 288-302).

186. See Hawkes, *Structuralism*, 48; Lévi-Strauss, *Structural Anthropology*, 213-19.

187. E. Leach, "Structuralism," *ER* 14:56; Lévi-Strauss, *Structural Anthropology*, 20-21, 33, 208-12, 230.

188. See Weger, *Rahner*, 24-26.

189. Rahner's thought in this regard is to be found primarily in his early work entitled *Spirit in the World*. Francis P. Fiorenza's introduction to this work is one of the best (Ibid., xix-xlv). On this aspect of Rahner's thought, see also: Lindbeck, "The *A priori* in St. Thomas' Theory of Knowledge," 41-63; Lindbeck, "The Thought of Karl Rahner, S.J.," *Christianity and Crisis* (October 18, 1965): 211-15; Gerald A. McCool, "The Philosophy of the Human Person in Karl Rahner's Theology," *Theological Studies* XXII (1961): 537-62; McCool, "The Primacy of Intuition," *Thought* XXXVII (1962): 57-73; Anne E. Carr, "Starting with the Human," in *A World of Grace*, ed. by Leo J. O'Donovan (New York: Seabury Press, 1980), 17-30; Michael J. Buckley, "Within the Holy Mystery," in Ibid., 31-63; R. Kress, *A Rahner Handbook* (Atlanta: John Knox Press, 1982), 27-32, 74-80, 104-106; Weger, *Rahner*, 1-34.

190. See Lindbeck, "*A priori* in Thomas," 45-46, 51; Weger, *Rahner*, 12.

191. Lindbeck, "*A priori* in Thomas," 43.

192. Rahner, *Spirit in the World*, 237-379. "*Conversio intellectus ad phantasma*" is treated by Thomas in the *Summa Theologica* I, 84, 7, and refers to the way the "universal" is converted into a "phantasm" or sensible image.

193. See Fiorenza's "Introduction," Ibid., xxiii.

194. See Ibid., xxix-xxx.

195. See Ibid., xxxiv.

196. See Lindbeck, "*A priori* in Thomas," 55, 62; Carr, "Starting with the Human," 20-21; McCool, "Philosophy of the Human Person," 539-42; Weger, *Rahner*, 22-54. As all these authors point out, Rahner's thought in this regard is also influenced considerably by the Belgian philosopher Joseph Maréchal, and especially the latter's *The Starting Point of Metaphysics*. Another modern metaphysician and theologian influenced by Maréchal, and developing a line of thought about the ontological "horizon" of all human knowledge, albeit, perhaps, without Rahner's Heideggerian appreciation of Kant's own understanding of the existential import of synthetic judgments, is Bernard Lonergan (See Lonergan's review of and commentary on Emerick Coreth's *Metaphysik*: "Metaphysics as Horizon," in Lonergan, *Collection* [New York: Herder and Herder, 1967], 202-20; see also: Lonergan, *Insight: A Study of Human Understanding* [London, New York, Toronto: Longmans, Green, 1958], 339-42, 634-730).

197. See Lindbeck, "*A priori* in Thomas," 43.

198. See Fiorenza's comments, in Rahner, *Spirit in the World*, xxxvi. This conclusion is based to some extent on Heidegger's re-interpretation of Kant's later understanding of "synthetical judgments" as "go[ing] beyond the concept and stat[ing] more than was thought in this concept, namely, that there is an object outside of the understanding" (Ibid., xxxix).

199. Lindbeck," *A priori* in Thomas," 43-44. Fiorenza notes that Rahner "denies explicitly that the absolute is known as some object or that the human mind could form an adequate objective concept of God. Instead he proposes a transcendental understanding of God, who is not known by man as an object of reality, but as the principle of human knowledge and reality" (Rahner, *Spirit in the World*, xliii-xliv).

200. See Weger, *Rahner*, 47-50

ABBREVIATIONS

DPP   *Dictionary of Philosophy and Psychology.* Edited by James Mark Baldwin. Gloucester, Mass.: Peter Smith, 1960.

EP   *Encyclopedia of Philosophy.* Edited by Paul Edwards. New York: Macmillan and Co., and The Free Press, 1967.

ER   *Encyclopedia of Religion.* Edited by Mircea Eliade. New York: Macmillan, 1987.

ERE   *Encyclopedia of Religion and Ethics.* Edited by J. Hastings. New York: Charles Scribner's Sons, 1928.

ES   *Encyclopedia of Sociology.* Edited by Edgar F. Borgatta and Marie L. Borgatta. New York: Macmillan Publishing Co., 1992.

GB   *Great Books of the Western World.* Edited by R. M. Hutchins. Chicago: Encyclopedia Britannica, 1952.

IESS   *International Encyclopedia of the Social Sciences.* Edited by David L. Sills. N.P.: The Macmillan Company and The Free Press, 1968.

NCE   *New Catholic Encyclopedia.* Edited by W. J. McDonald. New York: MacGraw-Hill, 1967.

NSHE   *New Schaff-Herzog Encyclopedia of Religious Knowledge.* Grand Rapids: Baker Book House, 1963.

SM   *Sacramentum Mundi.* Edited by Karl Rahner and others. New York: Herder and Herder, 1968.

BIBLIOGRAPHY

Abe, Masao. "Kenotic God and Dynamic Sunyata." In *The Emptying God*, 3-68. See Cobb, John B.

Abe, Masao. "Beyond Buddhism and Christianity — 'Dazzling Darkness'." Unpublished.

Alland, Alexander, Jr. *Evolution and Human Behavior*. Garden City, N.Y.: The Natural History Press, 1967.

Almond, Philip C. *Rudolf Otto: An Introduction to His Philosophical Theology*. Chapel Hill and London: The University of North Carolina Press, 1984.

Alston, William P. "Religious Diversity and Perceptual Knowledge." *Faith and Philosophy* 5, no. 4 (October, 1988): 433-48.

d'Aquili, Eugene and Laughlin, Charles D., Jr., "The Neurobiology of Myth and Ritual." In *The Spectrum of Ritual*, 152-82.

d'Aquili, Eugene. *The Spectrum of Ritual*. New York: Columbia University Press, 1979.

Armstrong, Robert L. "Cambridge Platonists and Locke on Innate Ideas." *Journal of the History of Ideas* 30 (1969): 187-202.

Ashbrook, James B. "Neurobiology: The Working Brain and the Work of Theology." *Zygon* 19, no. 3 (1984): 331-50.

Austin, William. "Are Religious Beliefs 'Enabling Mechanisms For Survival'"? *Zygon* 15, no. 2 (June, 1980): 197.

Ayala, Francisco and Dobzhansky, Theodosius. *Studies in the Philosophy of Biology*. London: Macmillan, 1974.

Bachrach, Arthur J. "An Experimental Approach to Superstitious Behavior." *Journal of American Folklore* 75 (1962): 1-9.

Baillie, John. *The Interpretation of Religion*. New York: Charles Scribner's Sons, 1928.

Banton, Michael, ed. *Anthropological Approaches to the Study of Religion*. London: Tavistock, 1966.

Banton, Michael, ed. *Darwinism and the Study of Society*. London: Tavistock; Chicago: Quadrangle, 1961.

Barringer, Herbert R., Blanksten, George I., and Mack, Raymond W. *Social Change in Developing Areas*. Cambridge, Mass.: Schenkman Publishing Co., 1965.

Bastow, David. "Otto and Numinous Experience." *Religious Studies* 12 (1976): 159-76.

Bateson, Gregory. *Mind and Nature*. New York: E. P. Dutton, 1979.

Bateson, Gregory and Mary Catherine. *Angels Fear: Towards an Epistemology of the Sacred*. New York: Macmillan, 1987.

Bellah, Robert N. *Beyond Belief*. New York, Evanston, and London: Harper and Row, 1970.

Bellah, Robert N. "Religion: The Sociology of Religion." *IESS* 406-13.

Benz, Ernst, ed. *Rudolf Ottos Bedeutung fuer die Religionswissenschaft und die Theologie Heute*. Leiden: E. J. Brill, 1971.

Bergson, Henri. *Creative Evolution*. New York: The Modern Library, 1944.

Bianchi, Ugo. *The History of Religions*. Leiden: E. J. Brill, 1975.

Bianchi, Ugo. "History of Religions." *ER* 6: 399–408.

Bidney, David. "The Ethnology of Religion and the Problem of Human Evolution." *American Anthropologist* 56, no. 1 (February 1954): 1–18.

Blasi, Anthony J. and Cuneo, Michael W. *Issues in the Sociology of Religion: A Bibliography.* New York: Garland, 1986.

Bonhoeffer, Dietrich. *Letters and Papers from Prison.* New York: Macmillan, 1971.

Bornhausen, Karl. "Das religiöse Apriori bei Ernst Troeltsch und Rudolf Otto." *Zeitschrift fuer Philosophie und philosophische Kritik* 139 (1910): 193–206.

Bovet, Pierre. *The Child's Religion.* New York: E. P. Dutton, 1928.

Bowler, Peter. "The Changing Meaning of Evolution." *Journal of the History of Ideas* 36 (1975): 95–114.

Bradie, M., "Assessing evolutionary epistemology." *Biology and Philosophy* 1: 401–59.

Bremmer, Jan. "Soul, Greek and Hellenistic Concepts of." *ER* 13: 434–38.

Broad, C. D. *Leibniz, An Introduction.* London: Cambridge University Press, 1975.

Brockman, John, ed. *About Bateson.* New York: E. P. Dutton, 1977.

Brockway, Robert W. "The Origins of Religion Debate and its Implications: A Psychological Perspective." In *International Symposium on the Intellectual Expressions of Prehistoric Man: Art and Religion*, edited by Antonio Beltran and others, 55–61. Capo di Ponte and Milan: Edizione del Centro and Editoriale Jaca Book Spa, 1979.

Buckley, Michael, J. "Within the Holy Mystery." In *A World of Grace*, 31–63. See O'Donovan, Leo J.

Burhoe, Ralph W. "Five Steps in Evolution of Man's Knowledge of Good and Evil." *Zygon* 2 (1967): 77–96

Burhoe, Ralph W. "Religion's Role in the Context of Genetic and Cultural Evolution — Campbell's Hypotheses and some Evaluative Responses." *Zygon* 11, no.3 (September, 1976): 156–66.

Burhoe, Ralph W. "Religion's Role in Human Evolution: The Missing Link between Ape-man's Selfish Genes and Civilized Altruism." *Zygon* 14 (1979): 135–62.

Burr, John R. and Goldfinger, Milton, eds. *Philosophy and Contemporary Issues.* New York: Macmillan, 1984.

Callebaut, Werner, and Pinxten, Rik. *Evolutionary Epistemology.* Dordrecht: D. Reidel Publishing Co., 1987.

Campbell, Donald T. "Blind Variation and Selective Retention in Creative Thought as in Other Knowledge Processes." *Psychological Review* 67, no. 6 (1960): 380–400.

Campbell, Donald T. "Comment on 'The Natural Selection Model of Conceptual Evolution'." *Philosophy of Science* 44 (1977): 502–507.

Campbell, Donald T. "The Conflict between Social and Biological Evolution and the Concept of Original Sin." *Zygon* 10, no. 3 (September, 1975): 234–49.

Campbell, Donald T. "On the Conflicts between Biological and Social Evolution and between Psychology and Moral Tradition." *Zygon* 11, no. 3 (September, 1976): 167–207.

Campbell, Donald T. *Descriptive Epistemology: Psychological, Sociological, and Evolutionary* (unpublished William James lectures, given at Harvard University).

Campbell, Donald T. "Evolutionary Epistemology." In *The Philosophy of Karl Popper*, 413–63. See Schlipp, Paul.

Campbell, Donald T. "Selection Theory and the Sociology of Scientific Validity." In *Evolutionary Epistemology*, 139–58. See Callebaut, Werner.

Campbell, Donald T. "Social Morality Norms as Evidence of Conflict between Biological Human Nature and Social System Requirements." In *Morality as a Biological Phenomenon*, 67–82. See Stent, G. S.

Campbell, Donald T. "Unjustified Variation and Selective Retention in Scientific Discovery." In *Studies in the Philosophy of Biology*, 147–58. See Ayala, Francisco.

Campbell, Donald T. "Variation and Selective Retention in Socio-Cultural Evolution." In *Social Change in Developing Areas*, 19–49. See Barringer, Herbert R.

Caplan, Arthur L., ed. *The Sociobiology Debate*. New York: Harper and Row, 1978.

Carmody, Denise Lardner. *The Oldest God: Archaic Religion Yesterday and Today*. Nashville: Abingdon, 1981.

Carmody, Denise L. and Carmody, John T. *Ways to the Center*. Belmont, Calif.: Wadsworth Publishing Company, 1981.

Carr, Anne E. "Starting with the Human." In *A World of Grace*, 17–30. See O'Donovan, Leo J.

Child, Arthur. "On the Theory of the Categories." *Philosophy and Phenomenological Research* 7 (1946): 316–35.

Christian, C. W. *Friedrich Schleiermacher*. Waco, Texas: Word Books, 1979.

Cicero. *Selected Works of Cicero*. New York: The Classics Club, 1948.

Cicero. *Tusculan Disputations*. London: W. Heinemann, 1927.

Cobb, John B., Jr. and Ives, Christopher. *The Emptying God: A Buddhist-Jewish-Christian Conversation*. Maryknoll, N.Y.: Orbis, 1991.

Cobb, John and Griffin, David. *Process Theology: An Introductory Exposition*. Philadelphia: Westminster Press, 1976.

Coles, Robert. *The Spiritual Life of Children*. Boston: Houghton Mifflin Co., 1990.

Collingwood, R. G. *The Idea of History*. London: Oxford University Press, 1969.

Cooper, D. E. "Innateness: Old and New." *The Philosophical Review* LXXXI (October, 1972): 465–83.

Copleston, Frederick. *A History of Philosophy* IV, *Descartes to Leibniz*. Garden City, N.Y.: Doubleday, 1963.

Copleston, Frederick. *A History of Philosophy* I, *Greece and Rome*, Part II. Garden City, N.Y.: Doubleday, 1962.

Copleston, Frederick. *A History of Philosophy* II, *Medieval Philosophy*, Part

I, *Augustine to Bonaventure*. Garden City, N.Y.: Doubleday, 1962.

Copleston, Frederick. *A History of Philosophy V, Modern Philosophy: The British Philosophers*, Part I: *Hobbes to Paley*. Garden City, N.Y.: Doubleday, 1964.

Copleston, Frederick. *A History of Philosophy VII, Modern Philosophy*, Part I: *Fichte to Hegel*. Garden City, N.Y.: Doubleday, 1965.

Copleston, Frederick. *A History of Philosophy VI, Modern Philosophy*, Part II: *Kant*. Garden City, N.Y.: Doubleday, 1964.

Critchley, Macdonald. *The Divine Banquet of the Brain and Other Essays*. New York: Raven Press, 1979.

Cullmann, Oscar. *The Earliest Christian Confessions*. London: Butterworth Press, 1949.

Cushman, R. E. and Grislis, E., eds. *The Heritage of Christian Thought*. New York: Harper and Row, 1965.

Darwin, Charles. *The Descent of Man*. Volume 49 of *Great Books of the Western World*. See Abbreviations.

Darwin, Charles. *Origin of Species*. Volume 49 of *Great Books of the Western World*. See Abbreviations.

Davidson, H. R. Ellis. *Gods and Myths of Northern Europe*. London: Penguin, 1964.

Davidson, Robert F. *Rudolf Otto's Interpretation of Religion*. Princeton: Princeton University Press, 1947.

Dawkins, Richard. *The Selfish Gene*. Oxford: Oxford University Press, 1976.

Descartes, Rene. *Meditations on First Philosophy*. Volume 31 of *Great Books of the Western World*. See Abbreviations.

Descartes, Rene. *The Philosophical Works of Descartes*. Cambridge: Cambridge University Press, 1983.

Despland, Michel. *Kant on History and Religion*. Montreal and London: McGill-Queen's University Press, 1973.

Dickson, D. Bruce. *The Dawn of Belief: Religion in the Upper Paleolithic of Southwestern Europe*. Tucson: The University of Arizona Press, 1990.

Diel, Paul. *The God Symbol: Its History and Its Significance*. San Francisco: Harper and Row, 1986.

Dillenberger, John and Welch, Claude. *Protestant Christianity*. New York: Charles Schribner's Sons, 1954.

Diogenes Laertius. *Lives of Eminent Philosophers*. London: W. Heinemann, 1965.

Dobzhansky, Theodosius. *The Biology of Ultimate Concern*. New York: New American Library, 1969.

Dobzhansky, Theodosius. "Chance and Creativity in Evolution." In *Studies in the Philosophy of Biology*, 307-308. See Ayala, Francisco.

Dobzhansky, Theodosius. "Ethics and Values in Biological and Cultural Evolution." *Zygon* 8, nos. 3-4 (September- December, 1973): 261-81.

Dobzhansky, Theodosius, Ayala, Francisco J., Stebbins, G. Ledyard, and Valentine, James W. *Evolution*. San Francisco: W. H. Freeman, 1977.

Durant, John, ed. *Darwinism and Divinity*. Oxford: Basil Blackwell, 1985.

Durant, John. "Innate Character in Animals and Man." In *Biology, Medicine, and Society 1840-1940*, edited by Charles Webster, 157-92. Cambridge: Cambridge University Press, 1981.

Durkheim, Emile. *The Elementary Forms of the Religious Life*. New York: The Free Press, 1965.

Durkheim, Emile and Mauss, M. *Primitive Classification*. Chicago: The University of Chicago Press, 1963.

Eccles, John C. *Evolution of the Brain: Creation of the Self.* London and New York: Routledge, 1989.

Eccles, John C. *The Human Mystery*. Berlin: Springer International, 1979.

Eccles, John C. *The Human Psyche*. Berlin: Springer International, 1980.

Eister, Allan W. *Changing Perspectives in the Scientific Study of Religion*. New York: John Wiley and Sons, 1974.

Eliade, Mircea. *A History of Religious Ideas*. Chicago: The University of Chicago Press, 1978.

Eliade, Mircea. *Myth and Reality*. New York and Evanston: Harper and Row, 1963.

Eliade, Mircea. *The Quest: History and Meaning in Religion*. Chicago and London: The University of Chicago Press, 1969.

Eliade, Mircea. *Patterns in Comparative Religion*. Cleveland and New York: The World Publishing Co., 1967.

Eliade, Mircea. *From Primitives to Zen: A Thematic Sourcebook in the History of Religions*. New York and Evanston: Harper and Row, 1978.

Eliade, Mircea. *Rites and Symbols of Initiation*. New York: Harper and Row, 1965.

Eliade, Mircea. *The Sacred and the Profane*. New York: Harper and Row, 1961.

Eliade, Mircea. *The Two and The One*. New York and Evanston: Harper and Row, 1965.

Eliade, Mircea and Kitagawa, Joseph M. *The History of Religions: Essays in Methodology*. Chicago: The University of Chicago Press, 1959.

Elkind, David. "The Development of Religious Understanding in Children and Adolescents." In *Research on Religious Development*, edited by Merton P. Strommen, 656-85. New York: Hawthorn Books, 1971.

Emerson, A. E. "Some Biological Antecedents of Human Purpose." *Zygon* 8, nos. 3-4 (September-December, 1973). 294-309.

Emerson, A. E. and Burhoe, R. W. "Evolutionary Aspects of Freedom, Death, and Dignity." *Zygon* 9, no. 2 (June, 1974): 156-82.

Epictetus. *The Discources of Epictetus*. Volume 12 of *Great Books of the Western World*. See Abbreviations.

Erickson, Erik H. "The Development of Ritualization." In *The Religious Situation, 1968*, edited by Donald R. Cutler, 711-33. Boston: Beacon Press, 1968.

Evans-Pritchard, Edward E. *Theories of Primitive Religion*. Oxford: Clarendon Press, 1959.

Farb, Peter. *Man's Rise to Civilization*. New York: E. P. Dutton, 1968.

Flannery, R. "Ethics in Primitive Societies." *NCE* 5: 578-83.

Fowler, James. *Stages of Faith*. San Francisco: Harper and Row, 1981.

Fries, Jakob Friedrich. *Dialogues on Morality and Religion*. Totowa, N.J.: Barnes and Noble, 1982.

Geertz, Clifford. *The Interpretation of Cultures*. New York: Basic Books, 1973.

Geertz, Clifford. "Religion: Anthropological Study of." *IESS* 13: 398-406.

Geertz, Clifford. "Religion as a Cultural System." In *Anthropological Approaches to the Study of Religion*, 1-46. See Banton, Michael.

Ginsberg, Morris. "Social Evolution." In *Darwinism and the Study of Society*, 95-127. See Banton, Michael.

Goethe, Johann Wolfgang. *Gesammelte Werke*. Edited by Bernt von Heiseler. Guetersloh: Sigbert Mohn Verlag, 1960.

Goldenberg, Naomi R. *Changing of the Gods: Feminism and the End of Traditional Religions*. Boston: Beacon Press, 1979.

Goldman, Ronald. *Religious Thinking From Childhood to Adolescence*. New York: Seabury Press, 1968.

Goodenough, Ward H. "Right and Wrong in Human Evolution." *Zygon* 2, no. 1 (March, 1967): 59-76.

Gould, Stephen Jay. "Biological Potential vs. Biological Determinism." In *The Sociobiology Debate*, 343-51. See Caplan, Arthur L.

Greg, W. R. "On the Failure of 'Natural Selection' in the Case of Man." *Fraser's Magazine* 78 (1868): 353-62.

Guttler, C. *Eduard, Lord Herbert von Cherbury*. Munich: C. H. Beck'sche Verlagsbuchhandlung, 1897.

Gysi, Lydia. *Platonism and Cartesianism in the Philosophy of Ralph Cudworth*. Bern: Verlag Herbert Lang, 1966.

Hamlyn, D. W. "A Priori and A Posteriori." *EP* I: 140-44

Hampdem-Turner, Charles. *Maps of the Mind*. New York: Macmillan, 1981.

Hardin, Garret. *Biology: Its Human Implications*. San Francisco: W. H. Freeman, 1959.

Hardy, Alister. *The Biology of God*. London: Jonathan Cape, 1975.

Hardy, Alister. *The Spiritual Nature of Man*. Oxford: Clarendon Press, 1979.

Harms, Ernest. "The Development of Religious Experience in Children." *American Journal of Sociology* 50 (1944-45): 112-21.

Harris, Marvin. *Cannibals and Kings: The Origins of Cultures*. New York: Random House, 1978.

Harris, Marvin. *Cows, Pigs, Wars, and Witches*. New York: Random House, 1974.

Harris, Marvin. "The Cultural Ecology of India's Sacred Cattle." *Current Anthropology* 7 (1966): 51-66.

Harrison, Peter. *'Religion' and the Religions in the English Enlightenment*. Cambridge: Cambridge University Press, 1990.

Hartshorne, Charles and Reese, William L. *Philosophers Speak of God*. Chicago and London: The University of Chicago Press, 1953.

Hawkes, Terence. *Structuralism and Semiotics*. Berkeley and Los Angeles: University of California Press, 1977.

Hegel, G. W. F. *The Philosophy of History*. Volume 46 of *Great Books of the Western World*. See Abbreviations.

Heller, David. *The Children's God*. Chicago and London: The University of Chicago, 1986.

Herbert, Edward, Lord Herbert of Cherbury. *De Religione Laici*. New Haven: Yale University Press, 1944.

Herbert, Edward, Lord Herbert of Cherbury. *De Veritate*. Bristol: University of Bristol, 1937

Hick, John. *An Interpretation of Religion*. New Haven: Yale University Press, 1989.

Hick, John. *Philosophy of Religion*. Englewood Cliffs, N.J.: Prentice-Hall, 1983.

Hick, John and Askari, Hasan. *The Experience of Religious Diversity*. Brookfield, Vt.: Gower Press, 1985.

Hick, John and Knitter, P.F., eds. *The Myth of Christian Uniqueness*. Maryknoll, N.Y.: Orbis, 1988.

Hoagland, Hudson. "Ethology and Ethics — The Biology of Right and Wrong." *Zygon* 2, no.1 (March, 1967): 43-59.

Holm, Soren. "Apriori und Urphaenomen bei Rudolf Otto." In *Otto's Bedeutung*, 70-83. See Benz, Ernst.

Huegel, Friedrich von. *Essays and Addresses on the Philosophy of Religion*. First Series. New York: E. P. Dutton; and London: J. M. Dent and Sons, 1921.

Hume, David. *The Natural History of Religion*. New York: Macmillan, 1992.

Huxley, Julian. *Religion without Revelation*. London: Max Parrish, 1957.

Huxley, Thomas Henry. "Evolution." *Encyclopaedia Britannica*. 20th century edition. New York: The Werner Company, 1903: VIII: 744-51.

James, E. O. *The Beginnings of Religion*. Westport, Conn.: Greenwood Press, 1973.

James, E. O. *Prehistoric Religion: A Study in Prehistoric Archaeology*. New York: Frederick A. Praeger, 1957.

James, William. "Great Men, Great Thoughts, and the Environment." *Atlantic Monthly* XLVI (October, 1880): 441-59.

James, William. *Principles of Psychology*. Volume 53 of *Great Books of the Western World*. See Abbreviations.

James, William. *The Varieties of Religious Experience*. New York: The New American Library, 1958.

James, William. *The Will to Believe*. New York: Dover Publications, 1956.

Jastrow, Morris. *The Study of Religion*. London: Walter Scott, 1901.

Jaynes, Julian. *The Origin of Consciousness in the Breakdown of the Bicameral Mind*. Boston: Houghton Mifflin, 1976.

Jensen, U. J. and Harre, R. *The Philosophy of Evolution*. Brighton, Sussex: The Harvester Press, 1981.

Jolley, Nicholas, "Leibniz and Malebranche on Innate Ideas." *The Philosophical Review* XCVII, no. 1 (January, 1988): 71-91.

Jung, Carl G. *The Archetypes and the Collective Unconscious.* In *The Collected Works of C. G. Jung*, Volume 9, Part I. Princeton: Princeton University Press, 1959.

Jung, Carl G. *Man and his Symbols.* New York: Doubleday, 1964.

Jung, Carl G. *Psychology and Religion.* New Haven and London: Yale University Press, 1968.

Kainz, Howard P. *Hegel's Phenomenology*, Part II: *The Evolution of Ethical and Religious Consciousness to the Absolute Standpoint.* Athens, Ohio: Ohio University Press, 1983.

Kant, Immanuel. *Critique of Pure Reason.* Volume 42 of *Great Books of the Western World.* See Abbreviations.

Kimball, J. W. *Biology.* Ready, Mass.: Addison-Wesley, 1983.

Kitagawa, Joseph M., ed. *The History of Religions: Retrospect and Prospect.* New York and London: Macmillan, 1985.

Kitagawa, Joseph M. *The History of Religions: Understanding Human Experience.* Atlanta: Scholars Press, 1987.

Kitagawa, Joseph M., Eliade, Mircea, and Long, C. H. *The History of Religions.* Chicago and London: University of Chicago, 1967.

Klubertanz, G. P. "Estimative Power." *NCE* 5: 558.

Kohlberg, Lawrence. *The Philosophy of Moral Development.* San Francisco: Harper and Row, 1981.

Kottich, R. G. *Die Lehre von den angeborenen Ideen.* Berlin: R. Schoetz, 1917.

Kress, Robert. *A Rahner Handbook.* Atlanta: John Knox Press, 1982.

Kroeber, A. L. "The Superorganic." *American Anthropologist.* 19, no. 2 (1917): 163-213.

Kueng, Hans. *Does God Exist?* Garden City, N. Y.: Doubleday, 1980.

Kueng, Hans. *Freud and the Problem of God.* New Haven: Yale University Press, 1979.

Kueng, Hans. *Theology for the Third Millennium.* New York: Doubleday, 1988.

Lane, Beldon C. *Landscapes of the Sacred.* Mahwah, N.J.: Paulist, 1988.

Lang, G. O. "Culture." *NCE* 4: 522-32.

Laughlin, Charles, Jr. and McManus, John. "Mammalian Ritual." In *The Spectrum of Ritual*, 86-107. See d'Aquili, Eugene.

Leach, Edmund. "Structuralism." *ER* 14: 54-64.

Leeuw, Girardus van der. *Religion in Essence and Manifestation.* New York and Evanston: Harper and Row, 1963.

Leibniz, G. W. *New Essays Concerning Human Understanding.* New York: Macmillan, 1896.

Leroi-Gourhan, Andre. *Prehistoric Man in Western Europe.* London: Thanes and Hudson, 1968.

Lévi-Strauss, Claude. *Structural Anthropology.* New York: Basic Books, 1963.

Lewis, John, ed. *Beyond Chance and Necessity.* London: Garnstone Press, 1974.

Lewontin, R. C., Rose, Steven, and Kamin, Leon J. *Not in Our Genes.* New York: Pantheon Books, 1984.

Lex, Barbara W. "The Neurobiology of Ritual Trance." In *The Spectrum of Ritual*, 117-51. See d'Aquili, Eugene.

Lindbeck, George, A. "The *A Priori* in St. Thomas' Theory of Knowledge." In *The Heritage of Christian Thought*, 41-63. See Cushman, R. E.

Lindbeck, George, A. "The Thought of Karl Rahner, S.J." *Christianity and Crisis* (October 18, 1965): 211-15.

Locke, John. *Essay Concerning Human Understanding.* Volume 35 of *Great Books of the Western World.* See Abbreviations.

Loewen, Harry. *Goethe's Response to Protestantism.* Bern and Frankfurt: Verlag Herbert Lang, 1972.

Lonergan, Bernard. *Collection.* New York: Herder and Herder, 1967.

Lonergan, Bernard. *Insight: A Study of Human Understanding.* London, New York, Toronto: Longmans, Green, 1958.

Long, Charles H. "Archaism and Hermeneutics." In *The History of Religions*, 67-74. See Kitagawa, Joseph M., Eliade, Mircea, and Long. C. H.

Long, Charles H. "A Look at the Chicago Tradition in the History of Religions." In *The History of Religions: Retrospect and Prospect*, 87-104. See Kitagawa, Joseph M.

Lorenz, Konrad. *Behind the Mirror.* New York: Harcourt Brace Jovanovich, 1978.

Lorenz, Konrad. *Evolution and Modification of Behavior.* Chicago: The University of Chicago, 1967.

Lorenz, Konrad. *King Solomon's Ring.* New York: Thomas Y. Crowell, 1961.

Lorenz, Konrad. *Man Meets Dog.* Harmondsworth: Penguin, 1988.

Ludwig, Theodore M. "Gods and Goddesses." *ER* 3: 59-66.

Lumsden, Charles and Wilson, Edward O. *Genes, Mind, and Culture.* Cambridge: Harvard University Press, 1981.

MacCormac, E. R. "Religious Metaphors: Mediators between Biological and Cultural Evolution that Generate Transcendent Meaning." *Zygon* 18, no. 1 (1983): 45-65.

Macintosh, Douglas C. "Troeltsch's Theory of Religious Knowledge." *American Journal of Theology* (July, 1919): 274-89.

MacLean, Paul D. *A Triune Concept of the Brain and Behaviour.* Toronto and Buffalo: University of Toronto, 1973.

Maddox, Randy L. "Hermeneutic Philosophy and Theological Studies." *Religious Studies* 21 (1985): 523-27.

Mandell, A. J. "Toward a Psychobiology of Transcendence: God in the Brain." In *The Psychobiology of Consciousness*, edited by Julian and Richard Davidson, 379-439. New York: Plenum, 1980.

Margulis, Lynn and Schwartz, Karlene W. *Five Kingdoms.* San Francisco: W. H. Freeman, 1982.

Maringer, Johannes. *The Gods of Prehistoric Man.* New York: Alfred A. Knopf, 1960.

Marty, Martin E. and Peerman, Dean G, eds. *A Handbook of Christian*

Theologians. Cleveland and New York: World Publishing Co., 1967.

Maslow, Abraham. *Religions, Values, and Peak-Experiences.* New York: The Viking Press, 1970.

Mattern, Ruth. "Altruism, Ethics, and Sociobiology." In *The Sociobiology Debate*, 462-75. See Caplan, Arthur L.

Maxwell, Mary. *Human Evolution.* New York: Columbia University Press, 1984.

McCool, Gerald, A. "The Philosophy of the Human Person in Karl Rahner's Theology." *Theological Studies* XXII (1961): 537-62.

McCool, Gerald, A. "The Primacy of Intuition." *Thought* XXXVII (1962): 57-73.

McDougall, William. *An Introduction to Social Psychology.* Boston: John W. Luce, 1926.

McInerny, R. *St. Thomas Aquinas.* Notre Dame, Ind.: University of Notre Dame Press, 1982.

McKenzie, John L. *Dictionary of the Bible.* New York: Bruce, 1965.

McKim, Robert. "Could God Have More Than One Nature?" *Faith and Philosophy* 5, no. 4 (1988): 378-98.

Meland, Bernard E. "Rudolf Otto." In *A Handbook of Christian Theologians,* 169-91. See Marty, Martin E.

Mensching, Gustav. *Die Religion: Erscheinungsformen, Strukturtypen, und Lebensgesetzen.* Stuttgart: Curt E. Schwab, 1959.

Miller, David L. "I Do Not Believe in Ghosts." *New York Times Book Review* (November 15, 1987): 48.

Mol, H. *Identity and the Sacred.* Oxford: Basil Blackwell, 1976.

Munro, Thomas. *Evolution in the Arts.* New York: Harry N. Abrams, n.d.

Munsey, Brenda, ed. *Moral Development, Moral Education, and Kohlberg.* Birmingham, Ala.: Religious Education Press, 1980.

Murphy, G. Ronald., S.J. "A Ceremonial Ritual: The Mass." In *The Spectrum of Ritual*, 318-41. See d'Aquili, Eugene.

Nash, Ronald H. *Ideas of History.* Two Volumes. New York: E. P. Dutton, 1969. "Natural and Supernatural Selection." *The Spectator* (October 3, 1868): 1154-55.

Niebuhr, H. Richard. "The Religious Philosophy of Ernst Troeltsch." Ph.D. diss., Yale University, 1924.

Niebuhr, Richard R. "Friedrich Schleiermacher." In *A Handbook of Christian Theologians*, 17-35. See Marty, Martin E.

Niebuhr, Richard R. *Schleiermacher on Christ and Religion.* New York: Charles Scribner's Sons, 1964.

Nietzsche, Friedrich. *The Joyful Wisdom.* New York: Russell and Russell, 1964.

Nogar, Raymond. "Evolution, Human." *NCE* 5: 682-84.

North, Robert. *Teilhard and the Creation of the Soul.* Milwaukee: Bruce, 1966.

Noss, John B. *Man's Religions.* London: Macmillan, 1969.

O'Donovan, Leo J., ed. *A World of Grace.* New York: Seabury Press, 1980.

Otto, Rudolf. *Goethe und Darwin: Darwinismus und Religion.* Göttingen:

Vandenhoeck and Ruprecht, 1909.

Otto, Rudolf. *The Idea of the Holy*. New York: Oxford University Press, 1967.

Otto, Rudolf. *Naturalism and Religion*. London: Williams and Norgate, 1913.

Otto, Rudolf. "Parallelisms in the Development of Religion East and West." *Asiatic Society of Japan. Transactions* 40 (1912): 153-58.

Otto, Rudolf. *The Philosophy of Religion*. London: Williams and Norgate, 1931.

Otto, Rudolf. *Religious Essays*. London: Oxford University Press, 1931.

Otto, Walter F. *The Homeric Gods*. New York: Pantheon, 1954.

Panikkar, Raimundo. "The Invisible Harmony: A Universal Theory of Religion or a Cosmic Confidence in Reality?" In *Toward a Universal Theology of Religion*, 118-53. See Swidler, Leonard.

Parijs, Philippe Van. "The Evolutionary Explanation of Beliefs." In *Evolutionary Epistemology*, 381-401. See Callebaut, Werner.

Parsons, Talcott. "On Building Social System Theory." *Daedalus* 99: no. 4 (Fall, 1970): 826-81.

Parsons, Talcott. *The Social System*. New York: The Free Press, 1951.

Parsons, Talcott. *Societies: Evolutionary and Comparative Perspectives*. Englewood Cliffs, N.J.: Prentice-Hall, 1966.

Partin, Harry B. "Classification of Religions." *ER* 3: 527-32.

Peacocke, A. R. *Creation and the World of Science*. Oxford: Clarendon Press, 1979.

Peters, Karl. "Religion and an Evolutionary Theory of Knowledge." *Zygon* 17, no. 4 (1982): 385-415.

Pettazzonni, Raffaele. "The Supreme Being: Phenomenological Structure and Historical Development." In *History of Religions*, 59-66. See Eliade and Kitagawa.

Pfeiffer, John. "Current research casts new light on human origins." *Smithsonian* (June, 1982): 91-103.

Pfeiffer, John. "Nature: The Radical Conservative." *New York Times Book Review* (April 29, 1979): 9, 52.

Piaget, Jean. *Biology and Knowledge*. Chicago and London: University of Chicago Press, 1971.

Piaget, Jean. *The Child's Conception of the World*. Totowa, N.J.: Rowman and Littlefield, 1983.

Piaget, Jean. *The Moral Judgment of the Child*. New York: The Free Press, 1965.

Piaget, Jean. *The Origins of Intelligence in Children*. New York: International Universities Press, 1975.

Piaget, Jean. *The Principles of Genetic Epistemology*. London: Routledge and Kegan Paul, 1972.

Piattelli-Palmarini, Massimo, ed. *Language and Learning, The Debate between Jean Piaget and Noam Chomsky*. Cambridge: Harvard University Press, 1980.

Plato. *The Dialogues of Plato*. Volume 7 of *Great Books of the Western World*. See Abbreviations.

Polanyi, Michael. "The Logic of Tacit Inference." *Philosophy* 40 (1966): 369-86.

Polanyi, Michael. *The Study of Man*. Chicago and London: The University of Chicago Press, 1959.

Polanyi, Michael. *The Tacit Dimension*. Garden City, N.Y.: Doubleday, 1966.

Preston, James. *Mother Worship*. Chapel Hill: University of North Carolina, 1982.

Rahner, Karl. "A Basic Interpretation of Vatican II." *Theological Studies* 40, no. 4 (December, 1979): 716-27.

Rahner, Karl. "Concerning the Relationship Between Nature and Grace." In *Theological Investigations*, I, 297-318. See Rahner, Karl.

Rahner, Karl. "Evolution: Theological." In *SM* II: 290-93.

Rahner, Karl. *Hearers of the Word*. New York: Herder and Herder, 1969.

Rahner, Karl. "Hominisation." In *SM* II: 294-97.

Rahner, Karl. *Hominisation: The Evolutionary Origin of Man as a Theological Problem*. New York: Herder and Herder, 1965.

Rahner, Karl. "Natural Science and Reasonable Faith." In *Theological Investigations* XXI: 16-55. See Rahner, Karl.

Rahner, Karl. "Priest and Poet." In *The Word: Readings in Theology*, edited by Carney Gavin, Charles Pfeiffer, and others, 3-26. New York: P. J. Kenedy and Sons, 1964.

Rahner, Karl. *Spirit in the World*. New York: Herder and Herder, 1968.

Rahner, Karl. *Theological Investigations*. Volume I. Baltimore and London: Helicon Press and Darton, Longman and Todd, 1961.

Rahner, Karl. *Theological Investigations*. Volume VI. London and New York: Darton, Longman and Todd and Seabury Press, 1974.

Rahner, Karl. *Theological Investigations*. Volume XXI. New York: Crossroad, 1988.

Rahner, Karl and Vorgrimler, Herbert. *Theological Dictionary*. New York: Herder and Herder, 1965.

Rappaport, Roy A. *Ecology, Meaning, and Religion*. Richmond, Calif.: North Atlantic Books, 1979.

Rappaport, Roy A. *Pigs for the Ancestors*. New Haven and London: Yale University Press, 1967.

Rappaport, Roy A. "The Sacred in Human Evolution." In *Annual Review of Ecology and Systematics*, edited by Richard F. Johnston, Peter W. Frank, and Charles D. Michener, 23-43. Palo Alto, Calif.: Annual Reviews Inc., 1971.

Raven, Peter H. and Johnson, George B. *Understanding Biology*. St. Louis, Toronto, Santa Clara: Times Mirror/Mosby College Publishing, 1988.

Read, C. *The Origin of Man and his Superstition*. Cambridge: Cambridge University Press, 1920.

Reeder, John P., Jr. "The Relation of the Moral and the Numinous in Otto's Notion of the Holy." In *Religion and Morality*, edited by G. Outka and J. P. Reeder, 267-79. Garden City, N.Y.: Anchor Press, 1973.

Reid, Thomas. *Philosophical Works*. Hildesheim: Georg Olms Verlagsbuchhandlung, 1967.

Rescher, Nicholas. *Leibniz: An Introduction to his Philosophy*. Oxford: Basil Blackwell, 1979.

Rescher, Nicholas. "A New Look at the Problem of Innate Ideas." *British Journal of Philosophy and Science* 17, no. 2 (1966): 205-18.

Rescher, Nicholas. *A Useful Inheritance, Evolutionary Aspects of the Theory of Knowledge*. Savage, Md.: Rowman and Littlefield, 1990.

Reynolds, V. and Tanner, R. E. S. *The Biology of Religion*. London and New York: Longman, 1983.

Reynolds, V. and Tanner, R. E. S. "The Effects of Religion on Human Biology." In *Darwinism and Divinity*, 131-54. See Durant, John.

Richards, Robert J. *Darwin and the Emergence of Evolutionary Theories of Mind and Behavior*. Chicago: University of Chicago Press, 1987.

Richards, Robert J. "Influence of Sensationalist Tradition on Early Theories of the Evolution of Behavior." *Journal of the History of Ideas* 40 (1979): 85-105.

Richards, Robert J. "The Innate and the Learned: The Evolution of Konrad Lorenz's Theory of Instinct." *Philosophy of the Social Sciences* 4 (1974): 111-33.

Richards, Robert J. *The Meaning of Evolution*. Chicago and London: The University of Chicago Press, 1992.

Richards, Robert J. "The Natural Selection Model of Conceptual Evolution." *Philosophy of Science* 44 (1977): 494-501.

Richards, Robert J. "Wundt's Early Theories of Unconscious Inference and Cognitive Evolution in their Relation to Darwinian Biopsychology." In *Wundt Studies*, edited by W. G. Bringmann and R. D. Tweney, 42-70. Toronto: C. J. Hogrefe, 1980.

Ricoeur, Paul. "The Hermeneutics of Symbols and Philosophical Reflection." *International Philosophical Quarterly* II, no. 2 (1962): 191-218.

Ruse, Michael. *The Darwinian Paradigm: Essays on its history, philosophy, and religious implications*. London and New York: Routledge, 1989.

Ruse, Michael. *Philosophy of Biology Today*. Albany: State University of New York Press, 1988.

Ruse, Michael. *Taking Darwin Seriously*. Oxford: Basil Blackwell, 1986.

Santayana, George. *Interpretaions of Poetry and Religion*. Cambridge, Mass.: The MIT Press, 1989.

Schleiermacher, Friedrich. *The Christian Faith*. New York and Evanston: Harper and Row, 1963.

Schleiermacher, Friedrich. *On Religion, Speeches to its Cultured Despisers*. New York: Harper and Row, 1958.

Schlipp, Paul, ed. *The Philosophy of Karl Popper*. Lasalle, Ill.: Open Court Press, 1974.

Schmidt, Roger. *Exploring Religion*. Belmont, Calif.: Wadsworth, 1988.

Schmidt, Wilhelm. *The Origin and Growth of Religion*. London: Methuen, 1935.

Schmitz-Moormann, Karl. "On the Evolution of Human Freedom." *Zygon* 22, no. 4 (December, 1987): 443-58.

Searle, J. R. *The Philosophy of Language.* London: Oxford University Press, 1971.

Segal, Robert A. "Victor Turner's Theory of Ritual." *Zygon* 18, no. 3 (September, 1983): 327-35.

Sharpe, Eric J. *Comparative Religion: A History.* London: Gerald Duckworth, 1975.

Simpson, George G. *The Meaning of Evolution.* New Haven: Yale University Press, 1949.

Simpson, George G. *Principles of Animal Taxonomy.* New York: Columbia University Press, 1961.

Skinner, B. F. "Superstition in the Pigeon." *Journal of Experimental Psychology* 38 (1948): 168-72.

Skinner, B. F. and Morse, W. H. "A Second Type of 'Superstition' in the Pigeon." *American Journal of Psychology* 70 (1957): 308-11.

Slater, Peter and Wiebe, Donald. *Traditions in Contact and Change: Selected Proceedings of the XIVth Congress of the International Association for the History of Religions.* Waterloo, Ontario: Wilfrid Laurier University Press, 1983.

Smart, Ninian. *The World's Religions.* Englewood Cliffs, N.J.: Prentice Hall, 1989.

Smith, Huston. *The Religions of Man.* New York: Harper and Row, 1958.

Smith, J. J. "Religious Development of Children." In *Child Psychology: Child Development and Modern Education,* edited by Charles E. Skinner and Philip L. Harriman, 273-98. New York: Macmillan 1941.

Smith, J. Maynard. "Evolution and History." In *Darwinism and the Study of Society,* 83-93. See Banton, M.

Smith, W. John. "Ritual and the Ethology of Communicating." In *The Spectrum of Ritual,* 51-79. See d'Aquili, Eugene.

Smith, Wilfred C. *Meaning and End of Religion.* New York: New American Library, 1964.

Smith, Wilfred C. "Traditions in Contact and Change: Towards a History of Religion in the Singular." In *Traditions in Contact and Change,* 1-4. See Slater, Peter.

Sokal, Robert R. and Sneath, Peter H. A. *Principles of Numerical Taxonomy.* San Francisco and London: W. H. Freeman, 1963.

Solmsen, Friedrich. "Plato and the Concept of the Soul (Psyche): Some Historical Perspectives." *Journal of the History of Ideas* 44 (July-September, 1983): 355-67.

Sperber, Dan. *Rethinking Symbolism.* London: Cambridge University Press, 1975.

Spiro, M. E. "Religion: Problems of Definition and Explanation." In *Anthropological Approaches,* 85-126. See Banton, Michael.

Stagner, Ross. "Homeostasis." *IESS* 6: 499-503.

Stanesby, D. *Science, Reason, and Religion.* London: Croom Helm, 1985.

Stanley, Steven M. *The New Evolutionary Timetable.* New York: Basic Books, 1981.

Stark, Werner. "Natural and Social Selection." In *Darwinism and the*

Study of Society, 49-61. See Banton, Michael.

Stent, G. S. *Morality as a Biological Phenomenon*. Berkeley: University of California Press, 1980.

Stich, Stephen P. *Innate Ideas*. Berkeley: University of California, 1975.

Stone, Merlin. *When God Was a Woman*. New York: The Dial Press, 1976.

Swidler, Leonard, ed. *Toward a Universal Theology of Religion*. Maryknoll, N.Y.: Orbis Books, 1987.

Swinburne, Richard. *The Evolution of the Soul*. Oxford: Clarendon Press, 1986.

Taylor, A. E. *Plato: The Man and His Work*. New York: The Dial Press, 1936.

Teilhard de Chardin, Pierre. *The Phenomenon of Man*. New York: Harper and Brothers, 1959.

Theissen, Gerd. *Biblical Faith: An Evolutionary Approach*. Philadelphia: Fortress Press, 1985.

Theissen, Gerd. *On Having a Critical Faith*. London: S CM Press, 1979.

Thomas Aquinas. *The Summa Theologica*. Volume 19 of *Great Books of the Western World*. See Abbreviations.

Thorpe, W. H. *Learning and Instinct in Animals*. London: Methuen, 1956.

Tiele, Cornelius Petrus. *Elements of the Science of Religion*. Edinburgh and London: William Blackwood and Sons, 1897.

Toulmin, Stephen. "The Charm of the Scout." *New York Review of Books* 27 (April 3, 1980): 38-42.

Toulmin, Stephen. "Human Adaptation" In *The Philosophy of Evolution*, 176-95. See Jensen, U. J.

Toulmin, Stephen. *Human Understanding*. Oxford: Oxford University Press, 1972.

Toynbee, Arnold J. *A Study of History*. New York and London: Oxford University Press, 1957.

Tracy, David. *The Analogical Imagination*. New York: Crossroad, 1981.

Tresmontant, Claude. *A Study of Hebrew Thought*. New York: Desclee, 1960.

Troeltsch, Ernst. *Writings on Theology and Religion*. London: Duckworth, 1977.

Turner, Viktor. "Color Classification in Ndembu Ritual." In *Anthropological Approaches*, 47-84. See Banton, M.

Turner, Viktor. *Dramas, Fields, and Metaphors: Symbolic Action in Human Society*. Ithaca and London: Cornell University Press, 1974.

Turner, Viktor. *On the Edge of the Bush*. Tucson: University of Arizona Press, 1985.

Turner, Viktor. *The Forest of Symbols*. Ithaca: Cornell University Press, 1967.

Turner, Viktor. *The Ritual Process*. Chicago: Aldine, 1969.

Urban, W. H. *The Intelligible World: Metaphysics and Value*. New York: Macmillan, 1929.

Verkamp, Bernard J. "Hick's interpretation of religious pluralism."

International Journal for the Philosophy of Religion 30 (1991): 103-24.

Verkamp, Bernard J. *The Indifferent Mean*. Athens, Ohio: and Detroit: Ohio University and Wayne State University Presses, 1977.

Verkamp, Bernard J. "Kueng's Ecumenical Dialectic." *Faith and Philosophy* 6, no. 3 (1989): 288-302.

Verkamp, Bernard J. *The Moral Treatment of Returning Warriors in Early Medieval and Modern Times*. Cranbury, N.J., London, and Toronto: University of Scranton and Associated University Presses, 1993.

Verkamp, Bernard J. "Recovering a Sense of Sin." *America* (November 19, 1983): 305-307.

Vallee, J. P. "The Search for Knowledge: Science versus Religion?" *Journal of the Royal Astronomical Society of Canada* 83, no. 1 (1989): 8-25.

Vollmer, G. "Mesocosm and Objective Knowledge." In *Concepts and Approaches in Evolutionary Epistemology*, 69-122. See Wuketits, F.

Vries, Jan de. *Perspectives in the History of Religions*. Berkeley, Los Angeles, and London: University of California Press, 1977.

Wach, Joachim. *The Comparative Study of Religions*. New York and London: Columbia University Press, 1966.

Wach, Joachim. *Introduction to the History of Religions*, edited by Joseph Kitagawa and Gregory Alles. New York: Macmillan, 1988.

Wach, Joachim. *Sociology of Religion*. Chicago and London: The University of Chicago Press, 1967.

Wach, Joachim. *Types of Religious Experience, Christian and Non-Christian*. Chicago: University of Chicago Press, 1951.

Waddington, C. H. *The Ethical Animal*. Chicago: The University of Chicago Press, 1960.

Wallace, Anthony F. C. *Religion: An Anthropological View*. New York: Random House, 1966.

Waller, James and Edwardsen, Mary. "Evolutionism." *ER* 5: 214-18.

Walsh, W. H. "Kant, Immanuel." *EP* IV: 319-20.

Walzman, Herbert M. "Question of Human Origins Debated Anew." *The Chronicle of Higher Education* (September 16, 1992): A7-A9.

Weber, Max. *The Sociology of Religion*. Boston: Beacon Press, 1964.

Weger, Karl-Heinz. *Karl Rahner: An Introduction to His Theology*. New York: Seabury Press, 1980.

Whitehead, Alfred North. *Religion in the Making*. New York: Macmillan, 1960.

Whitney, George Topley. *The Heritage of Kant*. New York: Russell and Russell, 1962.

Wilson, David Sloan. "Species of Thought: A Comment on Evolutionary Epistemology." *Biology and Philosophy* 5 (1990): 37-62.

Wilson, Edward O. "Academic Vigilantism and the Political Significance of Sociobiology." In *The Sociobiology Debate*, 291-303. See Caplan, Arthur L.

Wilson, Edward O. *On Human Nature*. Cambridge, Mass.: Harvard University Press, 1978.

Wilson, Edward O. *Sociobiology: The New Synthesis*. Cambridge, Mass.:

Belknap Press, 1975.

Windelband, W. *A History of Philosophy*. New York: Macmillan, 1960.

Wink, Walter. Review of Theissen's *Biblical Faith*. *Zygon* 21, no. 4 (December, 1986): 543.

Wispe, Lauren G. and Thompson, James N., Jr. "The War Between the Words: Biological Versus Social Evolution and Some Related Issues." *American Psychologist* (May, 1976): 341-85.

Wood, Ledger. "The Transcendental Method." In *The Heritage of Kant*, 3-35. See Whitney, George Topley.

Wuketits, F. *Concepts and Approaches in Evolutionary Epistemology*. Dordrecht: D. Reidel, 1984.

Wuthnow, Robert. *Meaning and Moral Order: Explorations in Cultural Analysis*. Berkeley: Univ. of California, 1987.

Wuthnow, Robert. "Religious Orientations." *ES* 3: 1651-56.

Yolton, John W. *John Locke and the Way of Ideas*. Oxford: Clarendon Press, 1956.

Yoon, Carol Kaesuk. "Social Castes Found to Be Not So Rare in Nature." *New York Times*. January 16, 1993: C1 and C6.

INDEX